A
PROVISION OF
HUMAN NATURE

ESSAYS ON FIELDING
AND OTHERS
IN HONOR OF
MIRIAM AUSTIN LOCKE

Miriam Austin Locke

A
PROVISION
OF
HUMAN
NATURE

ESSAYS ON
FIELDING AND OTHERS
IN HONOR OF
Miriam Austin Locke

EDITED BY
Donald Kay

The University of Alabama Press
University, Alabama

Library of Congress Cataloging in Publication Data
Main entry under title:

A Provision of human nature.

CONTENTS: Kay, D. Dedication to Miriam Austin Locke.—
Williamson, E. Guiding principles in Fielding's criticism of the critics.—
Durant, J. D. The "Art of thriving" in Fielding's comedies. [etc.]
     1. English literature—18th century—History and criticism—Addresses,
essays, lectures. 2. Fielding, Henry, 1707-1754—Addresses, essays, lec-
tures. 3. Locke, Miriam Austin. I. Kay, Donald. II. Locke, Miriam Austin.
PR442.P7   823'.03   76-40469
ISBN 0-8173-7425-6

✒ BILL OF FARE

AS WE DO NOT DISDAIN to borrow Wit or Wisdom from any Man who is capable of lending us either, we have condescended to take a Hint from these honest Victuallers, and shall prefix not only a general Bill of Fare to our whole Entertainment, but shall likewise give the Reader particular Bills to every Course which is to be served up in this . . . Volume.

The Provision then which we have here made is no other than HUMAN NATURE. Nor do I fear that my sensible Reader, though most luxurious in his Taste, will start, cavil, or be offended, because I have named but one Article. The Tortoise, as the Alderman of *Bristol,* well learned in eating, knows by much Experience, besides the delicious *Calipash* and *Calipee,* contains many different kinds of Food; nor can the learned Reader be ignorant, that in *Human Nature,* tho' here collected under one general Name, is such prodigious Variety, that a Cook will have sooner gone through all the several Species of animal and vege-table Food in the World, than an Author will be able to exhaust so extensive a Subject.

from Book I of
The History of Tom Jones,
A Foundling

67334

✍ CONTENTS

and Others

✒ MIRIAM
AUSTIN
LOCKE

IT IS WITH GRATITUDE that this honorific volume of essays is published by The University of Alabama Press as an especial tribute to Miriam Austin Locke upon her retirement as Professor of English in The University of Alabama. I am particularly happy to have been able to edit this *festschrift* for a warm friend and professional colleague who has always been most generous with her expert advice on matters large and small to everyone genuinely interested in the pursuit of knowledge. Of course a mark of the respect with which she is held on the Tuscaloosa campus and in the region is indicated by the outstanding scholars—both young and established—who have contributed fresh and considered essays for this book.

Miriam Austin Locke was born in Mobile, Alabama, during the first decade of this century, and she was educated at The University of Alabama, where she received both the B.A. and M.A. degrees, and at Northwestern University, where she was awarded the Ph.D. degree. She was an active member of Phi Beta Kappa and was a past president of the Tuscaloosa chapter. Upon her retirement in 1977, Professor Locke has the distinction of being the senior professor in the University, where she was for forty-eight years of teaching unusually successful in encouraging outstanding undergraduate students and M.A. students to pursue advanced degrees. Many of her former students are now teaching in colleges and universities across America. The graciousness she possesses and wears lightly as well as her example as an enlightened, humane individual are abundantly evident to all those who come into contact with her daily. We are all better for having had exposure to such a discerning scholar, provocative teacher, unselfish servant, and cordial companion. The stagecoach of our profession would be sadly limited without the Miriam Lockes, who contribute information for instruction and delight, who occasionally help to fight off bandits, and who stay on for stop after stop.

Most of the selections in this volume deal with Professor Locke's major scholarly interest—the works of Henry Fielding, whose *The True Patriot* she edited beautifully for The University of Alabama Press in

1964 and which is once more in print. Eugene Williamson writes a comprehensive and thorough analysis of Fielding's critical theories and practice; Jack D. Durant contributes an important—and unique, as far as I know—study of all eight "regular" comedies; John J. Burke, Jr., does a remarkable job of detailing Fielding's use of history in his fiction; George H. Wolfe surveys masterfully the moral imperative of *The Champion* essays; Susan Miller demonstrates the influence of the "game at play" in *Tom Jones;* and T. C. Duncan Eaves and Eleanor N. Hutchens concentrate more specifically on the characters of Amelia and Square even as they inform us about wider aspects of Fielding's novelistic techniques.

The other essays do not deal directly with Henry Fielding, but they all—save Aubrey Williams's "What Donne Did to Pope" and Calhoun Winton's "John Wilkes and 'An Essay on Woman' "—center upon the prose and drama of the Restoration and eighteenth century. Since prose and drama were Fielding's strong suits, I believe these essays indirectly (at least) help us gauge his accomplishments more accurately. The "And Others" essays need not, of course, be artifically attached to the "Fielding" essays, even as we note how they might be read profitably in conjunction with them. (Unity is not all, I suppose, in a *festschrift.*). Sue L. Kimball's essay on game playing in *The Way of the World* might, however, be read along with Professor Miller's on *Tom Jones;* Rebecca Armstrong's on the Great Chain of Being in *All for Love* and Robert E. Halli's rare essay on *The London Merchant* might be studied after Professor Durant's on Fielding's drama; David K. Jeffrey's lively comments about the epistolary techniques in *Pamela* and *Humphry Clinker* are stimulating on a general subject of novel making that could be considered alongside the commentaries of Professors Hutchens, Ware, Eaves, Burke, Williamson, and Miller; and surely Calhoun Winton's excellent—and quite unstale and unflat—study of "An Essay on Woman" might profitably be read along with Professor Eaves's essay on Amelia and Clarissa or Mrs. Kimball's remarks about the role of women in the game playing of *The Way of the World.*

This volume would not have been possible without generous assistance and contributions of advice and finances from individuals and organizations within and without The University of Alabama. I am most grateful to the following gracious PATRONS: Phi Beta Kappa, Mortar Board, Kappa Kappa Gamma Social Sorority, Chi Delta Phi English Honorary, Elizabeth Brock, Carol McGinnis Kay, Mr. and Mrs. James B. McMillan, Samuel Holt Monk, James L. Clifford, Moody E. Prior, Dwight L. Eddins, Mr. and Mrs. Fred Colby Hobson, O. B. Emerson, Jewel E. Hudgins, Anna Fleck Jacobs (for the design of the book), Mr. and Mrs. John Payne, Emerson R. Loomis, Mr. and Mrs. Carl Seebeck, Mr. and Mrs. Buckner B. Trawick, Joan North, Jan Wilson, Douglas E.

Jones, Richard Thigpen, Mr. and Mrs. I. Willis Russell, May Sims, Mr. and Mrs. Iredell Jenkins, Mr. and Mrs. John Luskin, Mary Gray Porter, Claude Stabler, Derek Milsom, Mr. and Mrs. Robert Halli, and F. David Mathews.

1 August 1976   DONALD KAY
Tuscaloosa, Alabama

A
PROVISION OF
HUMAN NATURE

ESSAYS ON FIELDING
AND OTHERS
IN HONOR OF
MIRIAM AUSTIN LOCKE

. . . if we judge according to
the Sentiments of some Critics,
and of some Christians,
no Author will be saved in
this World, and no
Man in the next
—*Tom Jones*

EUGENE WILLIAMSON 🙠 GUIDING PRINCIPLES
IN FIELDING'S
CRITICISM OF
THE CRITICS

A WRITER WHO INCORPORATES essays on the theory and practice of
literary criticism into his fictional masterpiece can hardly fail to arouse
interest in such matters as his sensitivity to criticism and his own efforts as
a critic. When the included remarks are as keenly phrased as the prolegomenous chapters of *Tom Jones*, we are the more interested in the
writer's understanding of his critical milieu and in his notions about how
literary works (including his own) should be read. Fortunately both
appreciation of Fielding's art and knowledge about his critical thought
have greatly advanced since the days when Shenstone found the wit in
this novel to be "ty'd up in Bundles at ye beginning of every *Book*."[1] An
examination of the principles that appear to have guided Fielding in
some twenty-five years of writing about critics and criticism, whether in
plays, novels, periodical essays, lucianic dialogues, poems, or in other
genres, is a logical development and extension of the available scholarship.[2]

Because Fielding's comments about critics were possibly conditioned
to some degree by critical responses to his novels and plays, some
preliminary account of the contemporary reception of his writings is
desirable. One might hope to learn what if any basis there was in his
own experience for his acid observation of 1740 that the world
obstructs no one seeking reputation so much as an aspiring writer and
that it withholds its approval as long as possible, "the Lawrel, like the
Cypress, being generally thrown into the Grave."[3] After a review of
aspects of Fielding's literary fortunes from 1728–54 that bear on his
outlook on the critics, I shall discuss his attack on the critical malpractices
of his day and his desiderata for adequate criticism, concluding with
attention to three instances of his own criticism that clearly reflect his
guiding principles.

I

Much of Fielding's dissatisfaction with the critical practices of his day would seem to have clear and direct relation to the kind of critical treatment given to his own dramas and novels. Although at the beginning of his literary career he made use of conventional strictures on critics that were the staple of Pope, Swift, and other neoclassic writers who preceded him, Fielding soon had a far more personal and immediate knowledge of the critical abuses to which he alluded in the prologues of his early dramas. Of the decade in which he was engaged in the writing of plays, only the first several years were relatively free from the close attention of the contentious, often hostile group of Grub-Streeters engaged in dramatic criticism. Fielding's first play, *Love in Several Masques*—it appeared in 1728, the same year as *The Beggar's Opera* and the first version of *The Dunciad*—contains ridicule of the stock figure of the dilettantish and critically irresponsible nobleman but less deliberately to arouse the ire of the Grub-Streeters than many of its successors (*Works,* VIII, 27). Indeed, before 1732, when Fielding became associated with Colley Cibber in the patent theater of Drury Lane, not even the highly satirical and greatly successful *Tom Thumb* (1730) had come under heavy fire. This association with the laureate occasioned much closer attention to Fielding's work, especially on the part of the writers for *The Grub-Street Journal.* Plays such as Fielding's *The Modern Husband* (1732) were criticized not merely for dramatic unskillfulness but also for immorality. Nettled by these attentions, Fielding retaliated in *The Covent-Garden Tragedy* (1732) by depicting the editor of the *Journal,* Richard Russel, a nonjuring clergyman, as a pimp. The result was a "frontal and sustained attack" for six months on Fielding as an obscene and immoral writer. This "bombardment" waned only when Fielding ceased trying to defend his personal character and his satiric intentions.[4] It is indeed ironic that Fielding, who admired Pope as a writer and who assumed the pseudonym "Scriblerus Secundus" for some of his plays, should suffer the most damaging criticism of his career from a paper operating under Pope's auspices.[5] These early criticisms of Fielding and his writings as indecorous, immoral, and "low" were to prefigure charges repeated throughout his career and to occasion some of his bitterest feelings about the possibility of justice in criticism. Partisan, *ad hominem,* and unsubstantiated criticisms are recurrent themes in Fielding's own critical pronouncements.[6]

Fielding's movement toward political satire in *Pasquin* (1736) and *The Historical Register for 1736* (1737) brought highly unsympathetic criticism from both old and new sources. *Pasquin,* the first of five plays produced by Fielding's own company of players at the Little Theatre in

Haymarket, was severely taken to task by Marforio (probably Russel) in *The Grub-Street Journal* for its confused allegory and its satire on clergymen, lawyers, and physicians.[7] This sharp criticism came in the face of the great popularity of the drama. Even more momentous than the *Journal*'s lengthy attack on *Pasquin,* however, was the reaction of a spokesman for the government (probably Lord Hervey) to *The Historical Register.* Writing in *The Daily Gazeteer,* 7 May 1737, this spokesman warned that affronts to Walpole's ministry contained in Fielding's play might well lead to governmental control of all theaters in order to prevent further abuses. Here Fielding saw all canons of criticism subordinated to naked political power. His rejoinder to this warning was in vain; the following month the independent theaters, including Fielding's own beloved Little Theatre, were closed under provisions of the Licensing Act of 1737.[8] Suddenly confronted with the loss of vocation, Fielding was compelled to turn to a second career in law, in journalism, and in the writing of novels.

His highly miscellaneous literary output from 1737 to the close of this second career included periodical essays, translations, occasional poems, pamphlets, novels, and other works. Because much of this work was politically controversial in nature, Fielding became well known to his adversaries and in a sense increasingly exposed to the scurrilous rough-and-tumble of contemporary journalism. In particular, his writings in *The Champion* (1739–41) and *The Jacobite's Journal* (1747–48) seem to have instigated much of the abuse with which virtually all of his later works were greeted. It is undoubtedly true that Fielding's considerable gifts for biting satire and invective had much to do with the virulence of the attacks on his writings. So too, however, did his shifts of political allegiance through these years. Both his political plays and his writings for the antiministerial *Champion* identified him with the Opposition cause and brought him the vilification of the Walpole press. *The Jacobite's Journal,* however, espoused the governmental cause and soon brought charges from the Opposition that Fielding was a turncoat and political tool. Fielding himself spoke of the heavy "Load of Scandal" that resulted from his editorship of the *Journal.* Whatever the merits of his various defenses of one's right to change his political opinions and his attempts to distinguish between adherence to cause rather than to party, these apparently did little to screen him from the highly personal attacks of his opponents and their highly negative reception of his other writings.[9]

Of these other writings only *Joseph Andrews* (1742), *Tom Jones* (1749), and *Amelia* (1751) elicited critical responses that need be considered. Though the reactions of the various critics of the novels differed considerably, most emphasized a theme that had appeared earlier in the criticism of the dramas: Fielding violated neoclassical decorum and was thus low; at the same time his writings were true to life and sometimes praiseworthy for being so (Paulson and Lockwood, p. 7).

Joseph Andrews was by far the slowest of the novels to gain the public notice of critics. Although it was popular enough to require three London editions (some 6500 copies) within thirteen months, at first it was largely ignored in the journals. Whether deterred by Fielding's reputation as scurrilous dramatist and political controversialist or by doubts concerning the legitimacy of the work's genre, most of the critics deferred comment. Most of the notices focused either on aspects of the work, such as the character of Parson Adams, or on the theory of the ridiculous set out in Fielding's Preface. After Fielding began *The Jacobite's Journal,* with its highly particular treatment of the political and literary opposition, *Joseph Andrews* came under sharp critical attack along with his other writings. The theme of this notice by such publications as *The London Evening Post* was the familiar one of "lowness," applied to the novel and the novelist alike and widely repeated. This abuse undoubtedly figured in later critical misapprehension of what the novelist was about and occasioned many of his own comments on the requisites of fair criticism.[10]

The political motive was still evident several years later in the criticism of *Tom Jones.* Perhaps partly because the dedication of the novel contained praise of Lyttelton and the Duke of Bedford and associated Fielding with the Pelham ministry, the Opposition criticism strongly attacked the "immorality" of the book. In addition to personal abuse, which had been a regular feature of Fielding criticism since the dramas of the 1730's, the novelist had to endure attacks on *Tom Jones* as "prejudicial to religion and offensive to chaste eyes." [11] Richardson's words in a letter of 1749 (before he had read *Tom Jones*) sum up the *ad hominem* tendencies of much of the public criticism: "But, perhaps, I think the worse of the Piece because I know the Writer, and dislike his Principles, both Public and Private. . . ." [12] Neither the popular success of the work (four London editions, some 10,000 copies printed in the first year) nor the affirmative reactions of friendly critics could do much to shut off the outpouring of critiques stressing the "lowness" and moral reprehensibility of Fielding and his fictional characters (Blanchard, pp. 35 ff.).

On a slightly more theoretical plane, Fielding also came under attack for his concept of the hero of mixed character and the exemplification of this concept in the character of Tom Jones. This issue, already evident in the criticism of *Joseph Andrews,* became focal in various contemporary assessments of *Tom Jones* that stressed the potential for moral harm in such characters. An essay of 1750 by Samuel Johnson makes clear the uneasiness that didactic literary theorists felt when confronted by realistic elements in such a work as Fielding's novel:

But when an Adventurer is levelled with the rest of the World, and acts in such Scenes of the universal Drama, as may be the Lot of any other Man, young Spectators fix their Eyes upon him with closer Attention, and hope by observing his Behavior and Success to regulate their own Practices, when they shall be engaged in the like Part. . . .

It is therefore not a sufficient Vindication of a Character, that it is drawn as it appears; for many Characters ought never to have been drawn. . . .

Many Writers for the sake of following Nature, so mingle good and bad Qualities in their principal Personages, that they are both equally conspicuous; and as we accompany them through their Adventures with Delight, and are led by Degrees to interest ourselves in their Favour, we lose the Abhorrence of their Faults, because they do not hinder our Pleasure, or, perhaps, regard them with some Kindness for being united with so much Merit.[13]

These views indicate a strong reluctance on the part of contemporary critics to accept Fielding's protestations in the dedication of *Tom Jones* of his moral purpose in attempting "to laugh Mankind out of their favourite Follies and Vices" (*TJ,* I, 8).

The highly unfavorable critical reception of *Amelia* (1751) was in certain respects reminiscent of that accorded Fielding's serious comedy, *The Modern Husband* (1732). This work had been severely received for the directness of its satire on contemporary morality, especially for the episode in which Mrs. Modern's husband persuades her to sell herself to Richly for a sum of money. Critics had also found much to object to in the fact that characters of higher social rank behaved if anything worse than those of lower.[14] Contemporary reactions to *Amelia* included similar charges and added others to them. For example, the hostile critics were particularly abusive about the notorious oversight by which Amelia, having suffered serious injury to her nose, was thereafter left noseless by the failure of the novelist to relate to the reader anything about the success of the surgical procedures undertaken to repair the damage. With their usual scurrilous ingenuity the Grub-Streeters soon initiated a highly discrediting attack on Fielding's virtuous heroine as a "common wench who had lost her nose in the service of Venus" (Cross, II, 339). Dr. Johnson surmised that it was this oversight more than anything else that led to declining sales of *Amelia* (Blanchard, p. 95). If it is true that Fielding did indeed model his heroine on Charlotte Cradock, the scurrilities must have been personally painful as well as harmful to the public acceptance of his novel.

If such feelings existed, however, they are not explicit in the apology for the novel that Fielding wrote for his newly founded *Covent-Garden Journal* (January-November 1752). Admitting the faults of his heroine before the Court of Censorial Inquiry, Fielding mildly contended that she did not "deserve the Rancour with which she hath been treated by the Public."[15] This apology was unavailing, however, and the revised edition prepared by Fielding was not called for until after his death. At the very close of his career as a fiction writer, he thus experienced the damaging results of critical usages that had dogged his career from the 1730's. It is perhaps entirely to be expected that an author who endured much at the hands of the critics should often be brought to reflection about what does and what does not constitute adequate criticism.

II

The large amount of writing that Fielding devoted to comment on the critical malpractices of his day advances three main points: the offending critics are (1) ignorant or otherwise unqualified for their work, (2) pedantic and mechanical in their approach to literary texts, and (3) unjust in their dealings with authors. Of these, perhaps the incapacity of critics was for Fielding basic and logically prior. Critics unable to grasp the design of literary works typically called for observance of rules and were unable to be just.[16]

The first of these three points, the lack of special qualifications in critics of the day, is made in oblique but telling fashion in one of the satiric glossaries that Fielding used to comment on the connection between the misuse of words and the state of contemporary values. The word "critic" is followed by the gloss, "Like *Homo,* a Name common to all human Race."[17] Elsewhere, in words only partly masked by satire, he speaks regretfully of the "Revolution" that has occurred by which the "Constitutions of Aristotle, Horace, Longinus, and Bossu, under which the State of Criticism so long flourished, have been entirely neglected, and the Government usurped by a Set of Fellows entirely ignorant of those Laws" (*CGJ,* I, 138). This statement reflects the disgust of one who was himself a classical scholar of surprising range and depth with ill-read moderns who professed to be critics yet lacked the learning essential to their task. The matter is brought to a *reductio ad absurdum* in his satiric remark on yet another occasion that the only learning to be insisted on in the critic is that he be able to read.[18]

The same emphasis on the essential ignorance of critics appears in several of Fielding's dramas of the 1730's. For example, in the burlesque dramatic preface to *The Tragedy of Tragedies* (1731), Scriblerus Secundus follows the example of his progenitor in Pope's *The Art of Sinking in Poetry* (1727) by ludicrously misreading and mistranslating his classical authorities. Among the "scholarly" notes to the drama is one translating the famous passage from Aristotle's *Poetics,* vi, about the primacy of plot as "A Ghost is the Soul of Tragedy."[19] *The Convent-Garden Tragedy* (1732) intensifies the attack on critical ignorance with its parody of a criticism "intended for the *Grubstreet Journal.*" Declining to trouble the reader with definitions drawn from *"Aristuttle* or *Horase,*" this critic proposes to base his remarks on his own definition of tragedy: ". . . a Thing of five Acts, written Dialogue-wise, consisting of several fine Similies, Metaphors, and Moral Phrases, with here and there a Speech upon Liberty. . . . it must contain an Action, Characters, Sentiments, Diction, and a Moral." In the play itself, Mother Punchbowl finds Leathersides fully qualified to be a judge of literary merit since he is able to read, has read playbills, and has written for *The Grub-Street Journal.*[20]

Both *The Champion* and *The True Patriot* continue the ridicule of unqualified critics. Among other sallies in the first of these against critical ignorance is the stipulation that no one "be allowed to be a perfect Judge in any Work of Learning, who, hath not advanced as far as the End of the Accidence. . . ." The same paper prohibits any man from communicating his critical opinions by shaking his head "who is universally known among his acquaintance to have nothing in it."[21] Similarly, in *The True Patriot* Fielding develops the same point, this time with particular emphasis on the ways in which ignorance in critics can inhibit artistic production. Both poets and prose writers are said to "labour under this Calamity of being try'd by Judges who never read the Laws over which they preside." The result is that some writers prefer not to write at all than to be tried in such a tribunal. To make matters worse, the critics who know least and are the least capable are "the most rigid Asserters of their own Jurisdiction" (*TP,* p. 159).

The ignorance and incomprehension of critics also receive notice in Fielding's lucianic dialogue *A Journey from this World to the Next* (c. 1742) and in *Tom Jones* (1749.) In Chapter viii of the former work the critic Addison is gently derided for pretensions to erudition that are proven to be unsubstantiated in fact. When Virgil is apprised of Warburton's discovery of the Eleusinian mysteries in *Aeneid,* vi, Addison does not recognize the allusion and asks why Virgil never mentioned these mysteries to him. Virgil's reply points the satire: "I thought it was unnecessary . . . to a man of your infinite learning: besides you always told me you perfectly understood my meaning." After this rebuff, Addison is "out of countenance" and forced to turn to Richard Steele for reassurance that "he had been the greatest man on earth . . ." (*Works,* II, 246–47). In *Tom Jones* one of the thrusts at critics also scores the lack of essential learning. "Fielding" observes that playwrights who give their female characters certain general traits which they share with, say, Dido are saved from charges of plagiarism only by the fact that "very few of our Play-house critics understand enough of *Latin* to read *Virgil.*"[22]

Along with this damaging ignorance of vital subject matter often went the complementary evil of pedantry and the mechanical application of critical rules. Fielding addressed some of his liveliest satire to this problem. Thanks to *A Tale of a Tub* (1704) and *The Dunciad* (1728, 1742), the names of certain critics and editors had by Fielding's time become part of the literary capital of the time, to be drawn on by anyone who wanted to ridicule pedantry. The names were those of John Dennis (1657–1734), Richard Bentley (1662–1742), and Lewis Theobald (1688–1744), all three of whom receive attention in Fielding's satires as horrible examples of how pedantry and its attendant mechanical outlook can blight criticism.[23] Allusions to one or more of these "pedants" appear in each of Fielding's extended satiric treatments of the problem, although in most of these his animadversions clearly go beyond the merely personal. His major target is of course the folly and the lack of proportion in criticism for which the names of Dennis, Theobald, and Bentley (perhaps not always justly) had become symbolic.

The pedantry of the textual annotators is brilliantly satirized in *The Tragedy of Tragedies,* with its burlesque editorial preface and apparatus of annotations. The notes to this work have been aptly called "little essays in obfuscation which darken rather than illuminate an already murky text" (Hatfield, p. 61). Even those that form part of the satire on various dramatic styles and speeches recall the pointless quotation of parallel passages by many commentators of the day. Other notes display conflicting emended readings of passages for which no emendation is needed or bring together arcane explanations for passages said to be unclear. Lines of uncommon flatness are said to reflect "The Beautiful Simplicity of the Antients."[24] Scriblerus Secundus thus becomes something of a composite figure incorporating most of the faults that Fielding found ridiculous "in Restoration and Eighteenth Century drama critics in general and John Dennis is particular."[25]

The same device of burlesque pedantry is employed in "The Vernoniad" (1741), a lengthy political satire in the form of a mock-epic poem. In this work Fielding praised Admiral Edward Vernon for his exploit at Porto Bello and criticized Walpole and his government for their "languid pursuit of the war with Spain."[26] Perhaps the most enduring interest of the work, however, is its lively satire on scholarly dullness. The editor and commentator on this "Homeric" work offers it to the public with a monstrous apparatus of emendations, explanatory notes, and scholarly conjectures that threatens to swallow up the text. The chief satiric target here is that archemender, Richard Bentley, together with Joseph Trapp (1679–1747), whose translation of Virgil was heavily and absurdly annotated (Cross, I, 292). In notes of spurious erudition that sometimes verge on the ribald (see *Works,* XVI, 46), Fielding offers a parody of the efforts of "that Laborious Tribe the Commentators" (Williams, p. 123). His opinion of such activities by the critics is perhaps best summed up by an acid comment in one long note that without Bentley's celebrated commentary on Milton, "it is more than possible few of us would have understood that poet in the same surprisingly fine manner with that great critic" (*Works*, XVI, 55).

Other notable treatments of pedantically absurd critical interpretations are to be found among Fielding's periodical essays and in *A Journey from this World to the Next*. The latter work includes an account of a dispute between the shades of the actors Betterton and Booth about the correct placement of accents in the line from *Othello*, V, ii, "Put out the light, and then put out the light." In the course of the argument the two are led to suggest various improvements (e.g., "Put out thy light, and then put out thy sight.") and are finally driven to consult the shade of the author himself about the proper reading of the line. When consulted, however, Shakespeare avers that he no longer remembers his meaning when he wrote the line and adds a fairly explicit evaluation of such critical activity: ". . . could I have dreamt so much nonsense would have been talked and writ about it, I would have blotted it out of my works; for I am sure, if any of these [readings] be my meaning, it doth me very little honour." When interrogated further, Shakespeare explicitly states the characteristically neoclassical position that "the greatest and most pregnant beauties are ever the plainest and most evidently striking." He therefore cannot understand why men trouble themselves to discover "obscure beauties in an author" (*Works*, II, 247–48). This remark implicitly questions the need for much of the insensitive and pedantic textual commentary of the day.

The satires on this topic in Fielding's periodical essays also draw on the nearly inexhaustible fund of Shakespearean commentary. A paper in *The True Patriot* largely devoted to political satire on the short-lived ministry of Granville and Bath also ridicules the emendations of Lewis Theobald. Some one and a half columns are devoted to editorial comment on Macbeth's words (*Macbeth*, V, v) beginning "Life's but a walking shadow" together with the two preceding lines. These latter are ludicrously corrected to "And all our Yesterdays have lifted Tools/The Way to Dusty Death. Out, out brief Cabal." The effect of the whole commentary is that imputed by Fielding to much critical activity of this kind: ". . . according to the usual Custom of Commentators, [it] reduces the Author's meaning to nothing" (*TP*, p. 145). Such is certainly the case in the brilliant satiric commentary in *The Covent-Garden Journal* on the soliloquy in *Hamlet*, III, i, beginning "To be, or not to be–that is the question." Having corrected the opening line to "To be, or not. To be! That is the Bastion," the commentator then goes on to emend each line, until he arrives at a kind of triumph over his text in the following "restoration": "—Thus the native Blue of Resolution,/Is pickled o'er in a stale Cask of Salt."[27]

In addition to thus satirizing pedantry among the commentators and textual critics, Fielding also gave attention to the mechanical application of the rules by contemporary judicial critics. Like Johnson and other neoclassic thinkers, Fielding was impatient with the prescriptive way in which the pseudo-Aristotelian unities of time and place were applied by dramatic critics.[28] Other considerations such as the five-act rule of Horace also seemed to him to be arbitrary and divorced from the practice of modern writers. In the concluding speech of *The Historical Register,* the author Medley calls on the critic Sourwit for assistance so that he "may have no elaborate treatise writ to prove that a farce of three acts is not a regular play of five" (*Works,* XI, 268). In *Tom Jones* "Fielding" questions the validity of both the unities and the five-act rule and suggests that such laws come into being because critics mistake accidentals in great literary works for things essential to the attainment of greatness. In time critics who begin as humble recorders of literary practices become lawgivers to writers. One result is that many rules are established that "curb and restrain Genius" much as a dancing master might be restrained "had the many excellent Treatises on that Art, laid it down as an essential Rule, that every Man must dance in Chains" (*TJ,* I, 211).

The same point is made in *The Covent-Garden Journal* with respect to Shakespeare. In what purports to be a letter from the pen of Tragicomicus, a Bedlam lunatic, there is mention of those "abominable Rules," the three unities of Aristotle. Though he concedes that Aristotle's principles might have been in accordance with the realities of Greek drama, Tragicomicus argues that they are no longer appropriate to modern plays. With a madness very close to the neoclassical good sense of Dryden and Johnson, he contends that had Shakespeare observed the unities, "he would have flown like a *Paper-Kite,* not *soar'd like an Eagle.*"[29] This statement approximates Fielding's own habitual aversion to those rules that seemed to him to be constrictive and out of touch with the practice of authors. Clearly when applied mechanically by some criticaster of the time, rules could be both a troublesome form of pedantry and an instrument of critical injustice.

The other malpractices to which Fielding devoted attention are even more obviously related to the problem of injustice in criticism. About such matters as partisan and *ad hominem* critical judgments he wrote with the dearly bought expertise of one whose writings had been thus condemned. Both his gift for stinging personal satire and his activism in political causes made it difficult for anything from his pen to be approached with impartiality. In view of much of the Grub-Street criticism of the plays and novels, it is therefore not surprising that Fielding should have concerned himself with the role of prejudice in critical judgments. Thus in the Advertisement to *The Universal Gallant* he comments on the prejudice that is all too clear when a play is condemned without being heard and points out the damage done to the livelihood of a working author by critics who "make a jest of damning plays" (*Works*, XI, 77). Again, in *The True Patriot* he satirizes the prejudice of the playhouse critics. Having gone to the theater, Fielding is struck by the vehemence and persistence with which two others present express their disapproval of the play. When he seeks an explanation, they reveal the ludicrously *ad hominem* character of their literary judgments. The catcalls of one critic are motivated by the fact that the playwright "was in possession of a very pretty Girl, for whom he had himself a violent Affection." The other critic is equally negative, though with a bias that is political rather than personal: "Ay damn him. . . . *I hate the Fellow, because he's a Whig.*" Fielding dryly observes that so many literary judgments now depend upon whether the author belongs to the critic's party that it will soon be necessary for an aspirant to literary greatness to request aid of a political leader: *"Sir, I desire you will let me be a great Poet, or be pleased to let me have a great deal of Wit and humor, in my Writings."* Perhaps thinking of the critical response to many of his own works, he says that those who refuse to be permanently identified with any one party can expect to have their writings abused by all.[30]

A critical shortcoming noticed by Fielding even more frequently than partisan bias was that of irresponsible condemnation of works, together with the attendant evil of critical vagueness. His concern with this problem is reflected in works written throughout the entire range of his career. In dealing with it in the dramas of the 1730's Fielding combined conventional references to fault finding with satire on the critical vagaries of ill-informed but fashionable lords and their capricious but equally splendid ladies. Vermilia in *Love in Several Masques* (1728) finds the world to be a "censorious, ill-natured critic" whose "cavillings" she despises. This opinion of critics appears also in the prologues, epilogues, and advertisements of several other plays as well as in dramatic speeches of Lovegirlo in *The Covent-Garden Tragedy* (1732) and Trapwit in *Pasquin* (1736).[31] In these references Fielding is making conventional comic and satiric use of established stage properties.

In a similar vein are several extended satiric treatments of fashionable critics who damn plays while knowing very little of them. A clear example is Lord Formal in *Love in Several Masques,* who discloses to Merital his manner of dealing with the critical problem: "By going to a bookseller's shop once a month, I know the titles and authors of all the new books; so when I name one in company, it is, you know, of consequence supposed I have read it; immediately some lady pronounces sentence, either favourable, or not, according as the fame of the author and her ladyship's cards run high or low—then good manners enrol me in her opinion." In reply Merital ironically speaks for the reader: "A very equitable court of justice truly" (*Works*, VIII, 27). In much the same way the "fine Gentleman" whose critique forms part of the satire in the Prolegomena to *The Covent-Garden Tragedy* arrives at his critical judgment without troubling himself to experience its object. He is considerably irritated at being kept from seeing his favorite "Shakespearean" play, *The Earl of Essex*, by a "damn'd farce" which he abominates so much that he has "never either seen it, or read it." [32] Equally irresponsible is Lord Dapper in *The Historical Register*, who concludes that the play he is judging is "damned stuff" without having seen it. For good measure he condemns the playhouse for its lack of mirrors, certainly a source of dissatisfaction for one who wishes to see not so much the play as himself. Dapper points out that he does usually see "something of the play" when passing from the greenroom to the boxes and therefore "perhaps may be as good a judge as another." [33] Clearly in these treatments of the theme of critical irresponsibility Fielding is thinking less of the depth of his analysis than of the farcical potentialities of the material.

His more serious analyses of the problem emphasize the tendency of critics to read out of context, to dwell upon inessentials, and to dismiss literary works with vague and defamatory terms such as "low" or "sad stuff." An early example of emphasis on critical malice is to be found in his defense (in a letter to *The Daily Post*, 31 July 1732) of his dramas against the attacks of *The Grub-Street Journal*. After noting the generally defamatory character of the criticisms of the plays, he examines particular instances in which the Grub-Streeters have convicted his works of indecency, immorality, and blasphemy. The critics have attempted to make their case by "tearing out several Passages, without inserting whole Speeches or making the Reader acquainted with the Character of the Speaker. . . ." [34]

The use by critics of such vaguely discrediting terms as "low" and "sad stuff" frequently receives attention in Fielding's works and seems to have been one of the main abuses that often led him to regard contemporary criticism as slanderous. A paper in *The Champion* comments on this practice in relation to the damaging effects of unjust censure on the livelihood of authors. To those who have no special interest in destroying the reputation of writers he recommends caution in the use of such words as "low," "dull," "stupid," "sad-stuff," and "Grub-street." Wishing all such words banished from the language, he nevertheless recognizes that this action might well impoverish the vocabulary of practicing critics. One of a number of Fielding's astringent parallels between critics and beaus underlines the point and establishes guilt by association: ". . . this [banishment] might be as fatal to Criticism, as the Banishment of indecent Words hath been to Gallantry; and . . . some Persons of admired Judgment would be as hard put to it to talk critically without the one, as some noted Beaus are to talk wantonly without the other." [35]

The matter is pursued in *Tom Jones* and in *The Covent-Garden Journal,* both of which point up the injustice of using general, vague, and loaded terms in place of a substantiated critical appraisal of the work in question. In "A Crust for the Critics," the introductory chapter to Book XI of *Tom Jones,* Fielding examines some ways in which critics fail to live up to the example set by such "proper judges of writing" as Aristotle, Horace, Longinus, Dacier, and Bossu. Among the more serious deficiencies noted is the slanderous use of pejorative though vague terms without accompanying comments on particular faults in the work being criticized (*TJ,* II, 569–70).

This attack on critical irresponsibility is continued in *The Covent-Garden Journal.* In a censorial instruction, Alexander Drawcansir lays down the requirement that critics fully substantiate their unfavorable judgments of works. He adds a specific prohibition against justifications that make use of expressions such as "low stuff." In a later number the same point is made obliquely as Amelia is tried, as character and as novel, before The Court of Censorial Inquiry. Counsellor Town contends that she is a "low" character and that the entire novel is "a Heap of *sad Stuff, Dulness, and Nonsense. . . .*" Town's charges are supported by the testimony of a witness, Lady Dilly Dally, who has stated that the work is "sad Stuff from Beginning to End." Under questioning, however, the witness is unable to remember even the title of the novel she is condemning. At length she admits that she has only been repeating what she overheard from another "critic." Not surprisingly the authorial parent of Amelia decides to extricate his child from this prosecution—in exchange for the promise to offer the world no more fictions.[36]

Other forms of critical irresponsibility also receive Fielding's notice. In a number of his works he is concerned with the tendency of critics to engage in minute fault finding that largely incapacitates them for proper appreciation of literary works. A related problem is that of criticism which does not take account of a work's total design and thus results in piecemeal censure. The first point is developed with special force in *The Jacobite's Journal, Tom Jones,* and *The Covent-Garden Journal,* all works of Fielding's later years. In a paper written while he was himself being "subjected to savage personal abuse by his political opponents and insulted as a literary hack" (Williams, p. 207), he argues that such great critics as Aristotle, Horace, and Quintilian did not write in order to discover flaws. Indeed, not even Scaliger, "the sourest of all good Critics," had such a conception of criticism. Yet modern critics merely point out faults and by saying nothing of the strengths of the work suggest that it has none. Fielding urges that judicial critics notice both strengths and weaknesses, "that the Public may judge which preponderates."[37]

The attack on one-sided criticism is continued in the introductory chapters of *Tom Jones*. There "Fielding" takes account of the equation of critic with censurer and critical judgment with condemnation (*TJ*, II, 566). In an ironic defense of his prolegomenous chapters he suggests that they serve to prepare the critic so that "he may fall with a more hungry Appetite for Censure on the History itself " (*TJ*, II, 833). Other prefatory chapters advocate a holistic and a balanced approach to the criticism of the novel. In one he admonishes a "little Reptile of a Critic" not to find fault with the parts of the work until he has seen how they fit into the whole (*TJ*, II, 525). Another chapter argues for a sense of proportion in literary judgments. Long works are not to be condemned for incidental faults. Similarly the flaws may be compensated for by the work's beauties. Fielding closes this chapter with a comment on the unreasonably harsh and ill-natured criticism that would damn whole works because of some offending detail: "To write within such severe Rules as these, is as impossible, as to live up to some splenetic Opinions; and if we judge according to the Sentiments of some Critics, and of some Christians, no Author will be saved in this World, and no Man in the next" (*TJ*, II, 571).

Critics blinded to positive literary values by minute fault finding are a target of the satire on pertness in literature in *The Covent-Garden Journal*. In a form similar to that of Pope's *Art of Sinking* (1728) the essay offers advice on how the aspiring writer can attain to "the Pinnacle of the true Pert." The disposition to find faults in the writing of others is presented as a great aid in this endeavor. Perhaps not surprisingly, the fault-finding Homeric criticaster, Zoilus, is invoked as the father of criticism. In language that is a near parody of Longinus on the Sublime, Misotharsus explains how "the Height of the Tharsus" (i.e., the pert) depends upon one's high opinion of oneself and how this "hopeful and profitable Disposition" is fostered by dwelling on the faults of other writers while ignoring the beauties of their works. The result of this course of action is analogous to the way in which the eye focused on small objects is unfitted to survey broad landscapes. Similarly, the critic engaged in discovering blemishes in a work "becomes incapable of perceiving the Beauties of its Disposition, and its principal Parts, they lying far beyond the Reach of his Discernment." This incapacity, here identified as a "Contractedness of Comprehension," is said to be most helpful to the aspirant to the pert in that it encourages him to think about the flaws in works by other writers instead of seeing just how far short of perfection his own writings are. The mention of John Dennis as one of the authors from whom the would-be fault finder can learn helps to make it clear that the satire is not wholly playful. Similarly, in the

closing remarks of his "letter to the editor," Misotharsus directs attention to the "numerous Army" of other contemporary critics from whom
the same lesson can be learned: "But let my hopeful Disciple herd with
the modish Majority; let him, with erected Ears, greedily drink in; let
him retain, meditate upon, and digest their free, easy, and airy Effusions;
Effusions not smelling of the Lamp but perfumed with a natural,
unlaboured Essence; quickened with a light volatile Spirit, and grate-
fully acidulated with the poignant Juice of Cavil." From this "modish
Majority" the disciple of the pert can expect to learn that slowness in
commendation but quickness at cavil which Fielding often attacked as
an impediment to critical justice (*CGJ*, II, 18–22).

III

Statements about how the shortcomings of contemporary criticism
might be overcome or avoided are relatively infrequent in Fielding's
works, for he "failed to establish a mode of analysis to compete with the
arbitrary system he had grown to hate." [38] Nevertheless, his attacks on
the critics and some of his own attempts at practical criticism enable us
to infer what he thought was needed. His desiderata for an adequate,
principled criticism correspond to his view that the critics were ignorant, pedantic, and unjust.[39] Both his literal and ironic statements
suggest that he saw the need for a criticism that was informed, genially
responsive to creative practice, and fair.

The vital importance of learning to adequate criticism is stated both
directly and with satiric obliqueness. For example, in *The Covent-
Garden Journal* he sets as one of the qualifications for admission to the
"Order of Critics" the reading and comprehension of Aristotle,
Horace, and Longinus in the originals. The same paper makes the point
ironically as follows: "To require what is generally called Learning in a
Critic, is altogether as absurd as to require Genius. Why should a Man
in this Case, any more than in all others, be bound by any Opinions but
his own? Or why should he read by Rule any more than eat by it? If I
delight in a Slice of Bullock's Liver or of Oldmixon, why should I be
confined to Turtle or to Swift?" [40] A later number of the *Journal* points
out the important relation between education and the improvement of
taste, that rare quality resulting from a "nice Harmony between the
Imagination and the Judgment." Fielding suggests that though all men
cannot hope to rival the imagination and judgment of a great critic such
as Longinus, the minds of most possess "some small Seeds of Taste" that
await the nurture of education (*CGJ*, I, 196–97). Although learning
cannot impart such innate characteristics as genius and power of imagi-

nation, it can greatly enhance critical efforts and can result in an informed criticism. In Fielding's view this criticism would be both adequately grounded in critical theory and so generally knowledgeable as to avoid the blundering interpretations and the ungrounded judgments that he knew firsthand in the criticism of his own dramas and novels.

In addition to knowledge of critical theory and general culture the critic needed a sensitivity to the actual practice of writers. Long before Coleridge's comments on "genial criticism" Fielding expressed the idea of an approach to the work that was in the spirit of its originative principle. His view of the matter is succinctly expressed by words that form a part of a well-known sally in *Tom Jones* about the relation between ale and the reading of history: ". . . every book ought to be read with the same spirit and in the same manner as it is writ." [41]

The same work half-seriously develops Fielding's concept of the author as fictional experimenter and "Founder of a new Province of Writing." In the introductory essay to Book II he asserts his consequent lack of accountability to "any Court of Critical Jurisdiction whatever" for variations in lengths of chapters and in the scale and pace of the narrative (*TJ,* I, 76–77). The implication of this line of thought is that the critic must be aware of the inventions of writers and allow them to broaden the horizon of his critical expectations.

This point is made explicit in the vigorous attack (Book V, Chapter i) on the legislative pretensions of critics. Here Fielding develops an account of criticism as founded originally on creative practice but in time seeking to become prescriptive in its dealings with authors: "Now, in Reality, the World have paid too great a Compliment to critics, and have imagined them Men of much greater Profundity than they really are. From this Complaisance, the Critics have been emboldened to assume a Dictatorial Power, and have so far succeeded that they are now become the Masters, and have the Assurance to give Laws to those Authors, from whose Predecessors they originally received them" (*TJ,* I, 210).

Instead of remaining a clerk and recorder of the laws derived from artistic practice, the critic advances dictates of his own (*TJ,* I, 211). Hence the pedantry of reference to now inapplicable rules such as the pseudo-Aristotelian unities. Such pedantry might be seen as the unfortunate result of a criticism that has lost touch with creativity.

An additional requisite for an adequate criticism was that it be fair and impartial in its appraisals. It is here that the connections between Fielding's views about criticism and his general moral outlook are most obvious. In a sense all that he wrote against unfairness in criticism can be seen as but one aspect of his critique of society from the standpoint of a Christian censor and moralist.[42] When he writes in *Tom Jones* that

". . . the Man of Candour and of true Understanding is never hasty to condemn" (*TJ*, I, 329), it is uncertain from the context whether the comment has more direct application to literature or to life. On the other hand, the fact that Fielding's criticism does reflect his general moral presuppositions need not prevent us from seeing that it is also in part the attempt by a critically maligned writer of dramas and novels to foster critical justice.

The emphasis on justice at the hands of critics becomes especially evident in the attention that Fielding gives to the solitary figure of the disinterested critic whose knowledge and integrity qualify him to render meaningful and just assessments. An example can be seen in the character of Honestus in *Eurydice Hissed* (1737). The appropriately named Honestus is depicted as an incorruptible judge of dramatic merit who decries the lack of impartiality in the reception of contemporary plays. Despite the efforts of the playwright Pillage to enlist his aid in boosting the play, Honestus remains true to his basic critical convictions. In blunt words that are anything but reassuring to Pillage, the critic states his position: "If you have merit, take your merit's due;/ If not, why should a bungler in his art/Keep off some better genius from the stage?" In a later speech he reaffirms his intent of both applauding and censuring justly.[43]

Fielding's playful discussion in *The True Patriot* of The Weather-Glass of Wit suggests a "scientific" alternative to playhouse critics less adequate and reliable than Honestus. In a letter dated from Crane Court, the home of the Royal Society, Torricelli, Jr., explains his remarkable discovery of an infallible (and of course completely just) method of assessing dramatic merit. This turns out to be a unique thermometer that indicates the "degree of *Heat* or *Coldness* in the *Understanding*" of authors as this is reflected in their writings. The device is calibrated in accordance with the general neoclassic emphasis on moderation and distrust of extremes. From Good-Sense at the midpoint, the scale extends upwards successively to Vivacity, True-Wit, Wildness, and Madness and downwards to Gravity, Pertness, Dullness, and Stupidity or Folly.[44] Among the advantages of such a device pointed out by Torricelli, Jr., is that it could inform dramatic audiences as to whether the wit in a new play more properly merited hisses or applause. Similarly, the Weather-Glass might prevent the ruin of many deserving authors by guiding readers who now have "no certain Rule" for judging new books. Fielding's "correspondent" argues that his instrument thus affords a better means of assaying literary worth than other widely used expedients such as judgment by the author's honorary titles, by the dedication of the work, or by the person for whom the work was printed (*TP*, p. [186]). Despite the comic tone of this extended *jeu d'esprit,* it is clear that Fielding is here addressing himself obliquely to the serious matter of the need for sensible and impartial criticism. The Weather-Glass is in fact yet another example of his propensity to make "significant critical observations in the guise of horseplay." [45]

Fielding's Courts of Criticism also occasionally reflect his emphasis on critical impartiality. Although some of the court proceedings and associated papers are used as a vehicle for invective and topical satire, others embody ideas about the need for a criticism free from the ills of critical unfairness and irresponsibility. In *The Jacobite's Journal*, for example, the Court is instituted for the express purpose of counteracting certain Grub-Street activities such as the puffing of undeserving works. [46] In a later number of the paper Fielding employs the device of a letter from a correspondent who commends the Court's favorable but impartial judgment of Richardson's *Clarissa* (1747). The letter expresses the hope that by good example the Court will foster disinterestedness in critical writing (*JJ*, p. 188). In these papers, as in the appearances of the Court of Censorial Inquiry in *The Champion* and *The Covent-Garden Journal*, there is the preoccupation with justice, which appears to have been one of Fielding's abiding concerns.

How well he was able to avoid critical injustice in several instances in which he himself evaluated writings by his contemporaries can be seen from his discussions of works by two friends, Edward Moore and Charlotte Lennox, and of a novel by his chief rival, Samuel Richardson. The guiding principles of his criticism of the critics emerge with particular clarity from these discussions. The critiques hardly fulfill present-day notions about the purposes of literary commentary; nevertheless, each clearly reflects the qualities of learning, sensitivity to creative practice, and fairness that Fielding held to be indispensable to good criticism. Though they do not manifest the judiciousness and power of style that send us again and again to *The Lives of the Poets*, Fielding's reviews are commendable exemplifications of his principles.

His criticism of Edward Moore's drama *The Foundling* (1748) was published in *The Jacobite's Journal* in one of the proceedings of The Court of Criticism. In dealing with this controversial play, from which he was later to appropriate the subtitle of *Tom Jones*, Fielding seems to have been unduly swayed neither by his friendship with Moore nor by the negative response to the work in the theater. [47] The Court's opinions are delivered in a balanced critique of the play's weaknesses and strengths, beginning with exceptionable plot elements and characters. Objections are made to aspects of the incident on which the plot of the play turns: the bringing by a male character of a young woman into his father's house under the pretext that she is the son's ward, "left to his Care by a Friend." Fielding objects to the improbable manner in which both this story and the young woman are accepted by other members of the family. In addition Faddle, one of the characters strenuously objected to by the contemporary audience, is found to exhibit his rascality too openly and to be dealt with by other characters in ways that violate the decorum of those characters. Balancing these defects are merits that lead the Court to a favorable judgment. These include affecting characterizations of the principals, Fidelia and Belmont, lively dramatic speeches, and the skillful management of plot. In addition, Fielding judges the play to be commendable for its depiction of "The Struggles between a virtuous Disposition and vitious Habits" and for its portrayal of the redemptive power of shame in ameliorating Belmont's character. Finally, the play is defended as an example of the comic genre against critics who objected that it led more often to tears than to laughter. In this defense Fielding both enlisted Horace's dictum, *"Interdum tamen et vocem comoedia tollit"* (*Ars Poetica,* l. 93), and also pointed to the actual practice of Steele in *The Conscious Lovers* (1722).[48] The critique strikes the reader as the work of a critic who is informed, sensitive to creative realities, and alert to both strengths and weaknesses.

These characteristics are also evident in his critique in *The Covent-Garden Journal* of a novel by Charlotte Lennox, an admirer of Richardson and later a friend to Johnson, Goldsmith, and Fielding himself. Although the work, *The Female Quixote* (1752), is now unread, Fielding's critique of it does well serve to point up his guiding principles. As the title suggests, the novel concerns the life of a girl who has "formed her idea of the life by reading the heroic romances. . . ."[49] After noting that the novel is an imitation of Cervantes's work, Fielding, speaking through proceedings of the Court of Censorial Inquiry, undertakes a "balance sheet" account of the various ways in which the work excels, equals, or fails to measure up to *The Life and Actions of that Ingenious Gentleman Don Quixote of the Mancha.* He finds the original superior to the imitation in originality, capacity to offer instruction as well as entertainment, and in the characters of Don Quixote and Sancho Panza. In addition, Cervantes's work is seen to have the advantages of dramatic presentment and of a main character who performs "Feats of Absurdity" himself rather than merely observing or provoking these in others (*CGJ,* I, 280).

After noting the success of both writers in creating endearing though flawed characters, Fielding then turns to points in which Lennox's work is seen to have the advantage. These include the perhaps theoretically negligible considerations of the Female Quixote's greater attractiveness because of her youth and beauty and of the greater interest of her situation. More substantive advantages are found in the English work's greater coherence and verisimilitude. On the basis of these strengths Fielding commends the work as a "most extraordinary and most excellent Performance" that is both diverting and instructive (*CGJ,* I,

281–82). Although posterity seems not to have endorsed this favorable assessment, the critique does show the extent to which he tried to take a new work on its own terms and to recognize its merits as well as its obvious defects.

Finally, Fielding's generous praise for his great rival, Samuel Richardson, further serves to illustrate his capacity to escape the limitations of personal bias. In the guise of a correspondent to *The Jacobite's Journal* he gives high praise to Richardson's *Clarissa* (1747), the work that was the chief competitor of *Tom Jones* for contemporary fame. The extent to which Fielding in December of 1747 was aware of Richardson's unfavorable opinions (many of them expressed in private letters) of his own writings is perhaps indeterminate, but as the author of *Shamela* and *Joseph Andrews* he could hardly have expected favor. Nevertheless, he gives remarkably high praise to Richardson's work for its affective power and artistry. In commenting on Richardson's mastery of the techniques by which the emotions of readers are engaged, Fielding quotes lines from Horace that were so satisfactory to Richardson that he appended them to the final volume of his novel:"—*Pectus inaniter angit, / Irritat, mulcet, falsis terroribus implet, / Ut Magus—.*" [50] Even more explicit praise of *Clarissa*'s affective power appears in a private letter that Fielding wrote to Richardson in October 1748. Although he acknowledges that the two are in rivalry for "that coy Mrs. Fame," Fielding gives unstinting recognition to the psychological penetration of Richardson's delineation of character and to the emotive impact of the fifth volume of *Clarissa*. It is revealing to compare Fielding's appreciations with the slighting, often unsubstantiated and unfair comments about Fielding that appear in Richardson's letters to his own circle of admirers.[51] Fielding's greater openness to artistic techniques and to values different from his own is immediately apparent. So too is his comparative freedom from the bias that he encountered in much contemporary criticism. In this respect as in others, the instances of Fielding's practical criticism underline principles that guided his criticism of the critics.

NOTES

[1] *Letters of William Shenstone,* ed. Duncan Mallam (Minneapolis, Minn.: Univ. of Minnesota Press, 1939), p. 140. Letter to Lady Luxborough, 7 April 1749. This letter is reprinted in part in *Henry Fielding: The Critical Heritage,* ed. Ronald Paulson and Thomas Lockwood (London: Routledge and Kegan Paul, 1969), p. 164; hereafter, Paulson and Lockwood. For arguments that the introductory chapters are integral to the complex effect of the novel, see Wayne C. Booth, *The Rhetoric of Fiction* (Chicago: Univ. of Chicago Press, 1961), p. 217; Fred Kaplan, "Fielding's Novel about Novels: The 'Prefaces' and the 'Plot' of *Tom Jones,*" *SEL,* 13 (1973), 535–49; John Preston, "*Tom Jones* and 'The Pursuit of True Judgment,' " *ELH,* 33 (1966), 315–26.

[2] I am indebted to the useful but overly general and fragmentary accounts in F. P. Van der Voorde, *Henry Fielding: Critic and Satirist* (1931; rpt. New York: Haskell House, 1966), pp. 89–91, 101–05, 199–200, and Richmond Croom Beatty, "Criticism in Fielding's Narratives and His Estimate of Critics," *PMLA*, 62 (1934), 1087–1100. See also John C. Metcalf, "Henry Fielding, Critic," *Sewanee Review*, 19 (1911), 137–54 (an undocumented study), and the inaugural dissertation by Bruno Radtke, *Henry Fielding als Kritiker* (Leipzig: Mayer and Müller, 1926), especially "Fieldings Anschauung über die Kritik," pp. 7–17. A more recent study of the relations among Fielding's moral concerns, irony, and convictions about language makes the excellent point that exposure of the debasement of critical language was for Fielding a habitual mode of attack on the critics. See G. W. Hatfield, *Henry Fielding and the Language of Irony* (Chicago: Univ. of Chicago Press, 1968, pp. 56–66.

[3] *The Criticism of Henry Fielding*, ed. Ioan Williams (New York: Barnes and Noble, 1970), p. 78; hereafter, Williams. For other editions cited, I have employed the abbreviations given below immediately following the titles to which they refer: Martin C. Battestin, ed., *The History of the Adventures of Joseph Andrews* (Oxford and Middletown, Conn.: Wesleyan Univ. Press, 1967) *JA;* Martin C. Battestin and Fredson Bowers, eds., *The History of Tom Jones: A Foundling*, 2 vols. (Oxford and Middletown, Conn.: Wesleyan Univ. Press, 1975) *TJ;* W. B. Coley, ed., *The Jacobite's Journal and Related Writings* (Oxford and Middletown, Conn.: Wesleyan Univ. Press, 1975) *JJ;* James T. Hillhouse, ed., *The Tragedy of Tragedies* (New Haven: Yale Univ. Press, 1918) T *of* T; Gerard Jensen, ed., *The Covent-Garden Journal*. 2 vols. (New Haven: Yale Univ. Press, 1915) *CGJ;* Miriam Austin Locke, ed., *The True Patriot* (University, Ala.: Univ. of Alabama Press, 1964) *TP;* Henry Knight Miller, ed., *Miscellanies Volume I* (Oxford and Middletown, Conn.: Wesleyan Univ. Press, 1972) *Misc.*); For works by Fielding not included in these editions, I have cited from William Ernest Henley, ed., *The Complete Works of Henry Fielding, Esq.*, 16 vols. (New York: Croscup and Sterling, 1903) *Works*.

[4] James T. Hillhouse, *The Grub-Street Journal* (Durham, N.C.: Duke Univ. Press, 1928), pp. 173–74, 185; Wilbur L. Cross, *The History of Henry Fielding*, 3 vols. (1918; rpt. New York: Russell and Russell, 1963), I, 123–41; Paulson and Lockwood, p. 2.

[5] For further evidence bearing on Fielding's early attitudes toward Pope (and towards Walpole), see Isobel M. Grundy, "New Verse by Henry Fielding," *PMLA*, 87 (1972), 213–45. Grundy points out that Fielding's attitudes towards both men were "fluctuating and difficult to define" (p. 213).

[6] It is now sufficiently clear that issues other than the moral one were involved in many of the negative critical responses to Fielding's plays. Political bias is all too apparent in much of the criticism. Moreover, Fielding's impetus towards the representational insured that when his focus was inelegant life, his works would be found to be "low." In addition, critics referring his drama to the models of sentimental comedy or the comedy of manners would be unlikely to credit his defense of farce as a satiric medium (see Prologue to *The Lottery*, 1732). It is probably also true that hostile critics deliberately confused the productions of Fielding's exuberant genius with biography. See Winfield H. Rogers, "Fielding's Early Aesthetic and Technique," *SP*, 40 (1943), 529–51; Paulson and Lockwood, pp. 1, 7; Hillhouse, p. 185.

[7] Hillhouse, p. 183; Paulson and Lockwood, pp. 83–95.

[8] Paulson and Lockwood, pp. 98–105; Cross, I, 205–37.

[9] I am indebted to W. B. Coley's masterly account of the backgrounds and impact of

Fielding's political journalism. See *JJ*, pp. lxi–lxxxii. Coley points out the defenses of changing one's party advanced by Fielding in *The True Patriot* (1746), his other "ministerial" paper (pp. xlvii–xlviii). See *TP*, pp. [133], [205]. For the ridicule by Fielding's antagonists of his marriage to his former housekeeper, Mary Daniel, see *JJ*, pp. lxxx–lxxxi and Cross, II, 60–62.

   ¹⁰ Frederic T. Blanchard, *Fielding the Novelist: A Study in Historical Criticism* (1926; rpt. New York: Russell and Russell, 1966), pp. 1–25; Paulson and Lockwood, p. 6. For some of the views expressed in private correspondence (including Samuel Richardson's ungenerous remarks about *Joseph Andrews*) see Paulson and Lockwood, pp. 120–43, 186.

   ¹¹ Paulson and Lockwood, pp. 10–11; Cross, II, 126; Blanchard, p. 31.

   ¹² Letter to Astraea and Minerva Hill, 4 Aug. 1749; rpt. in Paulson and Lockwood, pp. 174–75.

   ¹³ *Rambler* No. 4, 31 March 1750; rpt. in Paulson and Lockwood, pp. 232–33. Johnson does not mention Fielding's name or the title of the novel in this essay.

   ¹⁴ Paulson and Lockwood, pp. 2, 16–17; Beatty, p. 1097.

   ¹⁵ *CGJ* No. 8 (28 Jan. 1752), I, 186.

   ¹⁶ W. R. Irwin, "Satire and Comedy in Henry Fielding," *ELH*, 13 (1946), 171–72. Irwin's categories of critical incapacity, ill-temper, and pretence are suggestive but not sufficiently inclusive for my purposes.

   ¹⁷ *CGJ*, I, 155. Cf. I, 147.

   ¹⁸ *CGJ*, I, 149. For a brief account of Fielding's citations from classical authors, see Frederick Olds Bissell, *Fielding's Theory of the Novel* (1933; rpt. New York: Folcroft, 1970), pp. 20–21.

   ¹⁹ *T of T*, pp. 84–85, 127. Scriblerus hopes to do editorial justice to the play, having "for ten years together read nothing else" (p. 80).

   ²⁰ Williams, p. 14; *Works*, X, 113. Cf. similarly unflattering remarks about critics in *Euridice* (1737), *Works*, XI, 271–72.

   ²¹ Williams, p. 65. Cf. similar barbs directed at the ignorance and presumption of critics, Williams, pp. 59, 63–64; *Works*, XV, 121.

   ²² *Works*, II, 246–47; *TJ*, II, 526. See also *TJ*, I, 489; II, 739–40. Cf. Preface to *Familiar Letters* (1747), Williams, p. 133.

   ²³ For a brief account of contemporary literary reactions to these and other scholar-critics of the time, see A. Bosker, *Literary Criticism in the Age of Johnson*, 2d ed. (Groningen, Djakarta: J. B. Wolters, 1953). See also Bonamy Dobrée, *English Literature in the Early Eighteenth Century* (London: Oxford Univ. Press, 1959), pp. 303–05.

   ²⁴ *T of T*, pp. 90, 156, et passim.

   ²⁵ George R. Levine, *Henry Fielding and the Dry Mock: A Study of the Techniques of Irony in His Early Work* (The Hague: Mouton, 1967), p. 37. Cf. *T of T*. pp. 37–39.

   ²⁶ *JA*, p. xvii. See also Martin C. Battestin, "Pope's 'Magus' in Fielding's *Vernoniad:* the Satire of Walpole," *PQ*, 46 (1967), 137–38.

   ²⁷ *CGJ*, I, 315–20. Fielding's sense of the subjectivity and caprice that weakened much of the textual commentary of the time is humorously indicated by the commentator's insistence that in cases where the original reading seemed better than the suggested emendation, "the Reader must be left to his Choice."

   ²⁸ The validity of neoclassical rules and the relation of these to the writer's creative powers was a central issue of much early eighteenth-century critical writing. Dobrée points out that the discussions of the critics drew on both Lockean faculty psychology

and Longinus (p. 306). The latter was made generally available in 1712 by Leonard Welsted's translation. See also Samuel H. Monk, *The Sublime: A Study of Critical Theories in Eighteenth-Century England* (1935; rpt. Ann Arbor, Mich.: Univ. of Michigan Press, 1960).

[29] *CGJ*, II, 93. Along with many of his contemporaries Fielding customarily attributed all three unities (action, time, place) to Aristotle. Actually, of course, only the first of these was held by Aristotle to be necessary. Renaissance Italian commentators such as Cinthio and Castelvetro added the unities of time and place as requisites. Much of the legalistic spirit, the emphasis on rules, in the writings of Fielding's eighteenth-century antagonists was prefigured in the Renaissance literary theory of Vida and the Scaligers. In the early 1580's the three unities received attention in Sidney's *Apology for Poetry*. By the latter part of the seventeenth century, writings by Boileau, Rapin, Bossu (one of Fielding's favorite critics), and Dacier had established the doctrine as "an essential article of neo-classical orthodoxy." In England this view was represented in the critical writings of Thomas Rymer, John Dennis, and Joseph Trapp and was attacked by Dryden, Fielding, and Johnson. See Battestin, *TJ*, I, 209, n. 1; Walter Jackson Bate, ed., *Criticism: The Major Texts* (New York: Harcourt, 1970), p. 9; J.W.H. Atkins, *English Literary Criticism: Seventeenth and Eighteenth Centuries* (1951; rpt. London: Methuen, 1966), pp. 73–78, 369.

[30] *TP* No. 18, 25 Feb.–4 March 1746, p. [159].

[31] *Works*, VIII, 62, 189; IX, 281; X, 33, 119; XI, 77–78; XII, 130; *T of T*. p. 53. For similar comments in Fielding's poetry, see *Misc.*, pp. 24, 26, 64.

[32] Williams, p. 13. Fielding represents this critic as in some confusion as to the tone of *The Covent-Garden Tragedy*. Observing that more people laughed than cried at the play, the critic is disposed to regard it as a failed tragedy.

[33] *Works*, XI, 247–48. Several of Fielding's periodical essays admonish would-be critics not to issue unfavorable opinions of works without first having read them. See Williams, p. 65; *CGJ*, I, 149.

[34] Williams, p. 21. The letter is signed "Philalethes."

[35] Williams, p. 63. See also *Works*, XV, 335.

[36] *CGJ*, I, 149, 178–80.

[37] *JJ*, pp. 136–37. Such "balance-sheet" criticism is of course admirably exemplified in Johnson's *Prefaces Biographical and Critical* (later entitled *Lives of the English Poets*), 1779–81.

[38] George Watson, *The Literary Critics: A Study of English Descriptive Criticism* (Baltimore: Penguin Books, 1962), p. 80.

[39] For a similar approach to critical principles reflected in Pope's *Peri Bathous*, see Bertrand A. Goldgar, ed., *Literary Criticism of Alexander Pope* (Lincoln, Neb.: Univ. of Nebraska Press, 1965), pp. xviii–xix.

[40] *CGJ*, I, 148–50. John Oldmixon (1673–1742) published several historical works and an *Essay on Criticism* (1727). The latter defends critical rules as "in Nature and in Truth" (Dobree, p. 211). For other references by Fielding to Oldmixon, see *TJ*, I, 214–15, and Pat Rogers, "Fielding's Parody of Oldmixon," *PQ*, 49 (1970), 262–66.

[41] *TJ*, I, 151. Battestin (n. 2) points out earlier neoclassical parallels and possible sources in Pope's *Essay on Criticism* (1711), 233–34, and Swift's *Tale of a Tub* (1704), Preface. Cf. S. T. Coleridge, "On the Principles of Genial Criticism," Essay I (1814), *Biographia Literaria and Aesthetical Essays*, ed. J. Shawcross, 2 vols. (London: Oxford Univ. Press, 1907), II, 222. See also N.S. Tillett, "Is Coleridge Indebted to Fielding?"

SP, 43 (1946), 675–81; and Ernest Dilworth, "Fielding and Coleridge," *N & Q,* 203 (Jan. 1958), 35–37.

[42] Williams, pp. xiii–xiv. On Fielding's moral position see J.A. Work, "Henry Fielding, Christian Censor," in *The Age of Johnson: Essays Presented to Chauncey Brewster Tinker,* ed. F. W. Hilles (New Haven, Conn.: Yale Univ. Press, 1949), pp. 139–48; Martin C. Battestin, *The Moral Basis of Fielding's Art: A Study of Joseph Andrews* (Middletown, Conn.: Wesleyan Univ. Press, 1959).

[43] *Works,* XI, 301, 303. In *The Champion* Fielding cites Saint-Evremond (1616–1703) to the effect that "good judges are as scarce as good authors" and that there is real danger that their opinions will be stifled by "the ignorant and prepossessed multitude . . ." (*Works,* XVI, 86).

[44] *TP,* p. [185]. Williams notes Fielding's probable indebtedness to *Spectator* No. 281, 22 Jan. 1712, for this idea (p. 353).

[45] Maurice Johnson, *Fielding's Art of Fiction* (Philadelphia: Univ. of Pennsylvania Press, 1961), p. 15.

[46] *JJ,* pp. 127–28. Fielding's John Trott-Plaid, "Censor of Great Britain," relates the Court to that conducted earlier by Isaac Bickerstaff, the persona of Addison and Steele in *The Tatler* No. 162, 22 April 1710. See *JJ,* p. 90. Coley notes that much censure and some praise of the Court had a "personal basis" (*JJ,* p. lviii). This is, of course, incontestable, but what I wish to consider here is Fielding's use of the Court as a vehicle for his ideas about fair criticism.

[47] Cross, II, 90, 107. Cross speculates that Fielding might have based the account in *Tom Jones* of Sophia's fright at the disorder in the theater (XIII, xi) on the boisterous reception of Moore's play.

[48] *JJ,* pp. 207–09.

[49] Williams, p. 191; Cross, II, 414. The quixotic heroine is finally brought to her reason by "the arguments of a worthy divine" (Williams).

[50] *JJ,* pp. 119–20; Cross, II, 141–42. The quotation is from Horace, *Epodes,* II, i. 211–13. In the accompanying comment Fielding refers to witchcraft rather than the art of the magician.

[51] Williams, pp. 188–90. Cf. Paulson and Lockwood, pp. 174–75, 186, 215, 238, 334–36. Although the possibility that Fielding's remarks might be partly ironic cannot be entirely discounted, I have followed Battestin, Coley, Williams, and others in taking the praise at face value.

JACK D. DURANT ✑ THE "ART OF
THRIVING" IN
FIELDING'S
COMEDIES

CERTAINLY ONE OF THE MOST STRIKING PASSAGES in *An Essay on the Knowledge of the Characters of Men* (1743) is an early one in which Fielding defines what he calls the "Art of thriving," a capacity that "points out to every individual his own particular and separate advantage, to which he is to sacrifice the interest of all others; which he is to consider as his *Summum Bonum*, to pursue with his utmost diligence and industry, and to acquire by all means whatever."[1] Why some people devote themselves vigorously to this art and some do not is a question hard to answer. Perhaps the reason lies in an "unacquired original distinction in the nature or soul of one man, from that of another" (XIV, 282); but whatever the reason, the fact is that most people set out to perfect the art of thriving, and as a consequence "the world becomes a vast masquerade, where the greatest part appear disguised under false vizors and habits." Only a very few people show their own faces, and by doing so they become "the astonishment and ridicule of all the rest" (XIV, 283). These few, who by an "open disposition" reveal an "honest and upright heart," are, alas, the ones most liable to be "imposed on by craft and deceit" (XIV, 283). But with sufficient diligence even they can pierce the masquerades worn "on the greater stage" of life, and Fielding writes the *Essay* in behalf of this diligence.[2]

It is hard to imagine a handier or more comprehensive organizing principle for the study of Fielding's theatrical comedies—the eight "regular" comedies, as distinct from the farces and burlesques [3]—than this concept of the art of thriving. The world of his stage, like that "greater stage" he refers to in his *Essay,* is peopled with thrivers of the most accomplished sort. Some of them, like Lord Formal in *Love in Several Masques,* have sought their "particular and separate advantage" in pompous formalities and pseudo-urbanities. Others, like young Pedant in *The Temple Beau,* have bought absurd and useless knowledge at the expense of their own humanity; and yet others, like the utterly disarming Sotmore in *Rape upon Rape,* have chosen to "thrive" by just opting out, looking to 'rack punch and usquebaugh as the ultimate reality. Such thrivers as these, reprehensible and ridiculous as they are, threaten few people other than themselves. Of much greater significance to Fielding's comic concerns are the hard thrivers, the people whose particular advantages abuse and bemean others and bring all human relationships into the common marketplace.

Sir Avarice Pedant of *The Temple Beau* is such a one. He has long since disabused himself of any concern except money, and in this interest all people are for sale. A yet more savage avarice afflicts old Lovegold of *The Miser* (translating Moliere), who worships gold with votive fervor, and the most devastating instance of thriving for money occurs in *The Modern Husband,* where Mr. Modern arranges with his wife's full consent to sell her favors to the wealthy Lord Richly, a social predator who thrives arrogantly on lesser people's desperate and graceless zeal to thrive. Old Politic of *Rape upon Rape* finds his "separate advantage" in frenzied and fruitless preoccupations with national affairs. Consequently his private domestic affairs fall to chaos. And in this same play Justice Squeezum, the most determined artist of them all, pursues his advantage by classifying human character and conduct, studying the types of people likely to assist in and accede to his abuses of the law. The less sympathetic characters in Fielding's comedies, and of course the unsympathetic ones, function in fact as detailed studies in the art of thriving. Systematically and deliberately they "sacrifice the interest of all others" to their own selfish aims, obviously seeing these aims as a *summum bonum* to pursue with "utmost diligence and industry, and to acquire by all means whatever." They people a world fragmented by aggressive self-service, "separate advantage," where hostility and mutual resentment aggravate most relationships, where institutions flourish in behalf of wickedness, and where private interests vitiate community. It is a world largely menacing and unstable, its threat intensified by the dramatic medium itself, the play, which traffics but two hours and lacks the amiable reassurances of Fielding's narrative voice.

Many features of form in Fielding's comedies relate directly to his concept of the art of thriving. In pursuing their obsessive self-interests, the thrivers conceive a stunning variety of intrigues and stratagems, eavesdroppings, masquerades, blackmailings, and double dealings. Accomplished practitioners of the art display enormous daring and imagination, but they also run high risks of exposure and embarrassment. Hence their gifts must assist them in surviving discovery; for should their stratagems misfire, they must bring themselves off fully and gracefully, the better to thrive another day. Fielding never tires of comic evasion scenes. They function importantly for him in building suspense and tension and in controlling comic momentum and resolution. They give dramatic formulation to the art of thriving.

A lively instance of such a scene appears in *The Temple Beau* (IV. ii–vii), where Lady Gravely, just warming to the passion of Young Wilding, hears suddenly the approach of his father, Sir Harry. Quickly hiding her lover in the closet, which he locks from inside, she endures an interview with Sir Harry, then another with Lady Lucy Pedant, her spiteful sister-in-law, who suddenly pleads the vapors and asks a spoonful of ratafia. The ratafia, says Lady Gravely, is in the closet and the key lost. In fact, the bottle is broken. But "you have more," insists Lady Lucy, "for I drank some this morning" (IV. v). As they struggle at the door, Young Wilding suddenly emerges from it armed with the astonishing story that he was hidden there not at the urging of Lady Gravely but of Lady Lucy herself, who had engaged him in a wager about Lady Gravely's fear of ghosts. "If upon my stalking as frightful as possible, your ladyship shrieked out," he says, "I was to lose the wager." It is a masterpiece of evasion on the part of Wilding. By seeming to protect Lady Gravely's reputation at the expense of Lady Lucy's, it makes Lady Gravely receptive to his advances later on. It opens an opportunity in the following scene for him to convince Lady Lucy that he dallies with Lady Gravely only in the service of Lady Lucy herself, who wishes to expose the false honor of Lady Gravely. It keeps both ladies at his service so long as he wants them, and it opens the means by which he extricates himself at last from their claims upon him, a stratagem he effects by causing them to discover one another at his supposed apartments, to which he has deliberately sent them at the same hour of assignation.

Other of the comedies feature comparably daring and complex evasion scenes. When in *Rape upon Rape* Hilaret and Sotmore set the liberal conditions by which Justice Squeezum may extricate himself from charges of rape (IV. vii–ix), the wicked old jurist contrives to arrest his benefactors by means of their own instrument of conciliation, a letter releasing the innocent Constant from custody. In *The Universal Gallant,* Mrs. Raffler abuses her credulous husband simply by outcountenancing him, encouraging his stupid assumption that she has staged for humane purposes the episode in which he overhears her acknowledge infidelity to him (V. i). And in *The Wedding-Day,* Millamour assumes the role of a physician and claims credit for saving the life of Clarinda, who affects great illness on being discovered by her husband, old Stedfast, while she visits in Millamour's apartments. Millamour must permit the discovery because he has already secreted Charlotte Stedfast, old Stedfast's daughter, in his closet, but his talent for thriving makes him equal to the situation and even opens to him an opportunity to see Clarinda again later, when Stedfast summons him to attend as her physician. As it functions in Fielding's comedies, the art of thriving dictates innumerable scenes such as this, scenes in which aggressively self-serving characters extricate themselves from scrapes brought upon them by their own sheer effrontery. Counterstratagems alone can defeat them, ambushes laid against their privacy (as in *The Wedding-Day* and *The Fathers*) or spiteful double crosses (as in *Rape upon Rape*), and even then they seem to suffer only temporary setbacks, for nothing short of private reformation really damps their determination to thrive. They show a disturbing capacity to prevail.

Another feature of form dictated by the art of thriving, at least insofar as form relates to conflict, is the prevailing and usually vicious conflict in Fielding's comedies among members of the same family. Late in *An Essay on the Knowledge of the Characters of Men,* after he has "enumerated the principal methods by which deceit works its ends" and has pointed out "the symptoms by which [these methods] may be discovered," Fielding recommends "one more certain rule" that if followed will go far to "extirpate all fallacy out of the world." This rule, he says, is "carefully to observe the actions of men with others, and especially with those to whom they are allied in blood, marriage, friendship, profession, neighborhood, or any other connection" (XIV, 301). If someone is proposed for a trust, it is wise to "trace him into his private family and nearest intimacies." If he discharges well the duties of son, brother, husband, father, friend, master, or servant, he will likely merit a confidence, but "if he hath behaved himself in these offices with tyranny, with cruelty, with infidelity, with inconstancy, you may be assured he will take the first opportunity his interest points out to him of exercising the same ill talents at your expense" (XIV, 301). Since so forcefully felt a social principle is certain to make its mark upon Fielding's dramatic representations of experience, bitter familial discords, effects of the art of thriving, certainly pervade his comedies.

In *The Temple Beau,* for example, chicanery within the family not only blights the relationship of Lady Gravely and Lady Lucy but also that of Sir Avarice Pedant and his son, of Young Wilding and his father, of Veromil and his ruthless brother, who robs him of his patrimony by vilifying him in the eyes of their father. In *Rape upon Rape,* old Politic, having banished his son and placidly considered him hanged, chafes even to care for a dutiful daughter and complains that while "the bull, the horse, the dog, are not encumbered even with their own offspring," man "when once a gabbling priest hath chattered a few mischievous words over him, is bound to have and to hold from that day forward all the brats his wife is pleased to bestow on him" (V. i). Justice Squeezum, in the same play, contemplates the dangers of putting one's wife in the "power to hang" one—in which case "the sooner you are hanged the better" (II. iii)—and he consoles himself later to think that the advantage of cuckold's horns is "that he may shove his wife out of doors with them" (IV. i). *The Modern Husband* is everywhere a miasma of wicked familial infighting, where "marriage is traffic throughout" (II. vi), where fathers and sons have no cause to communicate, except when they "talk of money matters" (II. ii), where a wife's person, when "bought" lawfully in church, may be disposed of with profit (IV. i), where the household broods a dark prison of the spirit. "My children are my greatest enemies," says Lovegold in *The Miser* (I. vii). "A woman never acts as she should, but when she acts against her husband," says Lady Raffler in *The Universal Gallant* (V. i). "Severity is, in short, the whole duty of a parent," says Old Valence in *The Fathers* (IV. i). Fielding's comedies devote themselves to nothing more persistently than to spiteful and calculated divisions between husband and wife, parent and child, brother and sister.

And such divisions perforce give rise to institutional corruptions in the world of the comedies, for "a worthy discharge of the social offices of a private station" is according to the *Essay* the "strongest security which a man can give of an upright demeanour in any public trust" (XIV, 302). Hence Worthy, in *Rape upon Rape,* whose character dramatizes itself chiefly through his close concern for his sister Isabella, everywhere shows himself a jurist worthy of high trust, while Squeezum, who nurtures contempt for his wife, abuses the law unconscionably and sees its principles as comparable to those of whoring (IV. vi). Mr. Modern, the wife seller of *The Modern Husband,* conceives his moneylust in terms of religion, seeing gold in this world as covering "as many sins as charity in the next" (I. iv), and Lord Richly of that same play extends his abuse of his nephew Gaywit into all his social dealings. Far from honoring the obligations of his station, he gives preferment to the undeserving and lays designs against the dignity of people less fortunate than he, having arrived, as his nephew puts it, "at a happy way of regarding all the rest of mankind as his tenants" (II. vi). While Lord Richly, who looks upon religion as hypocrisy, wants to scrap the institution entirely, together with common sense (II. v), Lady Raffler, of *The Universal Gallant,* wants to keep it handy as a means to torment her husband, whom she can abuse only so long as she is "virtuous." Her suitor, Mr. Mondish, a leech upon unsteady marriages, argues for his part that "Virtue requires" her infidelity, that she can avenge her husband's suspicions of her only by sacrificing her virtue (V. i).

The moral phenomenon is the same throughout the comedies: Ethical and social institutions developed for human safety and comfort fall prey to the cruelties and sophistries of corrupt people, people void of concern even for their own families. In effect the comedies dramatize a significant political conviction, the conviction that anarchy within the family figures forth anarchy within the state, that the public good is best served by the devoted family man, that, in the words of the *Essay*, "the bad son, husband, father, brother, friend; in a word, the bad man in private, can never be a sincere patriot" (XIV, 303). As an effect of the art of thriving in Fielding's comedies, families and social institutions largely lack cohesiveness and stability. They serve better the ends of anarchy than of order, and when order establishes itself in the plays, however arbitrarily, it generally takes the form of newly found family harmony, as it does in the resolutions of *The Temple Beau, Rape upon Rape, The Wedding-Day,* and *The Fathers.*

If Fielding's basic impression of human social conduct, as formulated in his concept of the art of thriving, dictates significant elements of form in his comedies, it also presents him with significant problems of comic resolution, problems inhering in the only suitable moral response to the thriving mentality, the "good nature" that Fielding defines famously in his *Essay on the Knowledge of the Characters of Men* as "That benevolent and amiable temper of mind, which disposes us to feel the misfortunes, and enjoy the happiness of others" (IV, 285). Ironically, the world of Fielding's social ideal is a world without comedy, certainly without judgmental comedy. If everyone were good natured, enjoying "that heavenly frame of soul, of which Jesus Christ Himself was the most perfect pattern"—and Jesus "never was once seen to laugh, during His whole abode on earth" (XIV, 286)—there would apparently be no comedy. As Joseph Andrews says, it is impossible to turn a true good action into ridicule (Bk. III, Ch. vi). Good nature has the troublesome property of dulling witty language and canceling comic conflict, a property certainly troublesome to the playwright who would offer good nature as a recourse from the art of thriving, and Fielding's comedies provide something of a study in his efforts to cope with the dramatic problems posed by good nature.

Actually, his first comedy, *Love in Several Masques,* hits upon a reasonably effective strategy for handling the problem. Here Lady Matchless, as yet unwilling to forego the art of thriving, rejects the good-natured Wisemore at the outset of the play and accepts him at the close, after she perceives his true merit in contrast to the stupidity of her other suitors. Her "education" provides a comic momentum of sorts, one intensified by suspense in behalf of Wisemore and derision against his rivals.

The Temple Beau, however, which is morally much more complex than *Love in Several Masques,* evinces the worst effects of the problem. Since the principal romantic couple, Bellaria and Veromil, display mature good nature throughout, they simply arrest the comic action by rising above the conflict. Aggravated by his false friend, Valentine, to suspect Bellaria's constancy to him, Veromil confronts Bellaria with the offense. He hears her denial, sees it to square with his knowledge of her character, believes it without argument, and puts to rest a most threatening (and promising) conflict (III. vii). In furthering his own designs to win Bellaria, Valentine casts off the good-natured Clarissa, to whom he returns on realizing that Bellaria will not have him. Clarissa sustains the conflict a bit by forgiving Valentine only from Christian motives, not reinstating him as a lover (V. ii), but before the scene is out she reinstates him fully. The conflict rests. Earlier, Veromil reproaches Valentine for breeching friendship. Valentine accedes readily enough to the accusation, again canceling the conflict (IV. x); even when, at the close of the play, passion gets the better of Valentine and aggravates an unsuccessful attack on Bellaria, forgiveness born of good nature quickly dissipates all discord. Veromil and Clarissa decline to bear grudges against Valentine, despite his record of erratic conduct. The dynamic of the comedy derives throughout from the art of thriving. Good nature consistently damps the conflicts.

The next of the comedies, *Rape upon Rape,* busies itself constantly with the implications of its title: attempted rape, supposed rape, imagined rape, disappointed rape, rape upon rape. Rape excites the action, and this action, confused and darkened by a nocturnal setting, aptly dramatizes a world gone mad with thriving, a world so bent upon "separate advantage" that it denies and inevitably violates the sanctity of person. Nowhere, as Justice Worthy laments, does virtue now claim awe (V. v), and good nature seems to stand at odds with good sense, a fact Constant perceives when in trying to prevent a rape he is taken up as the rapist. "I begin to be of that philosopher's opinion," he complains, "who said, that whoever will entirely consult his own happiness must be little concerned about the happiness of others." Then he adds, "Good nature is Quixotism, and every Princess Micomicona will lead her deliverer into a cage" (III. ii).[4] The good-natured characters win out in the end, but from no resourcefulness of their own. Justice Worthy, albeit a grave moralist, cannot divine the treacheries of his colleague Squeezum, whose defeat comes only through the spiteful counter-treacheries of his own wife, her evidence corroborated by one Faithful, who just happens in times past to have served old Squeezum and can now incriminate him with authority. Providence receives credit for these happy turns, but the good-natured characters appear no less dull for these Providential services. Again, the art of thriving dominates events,and the play best succeeds as a lively warning to the good natured that thriving lays its snares for them everywhere. Arbitrary Providential intervention provides few if any comforts.

In *The Modern Husband,* which again finds good nature canceling significant conflict, as Mrs. Bellamant forgives without condition her husband's cruel infidelity to her (IV. ix), a new address to the dramatic problem of good nature develops in the "trial" of Mrs. Bellamant, a trial brought against her virtue by the wealth and effrontery of Lord Richly and by the stupid provocations of her husband.[5] Considerable dramatic energy also results from the confrontation between Lord Richly and Mr. Bellamant, once Bellamant repents his infidelities to his wife (V. vi). But while the moral force of good nature seems in this play to figure more directly in delivering the sympathetic characters than it does in *Rape upon Rape*, it does not allay the disconcerting sense that the thrivers will prevail. Although disappointed in his scheme to ruin Bellamant, Lord Richly will obviously ruin many another in days to come, and Mr. Modern, though possibly denied the profitable divorce he wants, suffers no permanent deflation of spirit. Moreover, the business of the play generates too little comic exhilaration. The issues of wife selling and vicious moral exploitation give rise at best to a defensive circumspection in the audience and perhaps, at the close, to the hollow sense of triumph that comes of winning one battle in a never ending war. A really satisfactory resolution to the problem of presenting good nature as a viable answer to the art of thriving, and of giving the presentation a suitable comic liveliness, comes only with *The Fathers; or, The Good-Natured Man*, a comedy completed in 1743, but not staged until 1778, long after Fielding's death.[6]

The solution for Fielding lay in the dialectical form he developed for three other of his later comedies, a form rising to notice in *The Modern Husband* and achieving structural dominance in *The Universal Gallant* and *The Wedding-Day*. In *The Modern Husband* Mrs. Bellamant functions obviously as a counterpoise to Mrs. Modern, the virtuous wife contrasted dramatically to the vicious one; but for complex reasons of structure and emphasis, reasons centering chiefly on Fielding's efforts to garner sympathy for Mrs. Modern at the close, making her the victim of her husband, who is not a striking counterpoise to Mr. Bellamant, the system of contrast lacks consistency and balance. It also lacks, rather to its credit, the self-consciousness apparent in the dialectical form of *The Universal Gallant*, a comedy appositely subtitled *The Different Husbands*. In this play Sir Simon Raffler represents the madly jealous husband, a buffoon invariably disappointed in his attempts to discover himself a cuckold, while his brother, Colonel Raffler, represents the stupidly credulous husband, a cuckold of long standing who declines to mistrust his arrogant and abusive wife. Of similar form, *The Wedding-Day* features conflicts between Mr. Stedfast, who has never broken a resolution, and Mr. Mutable, who has never kept one. Both these plays generate lively and complicated intrigues, actions woven between the poles of the dialectic and exposing in various ways the follies of both extremes, but the dialectic so dominates the form that the play comes across as a treatise analyzing a prefabricated moral issue.[7] Good nature does not touch the concerns of *The Universal Gallant;* and while, in *The Wedding-Day,* Millamour's sudden good-natured reformation (V. iii) certainly slacks the conflicts, its damage is minimal for coming late and for washing into the current of Mrs. Plotwell's Gilbert-and-Sullivan-like disclosure that Clarinda, whom Millamour loves, is Stedfast's lost daughter and cannot be his wife, though they are already partners in a yet unconsummated marriage. Since the play commits itself chiefly to the concerns of the dialectic, it suffers the less for these fortuitious resolutions.

In *The Fathers* good nature becomes the concern of the dialectic. Here Old Boncour, the good-natured parent, stands in contrast to Old Valence, the ill-natured one. Each father has a son and daughter to be matched to the daughter and son of the other, and the action of the play reveals the unsuitableness of the two matches, since the young Valences, as children of a thriving father, prove morally unworthy of the young Boncours. Questions arise about the good-natured conduct of Old Boncour, questions raised chiefly by his crusty and doubting, though thoroughly amiable, brother, Sir George. Is Boncour too indulgent to his wife? Is he too permissive and generous to his children? Has he encouraged acquisitiveness in his family? It turns out that he does need to impose greater authority on his wife. She actually wants him to. But the children, when put to the test by Sir George, who causes them to think their father financially ruined, ratify in their own exemplary conduct the effects of a good-natured upbringing. In rushing without hesitation to their father's support, they demonstrate that a generous and loving relationship within the family engenders the principles and spontaneous practices of high character and mature moral discernment. Moral certainty and independence also appear in Miss Boncour's address to her suitors, one of whom, Young Valence, she rejects for offering indecencies to her and the other, Young Kennel, for his boorishness and misapplied education, faults in which his booby of a father has encouraged him and from which he will eventually recover, ultimately to deserve her. No feature of resolution in *The Fathers* is wholly arbitrary or ill motivated. The lessons of good nature, nurtured in and emanating from family harmony, find suitable dramatization in the play. Here as nowhere before in Fielding's theatrical comedy does his affirmative moral statement fully balance his negative one.

This is to say, of course, that the negative statement is comparably well developed. Old Valence devotes himself vigorously to the art of thriving. He looks upon his children as commodities to be sold for his own advantage; he abuses unfeelingly his nearest neighbor, and when his designs fail he reviles his own family openly, despising them for acting after his own wicked example. The play amply dramatizes the domestic hostilities in which the thriving mentality breeds and flourishes; and by disallowing a conventional happy ending it condemns the art of thriving as a continuing social threat. Old Bancour and Sir George apologize that no wedding concludes the play (V. v); they can only appeal to the good nature of the audience to forgive the omission, for Fielding declines to contrive a conventional ending for them. In devising for the play a structural formula suitable to the presentation of good nature, he does not compromise his most persistent comment on the art of thriving, that it is subtle and persistent and hostile to sensibility and good will.

A general reflection on Fielding's comedies certainly brings to mind some of the broad thematic affirmations of the novels. The comedies acknowledge in their way the interposition of Providence, the merits of Christian charity, the imperatives of good nature;[8] but, lacking the amiable tone of the novels and addressing themselves immediately and scenically, without narrative distancing, to the conduct of a disillusioned urbane society, they clearly take shape in Fielding's mind as studies in the art of thriving. Peopled by thrivers of the most resourceful sort, they inform themselves after the thriver's art, devoting much of their action to complex evasion scenes and drawing their conflicts from bitter domestic hostilities, hostilities that expose the thriver's commitment to his own "separate advantage," irrespective of human relationships intimate or remote, and that dramatize in a most disconcerting way the irrepressible devotion of the thrivers to their art, their disturbing capacity to prevail. To understand the art of thriving is to be instructed, certainly, in the characters of men, and Fielding's comedies offer this instruction amply and in detail, but just as forcefully they send up an alarm sent up as well in *An Essay on the Knowledge of the Characters of Men,* a warning to the "honest undesigning man" that he can never be "too much on his guard against the hypocrite, or too industrious to expose and expel him out of society" (XIV, 305). In effect, Fielding's comedies are "comedies of warning." Generating severe laughter of ridicule and dramatizing the subtle and persistent successes of the thriver's art, they give little convincing treatment to the concerns of Providence, and they cause their happy resolutions, though attributed to Providence and virtue, to seem arbitrary and wildly fortuitous, mere chance occurrences of improbable good luck that happen outside the processes of causality and that accrue to the benefit of people who deserve them only indifferently.[9] Perhaps the audience can nurture a hope that in God's time all will be well, but it cannot escape the impression that the world of logical motive and control, the world of day to day experience, belongs to the thrivers and that anyone addressing himself to this world must do so with extreme caution and circumspection.[10]

NOTES

[1] Quotations from Fielding's texts cite *The Works of Henry Fielding,* ed. W. E. Henley (London: William Heinemann, 1903; rpt. New York: Barnes and Noble, 1967). When citing Fielding's *Essay,* parenthetical page references within this discussion indicate volume and page; and when citing passages from Fielding's comedies, parenthetical page references indicate act and scene. Because scene changes occur with each change of *dramatis personae* in most of Fielding's comedies, causing the scenes to be quite short, act and scene designations provide sufficient documentation for reference.

[2] For a splendid comprehensive discussion of the backgrounds and aims of the *Essay,* see Henry Knight Miller, *Essays on Fielding's Miscellanies* (Princeton: Princeton Univ. Press, 1961), pp. 189–228. An excellent concise statement of background is also available in Thomas R. Preston, "Disenchanting the Man of Feeling: Smollett's *Ferdinand Count Fathom,*" in *Quick Springs of Sense: Studies in the Eighteenth Century,* ed. Larry S. Champion (Athens, Ga.: Univ. of Georgia Press, 1974), pp. 224–28.

[3] The comedies drawn upon in this discussion, together with their dates of composition, are *Love in Several Masques* (1727); *The Temple Beau* (1728–29); *Rape upon Rape* (1730); *The Wedding-Day* (1730); *The Modern Husband* (1730–32); *The Miser* (1732); *The Universal Gallant* (1733–34); and *The Fathers* (1743). These dates of composition follow the datings offered in L. P. Goggin, "Development of Technique in Fielding's Comedies," *PMLA,* 67 (1952), 769–81. Goggin also supplies dates of performance.

[4] This concept of good nature as Quixotism finds full treatment in Fielding's three-act ballad opera *Don Quixote in England* (begun 1728, produced 1734), where various types of thrivers function in effect as the giants with whom Quixote tilts.

[5] This instance of temptation as a formal and thematic strategy very possibly foreshadows Fielding's more fully developed application of it in *Amelia.* See J. Paul Hunter, "The Lesson of *Amelia,*" in *Quick Springs of Sense,* pp. 161–64.

[6] For a concise comment on this production, see *The Dramatic Works of Richard Brinsley Sheridan,* ed. Cecil Price (Oxford: Clarendon Press, 1973), II, 780–82. At the time of the production, Sheridan was manager of Drury Lane Theatre.

[7] Mark G. Sokolanskij, in "Genre Evolution in Fielding's Dramaturgy," *Zeitschrift fur Anglistik und Amerikanistik,* 20 (1972), 280–95, labels these dialectical plays "dramatic pamphlets."

[8] The authoritative discussions of these matters appear, of course, in M. C. Battestin's *The Moral Basis of Fielding's Art: A Study of Joseph Andrews* (Middletown, Conn.: Wesleyan Univ. Press, 1959); Aubrey L. Williams's "Interposition of Providence and the Design of Fielding's Novels," *SAQ,* 70(1971), 265–86; and M. C. Battestin's *"Tom Jones:* The Argument of Design," in *The Augustan Milieu,* ed. Henry Knight Miller, Eric Rothstein, and George Rousseau (Oxford: Clarendon Press, 1970), pp. 289–319. Henry Knight Miller, in *Essays on Fielding's Miscellanies,* pp. 54–88, provides what is perhaps the best comprehensive discussion of good nature as it relates to Fielding's thought.

[9] "Providence" is specifically credited with the happy resolutions in *The Temple Beau, Rape upon Rape,* and *The Wedding-Day.* The other comedies celebrate the triumph of "virtue," but in every case the resolutions are so ritualized as to dissipate their thematic force.

[10] Fielding's burlesque plays relate interestingly to these "regular" comedies by making the thriver's art the received and openly acknowledged code of social and moral conduct within the world of the burlesque.

ELEANOR N. HUTCHENS ❧ O ATTIC SHAPE!
THE CORNERING
OF SQUARE

TOM JONES IS GENERALLY REGARDED as being geometrically conceived, despite its well-recognized thesis that goodness is unsystematic. The
symmetry of the novel, its parallels and intersections and circularity of
plot, together with the strong logical control exercised by the narrator,
suggests the demonstration of a theorem, although its very precision
works to exclude the idea that life is to be lived by rule and line. A
continual discounting process, moving gaily along in the brilliant interplay of Fielding's verbal and substantial irony, seems to be hunting the
straight Euclidean trail toward a truth that will rise in all the strict
formality of the demonstration itself. The typical problem ends, however, not with *quod erat demonstrandum* but with *quod est absurdum.*
Fielding is using Euclid against Euclid, showing by elimination that man
at his best is nonlinear. The absurdity of rationalized wrong yields one
kind of comedy in the book, while the independent triumph of good
provides the other.

It is obvious on first acquaintance with him that the squareness of the
philosopher Square will not do as a guide to the good life. Abstraction
that it is, its invisible lines can be applied hypocritically at will to any
situation so as to justify or rule out whatever Square wishes to assert or
deny. Fielding, after playing off such selfish applications in several
incidents against the theologian Thwackum's equally corrupt religious
authoritarianism, indulges in a bit of geometrical fun by placing Square
literally in a triangle—Molly Seagrim's attic—and contrasting the figure
he cuts there with the free-standing human form of Tom Jones:

> The Room, or rather Garret, in which *Molly* lay, being up one Pair of Stairs, that is
> to say, at the Top of the House, was of a sloping Figure, resembling the great
> *Delta* of the *Greeks*. The *English* Reader may, perhaps, form a better Idea of it, by
> being told, that it was impossible to stand upright any where but in the Middle.
> Now, as this Room wanted the Conveniency of a Closet, *Molly* had, to supply that

Defect, nailed up an old Rug against the Rafters of the House, which enclosed a little Hole . . . where among other female Utensils appeared . . . the Philisopher *Square*, in a Posture (for the Place would not near admit his standing upright) as ridiculous as can possibly be conceived.

. . . .

. . . *Jones*, though perhaps the most astonished of the three, first found his Tongue . . . and then saluting Mr. *Square*, advanced to take him by the Hand, and to relieve him from his Place of Confinement.

Square, being now arrived in the Middle of the Room, in which Part only he could stand upright, looked at *Jones* with a very grave Countenance. . . .[1]

Being led into the middle where he can stand upright has no immediate effect on Square's moral rectitude, though perhaps it is a faint foreshadowing of his deathbed reformation, when we learn not only that he has become religious but that he shares the Christian name Thomas with Allworthy and Jones. (Heartfree in *Jonathan Wild* is named Thomas too.) But the nature and meaning of this middle, to which Fielding has drawn attention so insistently as the only place one can stand upright, must be important.

It is not a golden mean, a position between the fallacies of Square and Thwackum or of any other opposed and equally wrongheaded pairs in the book (Squire Western and his sister, the Nightingale brothers, perhaps the Old Man of the Hill and Mrs. Fitzpatrick, and various minor disputants like the landlady and the lieutenant in VII, xiii, 288–93). Allworthy, in retaining Thwackum and Square while seeing some of their faults, has erroneously imagined this middle position to promise good:

> He thought indeed that the different Exuberancies of these Gentlemen, would correct their different Imperfections; and that from both, especially with his Assistance, the two Lads would derive sufficient Precepts of true Religion and Virtue. If the Event happened contrary to his Expectations, this possibly proceeded from some Fault in the Plan itself; which the Reader hath my Leave to discover, if he can. . . . (III, v, 102)

Even the nicest balance between two opposing doctrines will not produce human good; only good human beings will do that, and their goodness neither orginates nor manifests itself geometrically. As Tom says, there is "no Rule in the World capable of making such a Man" as Allworthy (III, v, 101).

The beautiful balances of the plot are similarly incapable of affirming good. Consider the correlation between Tom's affair with Lady Bellaston and his father's with his mother. Tom, a naturally good human being, is the product of an illicit union between a pleasing young man and an older woman who has disdained her brother's suggestion that she marry the youth. Like his unknown father, Tom in his turn has an affair with an older woman. He extricates himself by a proposal of marriage, which she indignantly rejects. While the two cases are not precisely parallel, they share enough oddity to hint that they may cast light on each other. Lady Bellaston's suspicion that Tom is a fortune hunter may explain his mother's anger, long ago, at the idea of a match with his father; both women perhaps know in their hearts that their young paramours do not love them, and both have sense enough to draw back from marriage (Bridget not knowing, of course, that she will have a child). Moreover, watching Lady Bellaston seduce Tom and understanding his surrender—

> Jones had never less Inclination to an Amour than at Present; but Gallantry to the Ladies was among his principles of Honour; and he held it as much incumbent on him to accept a Challenge to Love, as if it had been a Challenge to Fight. (XIII, vii, 547)

—illuminates the fall of his father, presumably another good human being led into error by "principle." This backward glance, in its turn, lends a ghostly inevitability to Tom's ignoble affair with Lady Bellaston. The two illicit mismatches not only balance but help to explain each other. Their chronological positions, one before the beginning and another near the end of Tom's misadventures, and their importance, one giving him life and the other nearly depriving him of it, stress their mutual relevance. Their neighboring positions in the narrative, the discovery of Tom's parentage coming when he is still suffering the consequences of the Bellaston amour, present them for ready comparison. Finally, whereas his proposal to Lady Bellaston almost loses him Sophia forever, the news of his parentage removes her father's objections to him as her suitor. All this neatness is pleasing as geometry and as a buttress to probability, but what does it reveal about good nature? Only that it is liable to imprudence and can be imposed upon, especially if it acts upon principle. Its origins remain unprobed, and there is no neat definition of its form.

Bad nature, on the other hand, does take on outline—the distorted shape of Square hiding in the angle of the attic. The middle of the room, the only place one can stand upright, is the place where the human form is not bent to accommodate itself to geometrical lines. In respect to Molly, Tom is at least as guilty as Square, but when caught he does not take refuge in an angle. Fielding's epic simile of the stag points to the naturalness of Tom's behavior when Thwackum and Blifil approach the thicket where he and Molly are disporting themselves; instead of hiding, he leaps into the open to meet the invaders. He does so again when surprised with Mrs. Waters in the Upton inn, and when Honour comes at an inconvenient moment to his room it is (necessarily, in this case) Lady Bellaston who hides. Is the middle of the room, then, simply openness as opposed to concealment? Probably not; Tom conceals facts for the benefit of others, even to the point of lying. The middle of the room, the only place allowing the full extension of humanity, is a natural freedom from the systems man constructs to trap and define goodness, then uses to give plausible housing to badness.

The figure of Allworthy lays the ground for this reading early in the novel. The asymmetrical, natural character of the good man is carefully established in the description of his house, which is not Grecian but Gothic, and his grounds, which are dominated by "a plentiful Spring, gushing out of a Rock covered with Firs, and forming a constant Cascade of about thirty Foot, not carried down a regular Flight of Steps, but tumbling in a natural Fall over the broken and mossy Stones, till it came to the Bottom of the Rock; then running off in a pebly [sic] Channel, that with many lesser Falls winded along, till it fell into a Lake . . . [out of which] issued a River, that, for several Miles, was seen to meander through an amazing Variety of Meadows and Woods, till it emptied itself into the Sea. . . ." A smaller valley is "adorned with several Villages," and there is a "View of a very fine Park, composed of very unequal Ground, and agreeably varied with all the Diversity that Hills, Lawns, Wood, and Water, laid out with admirable Taste, but owing less to Art than to Nature, could give." Beyond all this irregularity and variety rise "wild Mountains, the Tops of which were above the Clouds" (I, iv, 32).

No matter how much learning is brought to this passage, how much knowledge of midcentury landscape art, pre-Romantic aesthetics, and actual Somersetshire topography is justly applied to it, its significant function in *Tom Jones* remains intrinsic. It is an index to Allworthy's character and thence to the nature of human goodness as exemplified later in Tom, the true heir to the estate. The plentiful spring, constantly gushing, not geometrically guided, but taking its own way; the river that meanders through variety; the unequal ground agreeably diverse, where art yields to nature; the untamed mountains, reaching into the invisible heavens as the river eventually finds another grand profundity—all this suggests the image of good nature that qualifies Tom's vagaries. It is an image with no shape but its own, and no earthly measure encloses it.

The early books of *Tom Jones* can be misread as demonstrating the consistent gullibility of Allworthy and the baseness of practically everybody else. Fielding warns, but does not show, that the good squire is not at all stupid. What he shows, if read myopically, is that this well-meaning man has surrounded himself with rogues who deceive him again and again. Or, if the cast of characters is taken as a statistical sample of the human race, then the overwhelming majority are bad, and the good, a tiny minority, are unintelligent.

The error of these interpretations arises from putting Allworthy into the geometrical system with the other characters. Properly seen, he walks solitary and free, meditating benevolence, while the others from their angular hiding places calculate their own advantage, balance each other in competitive knavery, and cancel each other out. Their angles are largely formed by the neat lines of abstract doctrine. Mrs. Wilkins would get rid of the infant Tom in the name of Christianity, whereas Bridget Allworthy, who ordinarily would reject him in the name of Virtue, accepts him under pretense of martyrdom to her brother's wishes. Captain Blifil wins Bridget partly by his skill in theological discussion, and his brother Dr. Blifil, another lay theologian, tries to insure himself against Allworthy's displeasure at the match by feigning virtuous indignation at it himself. Such playoffs between systems of religion and virtue, really between schemers pretending to religion and virtue, culminate in the Thwackum-Square match, a long contest ending only with the death of one and the disgrace of the other. At its climactic points, this duel balances Square's exposure in the triangle of Molly's attic against the thwacking of the birch-rod pedagogue later in the same book, when Tom is surprised with Molly in the grove.

The geometry of *Tom Jones,* then, is the geometry of wrong. Like the best of its verbal irony, which works by invoking absurd connotations, its elegant geometrical patterns mock their own seeming truth.

Even Allworthy, when he is seen occasionally as one of a pair and thus part of a neat arrangement, is likely to be wrong. Although he is a conscientious magistrate and Western an irresponsible one, his judgment is remarkably fallible. When the two of them contemplate the affair of Sophia's bird, it is Western, prompted by his sense of property and his fondness for his daughter, who comes closer to the truth. Thwackum boasts of having formed Blifil's character by Christian instruction, Square of having taught him to tell right from wrong by the law of nature. (Blifil has made an expert apologia for his conduct, showing his precocious ability to hide in opposite angles at the same time.) Western is unimpressed. "So between you both," he says to Thwackum and Square, "the young Gentleman hath been taught to rob my Daughter of her Bird" (IV, iv, 123). He is only half right; the two have not taught Blifil malice, but they have provided him with the angles of deception. Allworthy is deceived, not because he is stupid but because the good heart is unable to imagine the crouching postures of the bad one. No rug has yet fallen away, as in time it will, to reveal the crookedness of those he trusts. In the meantime, whenever he is framed by their world, he is condemned to be wrong, that is, mistaken, as they are wrong in the other sense. Sophia, balanced by nobody, is right. Like Allworthy in his natural state, she stands free. To pair the two as Tom's judges, or to make a geometrical figure of the three, is to ignore the autonomy out of which each of them speaks and acts. They do not invoke rules and systems to justify their own behavior, nor do they bring other people to judgment thus; so far, they are alike. But they differ from one another in ways that are not antithetical. Sophia's correct reading of Blifil comes not from a bad heart but from intelligent casting up of probabilities suggested by observed fact, as Fielding explains in another connection (XI, x, 471). Circumstances playing upon the emotions, such as his sister Bridget's partiality to Tom and detestation of Blifil (III, vii, 105–06), sway Allworthy, whose pity appeals to the principle of justice for support, toward the side of Blifil, not out of stupidity but because "thus is the Prudence of the best of Heads often defeated, by the Tenderness of the best of Hearts" (XVI, vi, 662). Tom is unlike Allworthy and Sophia in the violence of his feelings and his animal spirits, but the other two certainly are not devoid of passion. The three of them present a variety of good, flourishing in their different ways like the features of Allworthy's grounds.

Tom is undoubtedly balanced against Blifil, however, and their fortunes make a neat chiasmus. But Fielding frankly admits that Tom's rise and Blifil's fall represent a violation of his own commitment to the truth of human affairs: "There are a Set of Religious, or rather Moral Writers, who teach that Virtue is the certain Road to Happiness, and Vice to Misery, in this World. A very wholesome and comfortable Doctrine, and to which we have but one Objection, namely, That it is not true" (XV, i, 600). And as for the opposition of the characters of the two boys, careful examination shows that when Tom is set in contrast to Blifil it is nearly always his own imprudence that brings him into the frame with his enemy. Like Allworthy with Western, Tom is usually in error when he is paired with Blifil. The seeming exceptions are dubious: in the incident of Sophia's bird Tom is kept in the background as Blifil speaks with forked tongue and the grown people take over the argument; and in breaking the news of Blifil's exile to him (XVIII, xi, 750) in a spirit opposite to that of Blifil's letter (VII, ii, 250) on the occasion of Tom's own banishment, he is carrying out the pattern of poetic justice Fielding has declared to be false to life. Early in the novel, Tom's impulsiveness in pursuing the partridge leads him to deceive Allworthy (on principles of honor) and thus to appear at a disadvantage—not to the reader, to be sure, but to the critics around Tom. He and Blifil are heavily contrasted as boys; but most of the time the contrast is drawn by bad judges, and the comic geometry works itself out at their expense. When Tom is at his best, Blifil becomes merely the third in a line of serpents of his name who have invaded

Paradise Hall. The two are not parts of one geometrical figure when the final assignments of value are made; Tom far transcends the linear world that contains Blifil.

"I am not writing a System, but a History," says Fielding (XII, viii, 499), and his technique bears him out. Human nature in *Tom Jones* is what is left after all the logical and formal representations of it have been discarded. Human goodness stands forth spontaneous, natural, and organic, while human badness crouches in the shelter of a rule. Human nature includes the bad and the good but is never defined; the impulse of the bad heart to rationalize itself is as unaccountable as the impulse of the good heart to forget itself in feeling for others. Human nature is manifest in the thoughts, words, and deeds of all kinds of people, and he who has observed these can set himself up as the historian of life. *Mores hominum multorum vidit*—in giving this epigraph to his masterpiece Fielding may have thought of the author even more than of the hero as the observer of many men's ways. Observation, not dogma, is the offering of the book, and it follows that to speak of a moral system in *Tom Jones* is risky.[2] One of its main statements, both expounded and illustrated, is that a systematized morality is immoral. As Fielding often says, he relies on the heart of the good-natured reader to distinguish between good and bad in the book; he despairs of communicating good to the bad heart,which can see only reflections of itself, and all he can teach the good heart is to beware of the bad.

Hence the theme of prudence. It is not only Tom, but the good-natured reader as well, who must acquire this self-defending quality. It is part of Fielding's comic method to apply the word "prudent" laughingly to those characters who put self-interest first; not only are its good connotations ludicrously inapplicable to them, but the use of the word suggests that they themselves would invoke it to justify their selfish policies. A system of prudential behavior, even without any intent to harm or deceive, is clearly unsatisfactory, as Fielding shows in the isolationism of the Man of the Hill and speaks of in the introductory chapter of Book XV. The good man must merely take prudence along to protect him as he goes his innocent and generous way. Allworthy speaks of it as something Tom must "add" to his character (V, vii, 185), and in the end Tom has freed himself from his tendencies to vice and also acquired prudence (XVIII, "Chapter the last," 761). Prudence is necessary to happiness in this world, but not to goodness.

But there is no cause for solemnity in all this. The brilliant satiric comedy of *Tom Jones* comes from the geometry of error and crime, which in its linear perfection makes every grade of wrong, from the affectation of prudent ladies to the black hypocrisy of prudent Blifils, delectably ridiculous, while the romantic comedy of the Foundling moves the hero beyond all the angular traps to victory. Mr. Allworthy on his hill is beyond geometry; Tom in Molly's attic is temporarily within it, though untouched and undeformed by its lines. Tom in the palace of Wisdom, Sophia's house whence impulsive excess in the person of Squire Western has removed itself to return only on visits of love—Tom in this undescribed habitation ("undetermined square or round"?) enters upon the fulfillment of his natural goodness. The geometry of *Tom Jones* does not encompass its whole conception but makes its negative points and operates all in fun, a structural mock formality wedded merrily to the verbal.

NOTES

[1] Henry Fielding, *Tom Jones,* ed. Sheridan Baker (New York: W. W. Norton & Co., 1973), Bk. V, Ch. v, pp. 173, 176. All subsequent references are to this text.

[2] This paper runs counter, in various respects, to a good deal of Fielding criticism, but I have not identified the persons with whom I take issue. It seems a bit unfair to mention them in a negative way when they can't reply through the same medium; besides, I think the dignity and permanence of a *Festschrift* call for positive and affirmative criticism that keeps its eye on the literature, not the competition.

JOHN J. BURKE, JR. ✑ HISTORY WITH-
OUT HISTORY
HENRY FIELDING'S
THEORY OF FICTION

SINCE THE ENGLISH NOVEL EMERGED as a distinct and distinctive
literary form in the early eighteenth century, the prose narratives of
Henry Fielding have a significance beyond their purely aesthetic merits.
Their chronological position alone indicates that they somehow affected
the direction prose fiction would take in the future. But if later novelists
had the advantage of precedents such as *Joseph Andrews* and *Tom Jones*,
Henry Fielding had not the same advantage, at least not with regard to
English models. For that reason Fielding scholarship has always taken a
major interest in the influences that helped what Fielding would call "a
new species of writing" take shape, whether they were the negative
influences of works by such contemporaries as Samuel Richardson,
Colley Cibber, and Conyers Middleton, or the positive influences of
Fielding's earlier apprenticeships in drama and in journalism. Though
such influences had an observable inpact on the way Fielding crafted his
narratives, they seem to have had less impact on his theory of fiction, that
basic rationale which Fielding thought would justify this "new species of
writing" "hitherto unattempted in English." On the level of theory, an
unlikely source—historiography—proved to be a major inspiration, for
Fielding seems to have perceived this new form of prose narrative as an
opportunity to create a new form of historiography, history without
historical content.[1]
   One clue to Fielding's interest in historiography during his transition
from dramatist to novelist can be found in the running polemic he
carried on with traditional historiographers in his early narratives,
especially in his *Life of Mr. Jonathan Wild, the Great.*[2] Attacks on
historiography, such as Fielding's *Jonathan Wild*, were not new.[3] Swift,
for instance, had indicated his displeasure with the practices of historiography by sending Lemuel Gulliver to the island of
Glubbdubbdrib where Gulliver found himself

chiefly disgusted with modern history. For having strictly examined all the persons of greatest name in the courts of princes for an hundred years past, I found how the world has been misled by prostitute writers, to ascribe the greatest exploits in war to cowards, the wisest counsel to fools, sincerity to flatterers, Roman virtue to betrayers of their country, piety to atheists, chastity to sodomites, truth to informers.[4]

Attacks on historiography, such as Swift's, were not based on the view that something was inherently wrong with historiography; they rather indicate a dissatisfaction with how the facts of history had been distorted by the spirit of partisanship. Presumably, if historians purified their motives, important truths could be accurately reported: courageous generals would be seen as courageous generals, cowardly generals as cowardly. Fielding's disenchantment with historiography was far more radical; something was inherently wrong with historiography. For Fielding, historiography meant something more inclusive than it does today: sometimes public affairs as opposed to private affairs, but also biography, particularly when an individual's life became a part of the world of public affairs.

First of all, Fielding was annoyed by the popular assumption that history was superior to a mere fiction. Since the facts of a history could be verified independently of the author and the facts of a fiction could not, a history was widely supposed to record the truth, while a fiction presented only a pleasing lie. Such a line of reasoning, in Fielding's view, was hopelessly naive. The historian's pretense of devotion to objective facts only masked his subjective dependence—a dependence he shared, willy-nilly, with all other writers—on compositional techniques such as unity, organization, selection, emphasis, and subordination. Though the facts might exist prior to and independently of the consciousness of any historian, they had to be shaped first by the historian's consciousness and then by the process of composition itself. In that sense, historiography was as subjective as fiction. The truth value of a history was not necessarily greater than that of a fiction, and it might be less.

If Fielding felt that the subjectivity of a history was no more realiable than the subjectivity of a fiction, he was even more disturbed by the inherent bias of the conventional subject matter of history, the notion that the affairs of the great constitute what is worth knowing about man's past. Theoretically at least, history should consist of the affairs of all the countless men and women who have ever lived. But history, so conceived, would be an unassimilable mass of data. So historiographers had to choose and exclude, mostly to exclude, if they were to write about the past at all. They had decided, wittingly or unwittingly, that the way to write about the past was to write about what was important.

Which events and which people were important seemed to involve vague norms that were both quantitative and qualitative. In other words, important persons or important events were those that had affected the lives of the greatest number of people in the most dramatic ways, within their own time or in the future.

Historiography, then, by necessity and by convention, drew its subject matter from the lives of the great—kings, queens, popes, leading statesmen, generals. The careers of an Alexander the Great or a Charles XII might be suitable subject matter for a history, but not the careers of an unknown Macedonian goatherder or an anonymous Swedish infantryman. If the subject matter was an event, such as the Pelopennesian War or the defeat of the Spanish Armada, the story would be told with a few important people in the foreground directing the action. The less great and the little would exist in the background of a historical narrative under a rubric such as "the people," when and if they were to exist at all.

This convention, which dictated that historiography concern itself with the affairs of the great, had further implications that were even more disturbing to Fielding. First of all, a great man came to the attention of his contemporaries and to later historians by means of his activities in the world of public affairs. But to be engaged in the world of public affairs, a man had to be motivated by ambition or else he would have been content with private life. Such a man must have an invulnerable ego, a strong belief that other men were made for him rather than he for other men. If he was to survive for long in the world of public affairs, he would have to be skillful in playing off whatever factions might develop around him to his own advantage. He would have to be hardhearted or cold-blooded enough to be able to encourage his followers, often in great numbers, to risk their lives in his service. Alfred the Great may have been a cultural hero to the English, but he did not preserve England from the Danes without Saxon corpses.

None of these qualities of the heroes of history were the human qualities Henry Fielding most admired. Fielding attacked historiography because he believed it encouraged people to admire and possibly imitate qualities he thought should be repressed. He wanted to discredit the notion that the great deserved the attention, much less the admiration, of posterity. The choice of a notorious prig or thief-taker for his subject matter, though a verifiable historical personality, did not meet the usual norms for historiographical greatness, but that was Fielding's rhetorical strategy: he reached down in order to go up. He could have directly attacked the great by choosing one of their number, an Alexander the Great, say, or a Charles XII. But, if he had, defenders would have immediately stepped forward, as had already happened in the case of Cicero.[5] That would have meant public controversy, and such controversy would only dissipate the force of his attack. So Fielding chose a subject for whom he could expect no defenders, much less admirers. Once he was able to assume universal detestation for his subject, he had only to convince his audience that this notorious criminal embodied the essential qualities of the great men of history.[6]

Fielding's burlesque of historiography was intended to discredit its target forcefully but indirectly. It is clearly a burlesque, for the world of Fielding's Jonathan Wild is a world apart from the ordinary world of historiography. Defoe, for example, in an earlier account, had reported that Jonathan Wild "was born about the year 1683, being at the time of his execution about two-and-forty years of age," that he was born in Wolverhampton in Staffordshire, and that his parents, "though Mean, had the repute of honest and industrious people." [7] Fielding's Wild, on the other hand, was born on the first day of the Great Plague in 1665 and was baptized by the infamous Titus Oates (p. 28), a suitable birth date and christening for a rogue who would later plague England. Fielding's mock genealogy shows a young Jonathan descended from an ancient line of Long-fingers. Wild's mother, instead of being "honest and industrious," had "a most marvelous glutinous quality attending her fingers, to which, as to birdlime, everything closely adhered that she handled" (p. 28). By the laws of heredity young Wild is thus ensured of the necessary anatomical equipment for picking other people's pockets. The historical Jonathan Wild was a notorious philanderer—a point made use of by John Gay in *The Beggar's Opera*. Defoe mentioned that, like Henry VIII, Wild had had six wives (p. 303). But the sexual appetite of Fielding's Jonathan Wild is divided between Tishy Snap and Mrs. Heartfree, and he is rather a failure with both women. Facts had to be adjusted to the larger design; otherwise the historiographer would become the slave of his facts.

Fielding was not, of course, concerned with revealing his own methods, but with suggesting by innuendo his unflattering estimate of the methods of his fellow historiographers. Seeming candor is ironic candor. So when Fielding includes a document, such as a letter, into his text, he is not the least embarrassed by the admission that he has tampered with the document in order to improve its style:

Again, if it should be observed that the style of this letter doth not exactly correspond with that of our hero's speeches, which we have here recorded, we answer it is sufficient if in these the historian adheres faithfully to the matter, though he embellishes the diction with some of his own eloquence, without which the excellent speeches recorded in ancient historians (particularly in Sallust) would have scarce been found in their writings. Nay, even among the moderns. . . . (p. 131)

The true historiographer would not only improve the documents when appropriate, he would also explain events even when hiatuses would seem to make explanation impossible. The final conversations between Wild and the Ordinary of Newgate, Fielding admits, were reconstructed from documents, even though crucial portions of these documents were either illegible or had been blotted out (p. 205). All of these admissions are clearly part of Fielding's burlesque of the compositional methods of historiographers, ancient and modern.

Nevertheless,the main target of Fielding's scorn was not the unreliable methods of historians, but the very subject matter of history, the affairs of the great. The great are the higher-ups, the Establishment, those people who by reason of their social position can suppress and oppress the little: emperors, kings, statesmen, ambassadors, bishops, judges, and, of course, prime ministers (pp. 66, 107, 145, 208). But the greater harm comes when these great become the subjects of historiographers, for their influence soon becomes extended as they become the subjects of other books, poems, plays, and operas. In the end, the great are perceived by an uncritical public as models of behavior.

Fielding refers to Julius Caesar, Aeneas, and Charles XII of Sweden as those among the great whose careers have been thus perniciously romanticized by historiographers, but his favorite example is Alexander the Great, from whom Wild supposedly borrowed his epithet:

> In these histories of Alexander and Caesar, we are frequently and indeed impertinently, reminded of their benevolence, of their generosity, of their clemency and kindness. When the former had with fire and sword overrun a vast empire, had destroyed the lives of an immense number of innocent wretches, had scattered ruin and desolation like a whirlwind, we are told, as an example of his clemency, that he did not cut the throat of an old woman and ravish her daughters, but was content with only undoing them. And when the mighty Caesar, with wonderful greatness of mind, had destroyed the liberties of his country, and with all the means of fraud and force had placed himself at the head of his equals, had corrupted and enslaved the greatest people whom the sun ever saw, we are reminded, as an evidence of his generosity, of his largesses to his followers and tools, by whose means he had accomplished his purpose and by whose assistance he was to establish it. (pp. 22–23)

Fielding clearly felt that the great, be they the heroes of history or reigning prime ministers, ought to be held in the same kind of contempt that society customarily reserves for murderers and other such outlaws. The only attribute that distinguishes an Alexander the Great or a Julius Caesar from a Jonathan Wild is rank in society. But that distinction is crucial, and Fielding's frustrated anger becomes evident when on occasion he drops his mask in an off-the-cuff remark:

> When I consider whole nations rooted out only to bring tears into the eyes of a
> GREAT MAN, not indeed because he hath extirpated so many, but because he
> had no more nations to extirpate, then truly I am almost inclined to wish nature
> had spared us this her masterpiece, and that no GREAT MAN had ever been
> born into the world. But to proceed with our history. . . . (p. 65)

Nature, however, has not spared us this her masterpiece. Great men
have been born, are being born, and will be born. This is the root of
Fielding's historical pessimism. The thin hope he retained for the future
was reserved for those writers who could shake themselves free from
the infection of hero worship, writers who would commit themselves,
with clear eyes, with courage and integrity, to exposing the true nature
of greatness, whatever the risk. Such writers could be a front-line
defense for the little against the depredations of the great. This seems to
be the point beneath the irony of a passage that reflects Fielding's own
difficulties with Prime Minister Walpole, whose Licensing Act had
effectively ended his ability to earn his living as a dramatist:

> There is one misfortune which attends all GREAT MEN and their schemes, viz.,
> that in order to carry them into execution they are obliged, in proposing their
> purpose to their tools, to discover themselves to be of that disposition in which
> certain little writers have advised mankind to place no confidence—an advice
> which hath been sometimes taken. Indeed, many inconveniences arise to the said
> GREAT MEN from these scribblers publishing without restraint their hints or
> alarms to society, and many great and glorious schemes have been thus frustrated,
> wherefore it were to be wished that in all well-regulated governments such
> liberties should be by some wholesome laws restrained, and all writers inhibited
> from venting any other instructions to the people than what should be first
> approved and licensed by the said GREAT MEN, or their proper instruments or
> tools—by which means nothing would ever be published but what made for the
> advancing their most noble projects. (p. 127)

Here Fielding seems to summarize an early rationale for his writing,
while he is also describing the narrative role he created for himself in
Jonathan Wild. He is the Juvenalian satirist whose *saeva indignatio* is a
world apart from the warm and tolerant smiles of the Horatian role he
creates for himself in *Joseph Andrews* and *Tom Jones*.

Grim as the tone of *Jonathan Wild* may sometimes be, there are
indications that Fielding was not entirely comfortable with a merely
negative social function. His introduction of Thomas Heartfree into the
narrative in Book II as a foil to Wild indicates that he was groping
towards a more positive role. Fielding's Heartfree represents the an-
tithesis of greatness, a heart free from guile of any sort. Heartfree is
sentimental, generous, kindly, trusting, and long-suffering; Wild, on
the other hand, is calculating, greedy, ambitious, bestial, hypocritical,

and cruel. The basis of Heartfree's superiority over Wild is supposed to be his pure-heartedness. However unsuccessful Heartfree might be in the ways of the world, his virtue guarantees him happiness (pp. 117, 127). Wild, on the other hand, is made to suffer the penalties of an evil heart: "Let me then hold myself contented with this reflection, that I have been wise though unsuccessful, and am a GREAT though an unhappy man" (p. 83). In the paradoxical world of Fielding's fiction, the happiness of the little becomes their means of looking down on the misery of the great.

Yet, it is difficult to admire, much less enjoy, Heartfree as a character. His virtues are effete, the virtues of a passive nature rather than an active, energetic one. What is worse, Heartfree is rigid and self-righteous. Perhaps, as some have argued, Fielding wanted us to see the ideal as a reconciliation of the heart and head, of Heartfree's virtue and Wild's energy, a marriage of heaven and hell. But if that was Fielding's intention, then his execution of it in *Jonathan Wild* is grievously flawed.[8] However, Fielding was probably more interested in polarizing than in reconciling. He himself argues early in *Jonathan Wild* that "no two things can possibly be more distinct from each other" than "goodness" and "greatness" (p. 22), and his fiction seems designed to illustrate just that thesis. It is an unpleasant dichotomy, though, for Heartfree is hardly more inspiring than Wild, and considerably less attractive.

Henry Fielding continued his polemic against historiography on into his *History of the Adventures of Joseph Andrews and of His Friend, Mr. Abraham Adams*,[9] a work he published in 1742, a year before publishing *Jonathan Wild* with his *Miscellanies*, though the latter was probably composed before the former.[10] For *Joseph Andrews* the immediate source of irritation was the false models of goodness Fielding believed had been proposed in Samuel Richardson's *Pamela; or, Virtue Rewarded* and in Colley Cibber's *Apology for the Life of Mr. Colley Cibber, Comedian.* But these were only the most recent rubs against a festering sore. Nevertheless, Fielding's disgust with Richardson and Cibber did force him to face up to the challenge of just how he proposed to communicate patterns more valuable than theirs and thus render a "service to mankind" (p. 13)—either that or be content with the role of the scoffer, that negative role he had adopted in *Jonathan Wild* and again in *Shamela.*

So *Joseph Andrews* reveals a new Fielding, a Fielding assuming a more positive and didactic role, a Fielding presenting a fiction with patterns of far greater value than was customary in historiography. The characters and events of this fiction were not drawn from the world of public affairs, as had even been the case in *Jonathan Wild,* but from the world of private affairs. The characters were selected from among the little, mostly from the lower ranks of English society. Such people and such incidents, even if they had been real, would never have received the attention of historiographers confined to their hero worship.

In so turning the world of history upside down, Fielding also chose to expand his own role as narrator beyond that of the authorial intrustions of *Jonathan Wild*. After all, if the lessons are to be taught, the teacher must be perceived as amiable, intelligent, and trustworthy. So Fielding added three introductory essays that allowed him to develop his narrative personality more fully. In these he carefully reveals himself as jolly, witty, and companionable, a man unerringly on the side of the angels. Biography and historiography were blended with autobiography, though autobiography of a special kind, since there is no obvious correspondence between the private historical Fielding and the public Henry Fielding of the narrative.[11]

These introductory essays are also vehicles for proposing the rationale by which Fielding hoped to be understood and appreciated. In the third Preface, "Matter Prefatory in Praise of Biography," Fielding explains why he felt his fiction constituted a new form of historiography, though his terminology is frequently confusing, and it is no easy matter to sort it out. In *Jonathan Wild,* Fielding is the mock biographer of greatness, and biography and historiography are equated because "the quintessence of history" is "the lives of great men." The term "biographer" is at best ambivalent, but mostly pejorative. In *Joseph Andrews,* Fielding poses as the biographer of goodness rather than of greatness, and "biographer" is now an honorable term. Historiographers are no longer biographers, but topographers or chorographers:

> Notwithstanding the preference which may be vulgarly given to the authority of those romance-writers who entitle their books "the History of England, the History of France, of Spain, &c.," it is most certain that truth is to be found only in the works of those who celebrate the lives of great men, and are commonly called biographers, as others should indeed be termed topographers or chorographers: words which might well mark the distinction between them; it being the business of the latter chiefly to describe countries and cities, which, with the assistance of maps, they do pretty justly, and may be depended upon; but as to the actions and characters of men, their writings are not quite so authentic, of which there needs be no other proof than those eternal contradictions occurring between two topographers who undertake the history of the same country: for instance, between my Lord Clarendon and Mr. Whitlock, between Mr. Echard and Rapin, and many others; where, facts being set forth in a different light, every reader believes as he pleases; and, indeed, the more judicious and suspicious very justly esteem the whole as no other than a romance, in which the writer hath indulged a happy and fertile invention. (p. 157)

In Fielding's eyes, of course, the term "romance" is an unequivocal insult, romancers being writers who, "without any assistance from nature or history, record persons who never were, or will be, and facts which never did, nor possibly can, happen; whose heroes are of their own creation the chaos whence all their materials are collected" (p. 158). In historiography, what is true is trivial, what is supposed to be significant is worthless.

Having reduced historiography to a species of romance, Fielding then argues that there are precedents for his new kind of history. He cites the works of Continental writers, such as Le Sage, Marivaux, and Scarron, as prose forms of "history," by which he seems to have meant that they are "antiromances," and as such more probable, more real, and closer to the truth. Nevertheless, the most important precedent had been provided by Cervantes. *Don Quixote,* he argues, deserves the title of "history," not only because, like *Gil Blas* or *La vie de Marianne,* it is an antiromance, but because it is "a general history of Spain." In fact, *Don Quixote* deserves that title more than does its historiographical counterpart, *Historia general de España* by the Jesuit historian Juan de Mariana. *Don Quixote* is the perfection of the form of history because it has universality in time and space—so much so, that it deserves to be called "the history of the world in general, at least that part which is polished by laws, arts, and science; and of that from the time it was first published to this day; nay, forwards as long as it shall so remain" (p. 159).

In other words, by linking his narrative form in *Joseph Andrews* to that of *Don Quixote,* Fielding is inviting his public to consider his fiction "a general history of England" at a minimum and "a history of the world in general" at a maximum. Though Fielding's claim may seem extravagant, it is not at all inconsistent with the literary theories of the time which maintained that the general or universal is best revealed through particulars. In any event, Fielding's version of this theory had at least two important consequences for the shape of his narratives. First of all, the narratives had to be inclusive enough to maintain the claim that his fiction constitutes "a general history of England." There would have to be a great many characters, drawn from the various classes and professions considered typically English. Secondly, the main characters could not be just particular individuals. They somehow had to be national. This requirement affected how Fielding chose his heroes. When this requirement of nationality is added to Fielding's earlier commitment to that greatness which is goodness, it is not surprising that he chose to embody England in a minor Anglican clergyman and then linked him up with an orphan footboy who is supposed to be the brother of Richardson's Pamela Andrews.

Another difference between the old and the new historiography is the question of time. Fielding argues that the new historians have "to imitate" nature, not merely "copy" her (p. 158); that is, historians should not base their representations of "the actions and characters of men" on what they have read in books, but rather on the depth and breadth of their experience in observing their fellow men. The old-fashioned historiographers, living in a time other than the one about which they wrote, could not observe the subjects of their narratives. Therefore, in reconstructing people and events from documents and other histories, they were, in essence, copying nature rather than imitating her. If observation is superior to erudition and essential to good narrative, then it follows that the new historiography has to go horizontally in time rather than vertically. It has to embody the past and the future in the present rather than reconstruct the past for the present.

The "Author's Preface" to *Joseph Andrews* is as much concerned with the rationale for this "new species of writing" as the Preface "Matter Prefatory in Praise of Biography," though its emphases are somewhat different. There Fielding is testing out other grounds for persuading his public of the legitimacy of this new kind of fiction. To that end, he challenges the prevailing literary dogmas that take a dim view of work in prose, particularly when that work is also comic. Fielding's ingenuity takes many turns, including an attempt to link his "low" narrative with the high dignity of the epic and the gambit that he is merely restoring a lost form, the comic epic, which has disappeared from the literary tradition only because the original model, Homer's *Margarites,* has also disappeared.

Perhaps the most significant remark in the "Author's Preface" [12] is made during Fielding's discussion of the distinctions between the comic and the burlesque. Here, he is justifying his own work in the theater by arguing from its personal and social benefits, but also providing the most satisfactory rationale for his fiction:

> [Laughter and mirth] are probably more wholesome physic for the mind, and conduce better to purge away spleen, melancholy, and ill affections, than is generally imagined. Nay, I will appeal to common observation, whether the same companies are not found more full of good-humour and benevolence after they have been sweetened for two or three hours with the entertainments of this kind, than when soured by a tregedy or grave lecture. (p. 9)

A man preoccupied with the effects of "melancholy" and "ill affections" is not a man who believes that life ordinarily works out for the best. Fielding's argument is the argument of a pessimist, not an optimist. It is the preoccupation with human happiness of the Fielding of *Jonathan Wild* emerging in another form. The Fielding of *Jonathan Wild* wanted to believe or at least wanted his public to believe that there is a correspondence between goodness and happiness. But Henry Fielding never really believed his own doctrine: "There are a set of religious or rather moral writers, who teach that virtue is the certain road to happiness, and vice to misery, in this world. A very wholesome and comfortable doctrine, and to which we have but one objection, namely, that it is not true." [13]

Fielding did believe, however, that happiness is the good man's most legitimate aspiration, one that could be encouraged and one that he had some chance of satisfying. A measure of happiness could buttress a good man's spirit against those buffetings of Fortune that he could expect as his share of the ordinary lot of men in this world. The sources of inner happiness in life, however, are lamentably few. To attend, for instance, to the public history of mankind, or even to the public history of England, is to contemplate pieces of earth soaked in the blood of deluded men. Such reflections depress and sour a man as much as, or more than, any tragedy or grave lecture. Consequently, Fielding moved away from the view that the writer should be a man who by hints and alarms could protect the little against the depredations of the great to the view of the writer as a man who could best serve his public by bringing them a measure of happiness by means of a new fictional model, a new kind of history. To that end, the comic mode is not a luxury, it is a necessity.

By the time of *The History of Tom Jones, a Foundling*, Fielding had refined and polished the theories he had been testing in his earlier fictions. The result is an even more marked shift in the direction of autobiography. If the public is to accept this new kind of history, it has to accept the new kind of historian. To win their acceptance more completely, Fielding shifts the focus in this new fiction even more towards the character of the narrator. That is why he expands the role of the narrator far beyond mere authorial intrusions and even beyond the three prefaces of *Joseph Andrews*. In *Tom Jones* there are, in addition to a dedication and the usual *obiter dicta* scattered through the tale, eighteen prefaces, one for each division of the story, thereby allowing for ample exposure and inspection of the character of the historian.

In the Preface "Of Those Who Lawfully May, and of Those Who May Not, Write Such Histories as This," Fielding lists four criteria by which his character and his tale should be judged: Genius, Learning, Conversation or Experience, Humanity or Goodness of Heart (IX, i, 415–18).[14] Fielding admits that a tale drawn from the scenes of private life can not enjoy the same credibility as one drawn from public transactions (VIII, i, 335), but this does not mean that, like the romancers, all his materials were collected from the chaos of his brain. Learning acts as a check on the idiosyncratic tendencies of the individual, and learning develops the native capacity of genius. The historian's mind and style have to be disciplined, though not enslaved, by a thorough acquaintance with the writers of the past: "A competent knowledge of history and of the *belles-lettres* is here absolutely necessary" (IX, i, 416). Undoubtedly the critical prefaces in *Tom Jones* are designed in part to demonstrate Fielding's competence on this score.

But just as learning acts as a check on genius, experience or conversation acts as a check on learning. Since a man who has no learning is unlikely to write books, the public is much more likely to receive histories from the hands of learned men who have little or no experience or conversation. Their histories, Fielding argues, should for that reason be suspect. For, from experience only "can the manners of mankind be known; to which the recluse pedant, however great his parts or extensive his learning may be, hath ever been a stranger" (XIII, i, 599).

Whether or not Fielding was justifying *ex post facto* what he wanted to do or what he was able to do by this principle of experience, it had an important influence on the way he practiced the art of fiction. It is clearly a principle appropriate to a narrative with the panoramic scope of *Tom Jones* rather than to one that would present a slice of life. This empirical strain in Fielding's rationale also helps to explain why he was alternately attracted and repelled by historiography. On the one hand, the materials of historiography seemed to guarantee secure and believable results because its data could be validated; on the other hand, the histories that had been published only produced results that were insecure and unbelievable. Ultimately, Fielding had to measure historiographers, not by what they said, but by what they did.

Fielding's principle of experience also led him to place an ever stronger emphasis on manners in his fictions. Since it is impossible, he felt, to get inside the head or heart of another man, a writer has to derive his understanding of him by careful observation of his external behavior and make his inferences therefrom. Any man's behavior, though to some extent unique, is largely shaped by whatever codes of conduct or modes of behavior there happen to be. Those codes or modes are summed up in the word "manners." Since manners are subject to variables of time and place, social and historical circumstances, it is essential to understand a man's manners, why he behaves the way he does, in order to assess and interpret his actions.

If that is so, then a writer seeking to imitate men in an aesthetic medium has to imitate their external behavior accurately. But to imitate those manners accurately, he has to, by the logic of empiricism, first observe those manners for himself. If he should try to render men without this first-hand acquaintance with their manners, he can only produce fanciful, unconvincing copies. Nor can he expect much better results if he merely copies the models of other writers who have observed for themselves the manners that he has not. Since manners change with circumstances and since circumstances change all the time, he will still produce unconvincing copies, the more so as the lag grows between the time of his own composition and that of the models he has copied. If Fielding can argue that his contemporaries produce only ridiculous stereotypes by copying the manners of the upper classes as they had been rendered forty years earlier by a Congreve or a Vanbrugh (XIV, i, 649–50), then, *a fortiori*, historiographers can only produce grotesques if they try to render the people of an entirely different era—say, of Tudor England—in their narratives, because they are precluded by time from ever having observed their manners for themselves. In other words, the logic of empiricism leads to the conclusion that a historian can only render in narrative the people of his own time, and then only those he has personally observed. *Tom Jones,* like *Joseph Andrews,* is deliberately set at a time close to the time of its composition.

The panoramic sweep of *Tom Jones* plus some seemingly casual hints in the text (I, ii, 5; VIII, i, 335) suggest that Fielding did intend *Tom Jones* to be a "History of England" in the sense he had described in his Preface "In Praise of Biography" in *Joseph Andrews. Tom Jones,* like *Joseph Andrews,* embodies the past and future of English history in the present, rendering the national experience through individual experiences. In *Joseph Andrews* Fielding places at the center of his tale a lowly Anglican clergyman, about the same age as Cervantes's Don Quixote, whose principal function is to guide the relationship between two youngsters to a chaste and happy conclusion in marriage.[15] Parson Adams's station in life is deliberately humble, in pointed contrast to the usual station of the great man. He is a clergyman because Fielding had apparently assumed that the clergy of the national Church tried to institutionalize what he considered the most desirable English—and hopefully human—trait: the idealistic impulse to act for the benefit of one's fellow human beings. This idealism or quixoticism of Parson Adams is then salted with what Fielding considered the characteristic earthiness of the English. The unpuritanical Adams enjoys his pipe and his ale, and, when abused, rarely turns the other cheek.

Although Fielding does populate the panorama of *Tom Jones* with the familiar types of *Joseph Andrews*—innkeepers, chambermaids, physicians, lawyers, busybody servants, effete and corrupt aristocrats—he does shift his focus. For one thing, the clergy disappear from the foreground, as though Fielding now felt that he had made a mistake in associating the central English experience with any one institution rather than with an individual without such ties. His new hero consequently has no professions. Goodness of heart is secularized. For another, Fielding may have felt that he had reacted too violently against the great man, so he moves his good characters up on the social scale, though not to the point where they are likely to affect the world of public affairs.[16] Since Fielding's own origins were connected with the upper class, he was also moving closer to his own direct experience.

Nevertheless, through most of the story we are supposed to presume that Tom is of lowly origin. So, even though Tom has noble blood in his veins, he combines the best characteristics of the upper and lower classes. Fielding certainly felt that such a combination would be desirable: "Besides, to say the truth, the manners of our historian will be improved by both these conversations; for in the [lower class] he will easily find examples of plainness, honesty, and sincerity; in the [upper class] of refinement, elegance, and a liberality of spirits which last quality I myself have scarce ever seen in men of low birth and education" (IX, i, 417). The way Tom combines high and low is one of the indications that Fielding has made a conscious effort to locate him at the center of the English experience. Though Tom's legitimate name would be Thomas Summer, he is always called Tom Jones. The name, of course, is necessary for the surprise at the end, but it is also appropriate. It would be difficult to think of a more typical, unallegorical English name, one less associated with any particular segment of English society.

The fourth criterion in the Preface "Of Those Who Lawfully May . . . Write Such Histories as This" is that of humanity or goodness of heart. Goodness of heart, of course, had been Fielding's persistent concern at least as far back as *Jonathan Wild*. Now, however, it becomes an indispensable quality in the teller of the tale—one more reason for expanding the role of the narrator. Now Fielding can defend love and goodness against those cynics, such as Mandeville (VI, i), who would deny their very existence, much less their value. But goodness of heart remains a problem in a history with an unconventional subject matter.

Apparently, Fielding did not feel that he had solved the problem of how to make goodness both attractive and believable. Heartfree had been neither attractive nor believable; his pure-heartedness made Wild's diabolism attractive by default. Parson Adams, on the other hand, had surely been attractive, though perhaps not easily believable because he was too good to be true. His worst flaws were the merest foibles. The worst Fielding could ever make the unworldly Adams do was bloody somebody's nose in self-defense, or, in his absent-mindedness climb into Fanny's bed only to snore chastely by her side through the night. His foibles were harmless; his virtues glaring. Fielding now seemed to feel that he should introduce more shadows, perhaps because no good purpose was served "by inserting characters of such angelic perfection," for "the mind of man is more likely to be overwhelmed with sorrow and shame than to draw any good uses from such patterns," "being ashamed to see a pattern of excellence in his nature, which he may reasonably despair of ever arriving at" (X, i, 447–48).

So, in *Tom Jones*, Fielding portrays his good-hearted characters with some flaws. Squire Allworthy, despite his name, has a few. Allworthy is splendidly oblivious to the emotional frustrations of his sister and to the machinations of his nephew Blifil. He judges poorly, even on the basis of the available evidence. He is unnecessarily stern to Partridge and to Jones. In Fielding's terms, Allworthy is more likely to be guided by his head than by his heart and only reforms when he begins to learn the truth. Sophia may mean wisdom in Greek, but Fielding's Sophia Western is not an incarnation of what the Greeks meant by wisdom, nor, for that matter, is she the embodiment of prudence. She is portrayed as young, inexperienced, sentimental, and naive—though she usually catches on quickly. But no young woman, single and pretty, with even a grain of prudence would travel the road from Somersetshire to London with only a female companion for protection. Moreover, Sophia too misjudges Tom on the basis of circumstantial evidence. But, unlike Squire Allworthy, Sophia usually follows the instincts of her heart rather than her head, and her heart always proves to be more right than her head. Tom's own flaws are several. He is as splendidly oblivious to the motivations of others as his patron Allworthy. He is too ready to yield to his animal spirits, though Fielding's Tom is never allowed to ruin anybody, for all of the maids he conquers had themselves been conquerors before. More seriously, Tom does not perceive how his actions might appear to those about whom he cares the most and so causes unnecessary pain. Since Tom rarely follows the dictates of his head, his redemption rests entirely on his good heart.

By introducing such shadows, Fielding effectively subverts the didacticism of those "valuable patterns" he thought he could communicate to the world. If his aim was to present a world where the people with good hearts are more attractive than the ones with wicked hearts, he succeeds only in bringing us to a foregone conclusion. If he was trying to teach more specific lessons, even that foregone conclusion could be in question. Are we to judge in real life according to our hearts and not according to our heads? Did Henry Fielding judge according to his heart when he presided as the Magistrate for Middlesex? Unlikely. Should teen-age girls run away from home when their fathers become obstinate? Hardly. In the end, Fielding's tale doesn't teach anything at all, or at least nothing useful. The characters in *Tom Jones* are saved from the consequences of their mistakes, not by their own actions, but by the providential interventions of the author. We cannot expect such interventions in our real lives, and Henry Fielding knew it. If history is not philosophy teaching by example, neither can fiction be morality teaching by example.

The evidence suggests that the ultimate meaning in *Tom Jones* is found in the frame, not in its tale, as a type of idealized autobiography—and that represents a considerable retreat from any earlier hopes of creating a new kind of historiography. The tale is merely part of a larger rhetorical strategy to engage us with the personality of the teller. The tale illustrates the kind of man Fielding was, or, better, wanted to be. By placing himself on the side of the angels—on the side of human warmth and goodness—he disposes us to be in his favor and draws us into his circle. As an author he offers us happiness—not the happiness that issues from a virtuous heart, but an aesthetic happiness. As he remarks in his "Farewell to the Reader": "If I have been an entertaining companion to thee, I promise thee it is what I have desired" (XVIII, i, 820). An entertaining companion Henry Fielding is. He sweetens our dispositions through mirth and laughter and thereby brings us a small measure of happiness, even though we remain locked into the world of history. It is this small measure of happiness that Fielding was finally willing to accept as the one certain benefit of his art (XIII, vi, 618). In this he has been proved right.

In the end, two major principles in Fielding's theory of fiction—experience and goodness of heart—are contradictory principles. Eventually, Fielding had to resolve this contradiction in favor of one or the other. In reacting against the worship of greatness in ordinary historiography, he assumed the responsibility of celebrating goodness in its place, as though he could reverse these age-old roles of victim and victimizer and engineer by means of his pen a victory for the good over the great. Experience, the world as we observe it, forced him to recognize this as unhistorical and eventually unreal. The patterns of human history—the tricks of the blind lady Fortune, as Fielding called them—are random and indifferent. Fortune, insofar as she works to the favor of any man or group of men, works to the advantage of the great and will continue to do so on into the vast stretches of the future. To construct a tale that imitates what he observed would be to abandon the comic mode.[17]

But rather than yield to historical pessimism and abandon the comic mode, Fielding adapts his tale to a form of idealized autobiography where he is free from some of the pressures of external fact. As the omnipotent author he can make events turn out right. The providential patterns that do not work out in the world of history can be made to work out in fiction, where he can effect a victory over the wicked and a happy outcome for the good. Providence is, after all, "a very wholesome and comfortable doctrine," to which one can have "but one objection," namely, that it is not true. Fielding, of course, realizes—as he expected his public to realize—that the tale he tells does not imitate either the observable world or the world of history. That is the ultimate irony in Fielding's theory of fiction: the new history turns out to be, not better history, but an escape from history.[18]

NOTES

[1] Robert M. Wallace, "Fielding's Knowledge of History and Biography," *SP*, 44 (1947), 89–107. Wallace argues that Fielding's "interest in history and biography has been insufficiently emphasized" and that "they rather than the epic may have been the chief influence on the form and purpose of the novels" (p. 90).

[2] Henry Fielding, *The Life of Mr. Jonathan Wild, the Great,* Signet ed. (New York: New American Library, 1961). All future references to Fielding's *Jonathan Wild* will be to this edition and will be included in the text.

[3] This topic has been surveyed in a chapter entitled "The Role of Historiography" in James William Johnson's *The Formation of English Neo-Classical Thought* (Princeton: Princeton Univ. Press, 1967), pp. 31–68.

[4] Jonathan Swift, *Gulliver's Travels and Other Writings,* ed. Louis A. Landa (Boston: Houghton Mifflin Co., 1960), p. 161.

[5] Addison Ward, "The Tory View of Roman History," *SEL*, 4 (1964), 413–56.

[6] Walter J. Farrell has argued this point in a different context: "The ultimate target of Fielding's mockery is not Wild but his counterparts in the respectable world. This means that the novel must do more than merely humiliate its already less than dignified hero; it must also identify the rogue in some way with the great conquerors and politicians that traffic in human misery." See "The Mock-Heroic Form of *Jonathan Wild*," *MP* (1966), 216, et passim.

[7] Daniel Defoe, "The Life and Actions of Jonathan Wild," with *The History of the Life of the Late Mr. Jonathan Wild, the Great* by Henry Fielding, ed. Wilson Follett (New York: Alfred A. Knopf, 1926), pp. 289–90.

[8] Even Fielding seems to have become annoyed with his own creation. He ridicules Heartfree's rigidity—not to mention his lack of human warmth—by reporting that Heartfree's first concern, once he has learned that his wife has been abducted, is not for her health and safety, but for her sexual purity (p. 141). He may have intended some additional ridicule by noting that, after their ultimate reunion as man and wife, Mrs. Heartfree "never had another child" (p. 219), implying that they never lay together as a couple again because of Heartfree's unconquerable suspicions that his wife had indeed yielded up her chastity during those adventures abroad. Nevertheless, these are slight and very subtle touches in Fielding's portrayal of Heartfree as a whole, and they seem a thin basis for arguing that Fielding seriously undercuts his own standard bearer.

[9] Henry Fielding, *Joseph Andrews and Shamela,* ed. Martin C. Battestin (Boston: Houghton Mifflin Co., 1961). All future references to *Joseph Andrews* will be to this edition and will be included in the text.

[10] Although I argue from *Jonathan Wild* to *Joseph Andrews* to *Tom Jones,* chronology of composition is not strictly necessary to my argument. It would be sufficient if these ideas were running through Fielding's mind, as it seems they were, when he started to consider a career as a writer of prose fictions. In any event, many scholars feel that Fielding had started work on *Jonathan Wild* as early as the late 1730's, even though he delayed publishing it. Martin C. Battestin has offered an unusual analysis of Fielding's reasons for the delay. See "Fielding's Changing Politics and *Joseph Andrews*," *PQ*, 39 (1960), 39–55. Wilbur Cross, while acknowledging that most Fielding scholars believed that the composition of *Jonathan Wild* antedated that of *Joseph Andrews,* accepts the minority view. See *The History of Henry Fielding,* 3 vols. (1918; rpt. New York: Russell & Russell, 1963), I, 409–10.

[11] Henry Fielding's public role as the jolly, witty, and congenial narrator dedicated to the defense of virtue and the stigmatizing of vice is not entirely consistent with those parts of his own biography that suggest a man who was—at least sometimes—improvident, lazy, ostentatious, addicted to begging favors and bitter when those favors were refused, as well as a man severely depressed by terrible personal tragedies that struck him more than once. See "The Life of Henry Fielding" by Sir Walter Scott, a warm admirer of Fielding, in his *Lives of the Eminent Novelists and Dramatists* (New York: Scribner, Welford, and Armstrong, 1887), pp. 420, 425, 428. See also Cross, I, 351–52.

[12] Alan Dugald McKillop cites this passage as "Fielding's most complete recognition of humor as an aesthetic experience rather than as a tool of didacticism, his theoretical recogntion of a genial tolerance that would cover Parson Adams, Tom Jones, and Squire Western." See *The Early Masters of English Fiction* (Lawrence: Univ. Press of Kansas, 1956), p. 112.

[13] Henry Fielding, *The History of Tom Jones, a Foundling* (New York: Modern Library, 1950), p. 690. All future references to *Tom Jones* will be to this edition and will be included in the text.

[14] Fielding discusses these criteria a second time in his Preface to Book XIII, 597–600.

[15]There has been an ongoing debate on how to interpret the thematic center of *Joseph Andrews,* a debate provoked, at least in part, by the way Fielding chose to title his book. My own view, implied in my argument, is that *Joseph Andrews* is not entirely successful as a work of art, if unity is to be the norm of success. The lack of unity is due to the presence of conflicting intentions in Fielding's mind at the time of composition. In my opinion, Fielding let the title stand because he wanted his novel to be taken as a wholesome alternative to the sickness of Richardson's *Pamela,* the idea with which he started *Joseph Andrews* and one he never entirely suppressed. At the same time, however, he wanted *Joseph Andrews* to open up the possibility of a new kind of historiography. He himself locates the center of interest, on this count, in the character of Parson Adams in the last paragraph of his "Author's Preface." Moreover, I agree with Sheridan Baker that, despite Fielding's loud protests to the contrary, the conventions and attitudes of the older prose romances linger on in Fielding's novels. In the case of *Joseph Andrews,* the attitudes of the older romances linger on most obviously in Fielding's portrayal of the characters of Joseph and Fanny. See "The Idea of Romance in the Eighteenth-Century Novel," *PMASAL,* 49 (1964), 517, et passim.

[16] In *Tom Jones* there are a few references to the world of public affairs, especially to the Jacobite Rebellion of 1745. At one point Tom wants to enlist in the army of the Duke of Cumberland, and Sophia is at another time thought to be Jenny Cameron. However, these are introduced only to be quickly filtered out.

[17] My conclusion here coincides, in part, with the thesis of Andrew Wright in *Henry Fielding: Mask and Feast* (Berkeley and Los Angeles: Univ. of California, 1966), where Wright argues that Fielding, in reaction to his own pessimistic fatalism, creates an art which is festive and celebratory, not satiric, and that Fielding's purpose is not to reflect life but to transfigure it by means of his comic art (e.g., pp. 15, 29, 30). However, Wright also insists that *Jonathan Wild* does not deserve an important place in the Fielding canon, because it is "neither a novel nor a philosophical work," but "a tract," "an entirely simple handling of one idea—or at most two" (p. 45).

[18] Philip Stevick has written on "Fielding and the Meaning of History," *PMLA,* 79

(1964), 561–68. There is no obvious correspondence between Stevick's position and my own. Stevick argues that "Fielding's interest in history and its meaning led him, contrary to the dominant thought of his age, away from doctrine and towards skepticism" (p. 561). Eventually, Fielding arrived at a notion of "history as development (in Raymond Aron's phrase)" so that Fielding "without a philosophy of history" could afford "a pleasure in the contemplation of his time that neither the progressivist nor the anti-progressivist could enjoy" (p. 565). My own view is that the meaning of history was never an issue for Fielding, that he had a philosophy of history, that it was pessimistic fatalism, summed up in his attitude towards Fortune. Fielding believed that events—and often the great—were in the saddle and rode mankind and that this would continue to be so as far as he could see into the future. This pessimistic fatalism was the reason why he filtered history out of his prose fictions. His fictions were not a celebration of his own time, because they were meant to take place outside of time.

GEORGE H. WOLFE *LESSONS IN EVIL*
FIELDING'S ETHICS IN
THE CHAMPION ESSAYS

BY THE TIME HENRY FIELDING came to write for *The Champion: or British Mercury* in the fall of 1739 he was already an educated, married (by elopement), loved and detested, admired and ridiculed, published, praised, and out-of-work playwright. And only thirty-two years old. Walpole's Licensing Act of 1737, for which Fielding had been at least partially responsible, had effectively shut him off from the stage, and his economic condition had reduced itself to precarious levels. Although admitted to read law at the Middle Temple in November 1737, he would not be called to the bar until June 1740; in the meantime his perennial distaste for Walpole's ministry, coupled with a pressing need for funds, conspired to involve him in this latest Opposition newspaper.[1]

It is worth noting at the outset exactly where in Fielding's career *The Champion* falls. The plays, with their energetic if often clumsy excoriations of social inequities and political enemies, were behind him; ahead lay the triumphs of his novels, the later journalism, and a notable public life as a police magistrate. *The Champion* essays appear, therefore, at a crucial juncture in the artist's life; still in his early thirties, but no longer the fashionable and controversial young playwright, and not yet the eminent (and controversial) man of letters, he is seeking throughout this period to organize and articulate a satisfactory ethical system for himself and, by extension, for mankind. Since the conception of evil and human malfeasance depicted variously in these essays becomes vintage Fielding in the novels, it is perhaps as a series of tentative moral forays into the real world that *The Champion* might best be regarded; these are, after all, his first attempts, outside the theater, to order an inchoate but pervasive fascination with ethical problems. What one ought to do, then, is to observe the kinds of behavior he embraces and rejects (and the reasons why) and to evaluate his choices as guides to the moral orientation of the subsequent fiction. In so doing, Fielding's moral schemes may be surprised in an embryonic state and thereby some light may be shed on their early development.

In a detailed examination of Fielding's uses of irony, George R. Levine, like others before and after him, focuses on the author's clever use of masks.[2] Under the general heading of "The Ironic Mask" are presented the four subheads of Editor, Public Defender, Politician, and Traveller, a breakdown that Levine uses to elucidate Fielding's political-moral attacks on Walpole's government and contemporary society. With respect to *The Champion,* Levine argues that "[Fielding's] chief incentive was not disgust with political ineptitude and misman-agement as such, but with the old problems of 'vice and imposture' in society as a whole. . . . Fielding was more concerned with perversions of morality than with specific political issues . . ." (p. 34). He goes on to deduce that Fielding very likely viewed the corruption of the political process as symptomatic of a pervasive moral degeneration then going happily forward in England under the watchful eye of Robert Walpole.

Although not altogether accurate, these observations are useful for the distinction they suggest between the self-serving concerns of an Opposition politician and Fielding's apparently genuine and sustained moral outrage. One of his lasting perceptions of human evil is the insidious manner in which an originally corrupt impulse often leads by slow degrees to misery, degradation, and larger evils for ever-increasing numbers of people. To be sure, Fielding was, as Sheldon Sacks ob-serves, "deeply committed to the notion that action should be judged according to the motives that led to it." [3] But it is equally true that he was committed to a corollary imperative: Action should be judged according to the good or evil it generates in the lives of men. Parson Adams's support of good works versus faith, in that familiar dialectic, meshes closely with Fielding's own sense (open to view throughout his work) of the proper grounds for judging both professing Christians and honorable politicians.

The problem in the first instance (judging action by motive) is a practical one: how do we ascertain the source and motive of human behavior? Fielding's answer is typically matter-of-fact. In an early *Champion* essay he observes: "The only ways by which we can come at any knowledge of what passes in the minds of others, are their words and actions; the latter of which, hath by the wiser part of mankind been chiefly depended on, as the surer and more infallible guide."[4] From the theater years onward he applied such reductive criteria to the negoti-able morality of English politics and society with the result that his life became a remarkable public and polemical ride through many of the more interesting events of his day.

In the year 1739 that ride brought him to *The Champion* and to the opportunity of speaking out openly on issues that troubled him. The plays and farces of his first creative decade had bristled with increasingly sardonic attacks on selected evils—as a comparison of *The Historical Register for the Year 1736* with a frivolous early piece like *Love in Several Masques* will immediately reveal. We might note, then, to what extent Fielding's literary preoccupations had become ethical (though certainly not solemn) by this time. James A. Work, in a brief but sweeping declaration of Fielding's fundamental Christianity, assesses the ex-playwright's moral orientation in 1739, and after: "It is clear that by the time of *The Champion* . . . Fielding was in all significant points an orthodox believer in the rational supernaturalism of such low-church divines as Tillotson, Clarke, and Barrow, and that he experienced no important changes in belief throughout the remainder of his life." [5] Martin C. Battestin takes essentially the same view in his excellent study of *Joseph Andrews*, [6] but what are the practical components of this strengthening Christian vision, and how do they apply to these essays?

In a real sense Fielding's ethical coming of age, prepared for among the vagaries of the theater, coincides with his *Champion* years, and it is not too much to say (as indeed Work does say) that "a major motive underlying his chief writings from that time [1739] on was to reform the individual and society, to exalt morality and to defend orthodoxy" (pp. 144–45). This element of reform, of identifying, then prescribing common sense antidotes for, the ailments of the body politic, increasingly preoccupies Fielding's attention henceforth. His assaults upon evil are based on the orthodox view that men are born with an inherent capacity for sinning, though capable simultaneously of great good. It is from this elective dilemma that moral instruction must seek to extract them. [7]

At the heart of the dilemma lies the problem of temptation. If we subscribe to a view of man that sees for him enormously wide ethical latitudes, and if we allow him to sin and still recover the fold, and if, finally, we care deeply about his fate (all of which Fielding does), then we must come to regard man's ability to handle temptation as a principal means of defining his virtue (which Fielding also does). Joseph, Adams, Amelia, Booth, Tom, Heartfree, and others are in a variety of ways seriously tempted. By and large they resist, and, to the extent that they do, prove estimable. However, when someone does succumb temporarily to the delights of lust or gambling, he must be redeemed, and he is, either by true contrition and confession, or a dark night of the soul, or trial by fire, or a combination of these. The whole shadowy problem of temptation in a real-world situation intrigues Fielding; he regularly confronts characters with tantalizing options for sin, allowing the pattern of their reactions to determine their suitability as human beings. Evil characters either fail to see or refuse to repent their crimes.

The temptation must, however, at least be tempting. Certainly, one major source of humor and humanity in Shamela, Parson Adams, and Tom, both for Fielding's contemporaries and ourselves, is the comparison constantly hovering in our minds between their recognizable if flawed character and the essentially unthreatened (because actually impervious) virtue of Pamela. If modest glory is due the military commander who successfully defends a naturally impregnable fortress, then for the same reason the absence of a properly threatening temptation must be ranked high among Fielding's objections to Pamela Andrews. She is unacceptable to him precisely because she is allowed to withstand the challenges to her formidable virtue without sufficient anxiety, backward glances, spirited moans, or heated blood. Fielding's response in *Shamela* is rife with allusions to the unprecedented commercial success of Richardson's novel, a success that Fielding found galling largely because it established in polite society a (for him) deficient moral reservoir for fiction. There just was not enough of this world, of truth to life, in Pamela's meeting with her devil. To pretend otherwise was an hypocrisy.

Had she fallen and been redeemed (like Clarissa), had she *almost* fallen, her plight would have interested Fielding considerably more. As she stands, Pamela, judged as a fictional creation, fails to engage our sensibilities or compassion because her attempted seduction is in the end unfeared and unfelt, never in fact a possibility. Both dramatically and morally, this situation was for Fielding falsely titillating, a concoction that answered his demands neither on art nor life.[8]

A preference for such real life ethics first emerges clearly in *The Champion,* where he began to lay out over a period of several months the initial prose codification of his ethical world, one in which virtually all judgments of men are at bottom moral and behavioristic. It is hardly necessary to say that such valuations need not be stuffy or dull—a point he made repeatedly beginning with the plays—nor that they serve merely to proscribe or limit behavior. In fact, Fielding's code takes a quite liberal view of Tom's natural exuberancies, Booth's fecklessness, Parson Adams's unconventional clericality. It is the state of the heart that interests Fielding, and the state of each of these hearts is exemplary, for each defines itself by its capacity for humanity and sympathy when it matters. The pitiable figures in Fielding's work are those whose behavior (narrow, vindictive, avaricious) violates a criterion of generosity and thus prohibits their entry into a loose federation of the elect. As Doctor Harrison says in *Amelia,* ". . . a wicked soul is the greatest object of compassion in the world."

Long before Harrison's sometimes trying goodness, however, Fielding had detailed more specifically a few components of the wicked soul. In two successive *Champion* essays, 27 and 29 December 1739, he calls covetousness a "vice, which carries with it a more especial mark of madness than all the rest" and goes on to pity the covetous man who sells his soul to the devil without getting anything for it. Then, in the voice of his persona, Mr. Nehemiah Vinegar (29 December), he sums up a dream-vision estimate of another similar evil: "It appeared to me, that wealth is of all worldly blessings the most imaginary; that avarice is at once the greatest tyrant, and the greatest object of compassion; and that the acquisition of over-grown fortunes, seldom brings the acquirer more, than the care of possessing them, and fear of losing them." Whether castigating contemporary politicians in these essays or inventing his own evil-doers afresh in the novels, Fielding delights in exposing warped, almost humoral, personalities running amuck within an eminently corruptible society. A measure of the compassion called for by Doctor Harrison, above, may indeed lurk in his portraits of political and religious pollution, but the sting of the denunciations remains. In fact, the author of *The Champion* reserves some of his sharpest language for attacks on political malfeasance, a category of human misconduct particularly irksome to him. The reasons for this preeminence are central to Fielding's ethical world and to an understanding of the organizing effect of these first journalistic essays on his views of human nature.

In the 11 December 1739 *Champion* Fielding declared the fallacy of proclaiming evil to be universal among men as much the fault of the viewer as the viewed. In a typical rhetorical tactic, he turns the enemy's argument against the enemy: "Those authors, who have set human nature in a very vile and detestable light . . . have often succeeded in establishing an infamous character to themselves." He goes on to conclude that such authors (meaning Hobbes and Mandeville particularly) draw such conclusions by studying outward appearances filtered through their own corrupt hearts. The outcome of this jaundiced estimate of mankind, says Fielding, is a pervasive immorality extending via the pulpit, books, and journalism to an entire nation: " 'Tis the worst abuse of the press to propogate doctrines that visibly tend to the entire extirpation of all society, all morality, and all religion" (11 December).

Clearly Fielding abhorred the political process as practiced by his contemporaries, and a part of that abhorrence springs from the politician's familiar contempt for man's frail virtue. To the political operative, people are bought and manipulated to convenient ends, and since every man has his price it only remains to establish and meet it. Election rigging, buying of votes, stuffing ballot boxes, all were common enough practices for Walpole and his friends (and enemies), but to a man of Fielding's relatively uncomplicated moral perspective utterly damning. For him, man was flesh and flesh is, as we know, weak; no great skill was required of those managing to subvert laws or suborn witnesses in court. What makes this process so odious for Fielding and what makes him cry out against the principle behind it repeatedly in novel, play, and essay is that men in power, men trusted with high office, men who in a free society are always (practically speaking) slightly above the law, take advantage of their position to abuse their trust. It is as much the violation of a delicate social balance as the resulting corruption that angers him.

In a curious way Fielding expects philosophers and religious or governmental leaders to exercise a proprietary control over their subjects, a benign and benevolent dictatorship of the gifted that will protect weak men from the ravages of their own evil proclivities. Had he been in a position to do so during his early thirties, he would, it appears, have exercised considerable restraints upon the public expression of philosophical ideas (atheism, deism, Mandeville's cynicism) inimical to his own notion of a virtuous society. He posits the ostrichlike assertion (in a 22 January *Champion*) that "An evil which admits of no remedy, a wise man would surely wish to remain in ignorance of," going on to note that non-Christian immoral writers of all sorts "do a real dis-service to mankind, even supposing [their] allegations were true, and religion as false as they would have it imagined." He, of course, does not happen to believe the allegations *are* true, but even if there were "no future state, it would be surely the interest of every virtuous man to wish there was one. . . ."

This essay, like others in the series, admits implicitly the frail uncertainties of human nature and the ease with which men are captivated by philosophical trinkets and alluring baubles of sin. To follow Hobbes, Fielding implies, while repudiating the latitudinarians is to take the downhill path of easy complicity—much the finer to bear up under the load of a spare (but true) Christian ethic and so save oneself and the nation in the process. But because we are unable to bear the full disclosure of certain false doctrines and often must be protected from ourselves, it is the role of society's leaders to afford that protection.

The origin of such profound responsibility derives from Fielding's notion of personal magnetism. In a 15 January *Champion* he continues the process so evident throughout these essays of assembling and streamlining a body of personal criteria for judging human actions. The subject here is that elusive quality which today we blandly term "leadership." Fielding prefers "authority": "By authority, then, I understand, that weight which one man bears in the mind of another, resulting from an opinion of any extraordinary qualities or virtues inherent in him, which prepares the latter to receive the most favourable impression from all the words and actions of the person thus esteemed." A man so endowed enjoys a privileged place in the world, quite obviously, for "Whatever he affirms, they will believe; whatever he affects they will hope; whatever he commands, they will execute." As one might expect, accompanying this power are solemn responsibilities, the violation or misuse of which threatens to sunder the thin tapestry of society.

The phenomenon of authority shades easily into popularity, of course, and into further questions of getting and maintaining control in a political world. Fielding lists in this same piece eleven aphorisms of evil that serve as the source of hatred and contempt among the people for their leaders.[9] The list constitutes a rogues catalog of accusations leveled by Fielding against the prime minister in earlier plays. It also indicts political corruption of all stripes and reveals at the same time Fielding's utter distaste for even the expedient compromise toward "beneficent" ends that he sees as the basis of all political maneuvering. The embroiling inequities of large scale systemic corruption, whether clerical, political, or randomly social, is a regular theme throughout *The Champion* and comes to inform the moral view taken by the later novels.

It is the dangerously poised balance between good and evil, the soul's no-man's land, that is undermined by an intentional and programmed system such as politics. In order best to criticize the system, though, one must remain outside it as much as possible, something Fielding did not always do, since *The Champion* itself was a political instrument. He does seem to have been aware of the possible compromises of partisan involvement in political controversies, however, and on at least one occasion seeks to dissociate himself from hard-core politicos. Speaking through one of his mask voices, Nehemiah Vinegar, he says:

> . . . I find I am no politician . . . I find this study is beyond my reach. A man must be born a politician as well as a poet. . . . I know some have thought that Eve was the first versed in politics which she is thought to have learnt from the devil, an opinion confirmed by Dr. South, who deduces it from the same fountain, and affirms the devil to be a very eminent politician. (14 February)

Vinegar-Fielding goes on to offer additional explanations for the source of this exploitative evil business, finally fixing the origin of politics as coeval with the construction of the Tower of Babel, "the attempting to build a tower up to Heaven, bearing an exact resemblance to most political schemes." Delighting in his metaphor, he carries on, touching upon another important means of human deceit—the violation of language to corrupt ends. Playing upon the familiar legend that the proliferation of tongues also originates with Babel, he asserts with mock seriousness that "the best critics" have argued that the builders were nothing less than a group of political ministers "which I suppose to have been collected from their confounding one another by their language, a circumstance in which all their successors have imitated them, it being the chief excellence, and earnest endeavor of a minister to avoid being understood by any of his fraternity" (14 February).

Fielding repudiates unscrupulous political activity principally because its goal is authority and power through deception. In a *Champion* essay attacking the criminal or deceitful use of language, he questions the idea that communication through words distinguishes man from all other creatures (as we boast) or that man communicates at all with his language. Quoting Locke's doleful assessment of men's speech in the *Essay Concerning Human Understanding* [10] he lists a number of professions that pervert and squander language in everyday use: physicians, merchants, bold swearers, cursers, polite gabblers, and lawyers are all arraigned for sloppy communication, their opacity reduced to the Gulliver-like nonsense word "Barababatha." But for his final and perhaps most telling complaint of "barbarous" usage, Fielding cites great men and politicians "who have peculiar phrases, which some persons imagine to have a meaning among themselves, but give no more idea to others than any of those unintelligible sounds which the beasts utter" (17 January). Among these he includes "upon my honour," "believe me," "depend on me," "I'll certainly serve you another time," and "this is promised," all of which apply to duplicitous politicians as he had demonstrated so brilliantly in *Pasquin* and *The Historical Register for the Year 1736* and would again in *The True Patriot* [11] and *Covent-Garden Journal*.

Of all their qualities, it is perhaps the false sincerity of these phrases that Fielding finds most offensive; that and a calculated deviousness inevitably associated with too ready compliance in political matters. As for the politician's well-known ease in shifting positions to accord with the ebb and flow of power, the author offers a finely ironic justification: "It must be granted, that no man is so good a judge of the true merits of a cause, as he who hath been on both sides of it" (12 January).

Despite the evil surrounding us, all is not lost in Fielding's cosmos, and the quality in our natures that saves the rest of us from the political operatives is sheer diversity. This strength he sees as the greatest stumbling block to political machination and the source of a people's power to resist tyrannical rule. Throughout the later fiction it is this diversity that he celebrates in his fullest characters, with perhaps Tom and Parson Adams the prime examples of gusto and scope joined to an independent self—the very combination best suited to their survival. But the range of personalities, from Peter Pounce, Black George, Lady Bellaston, Parson Trulliber, Wild, Mrs. Towwouse, and Ensign Northerton to Amelia, Dr. Harrison, Heartfree, and Joseph, demonstrates Fielding's commitment to human variety as the most versatile and finally most vital weapon of the innocent portion of mankind in its war against corruption of all sorts.

The tensions of ethical combat are fairly constant in all Fielding's work, and the presumption of roughly balanced aptitudes for good and evil in the human psyche demands from him a prominent role for the benevolent and generous as well as the depraved in man's nature. To be sure, although benevolence and generosity are core ingredients of his celebrated "Good Nature" (as are truth, honesty, dependability), all such virtues are simultaneously susceptible to radically different applications in different men. In the 3 January 1740 *Champion* Fielding reflects on the uses to which particular skills might be put: "There are certain qualities, which, notwithstanding the admiration the world hath been pleased to allow them, are, in themselves, quite indifferent, and may enable a man to be either virtuous or vicious, according to the manner in which they are exerted. . . ." Courage (valor) and wit, he suggests, are good examples of such qualities. When adequately modulated by comparable restraints within the mind, they render a man "truly amiable, and justly entitle him to the esteem of mankind; but, when they meet with a different disposition, only render the possessor capable of doing greater mischief and make him a more dangerous enemy to society than he could otherwise have been."

Valor and wit are misapplied, of course, when pressed into the service of evil. When wit attacks religion, virtue, honor, modesty, or innocence and when valor is exhibited in the defense of false principles, political or otherwise, then both constitute dangers for the individual and society, but, "when the defence of one's country, or friend, hath flowed from valour; or when wit hath been used, like that of Addison or Steele, to propogate virtue and morality; when, like that of Swift, to expose vice and folly; it is then only that these become commendable, and truly worthy of our praise and admiration."

This overriding sense of social responsibility informing Fielding's ethic requires him always to judge human characteristics in terms of their application to society at large. The political vices he attacks in the plays and essays, the foibles and evils he lampoons in the novels are approached warily, as threats of direst consequence to the frail network connecting individuals with each other and with church and state. The questions implicit in these cautionary *Champion* leaders are the same ones seen in all of Fielding: Who will watch the watchers? How do evils in the individual affect larger structures of family and nation? What are the bends sinister in human nature? How are men best taught to embrace virtue and abhor vice? What, finally are vice and virtue?

With respect to the last question, *The Champion* reveals early in his career that virtue, for Fielding, consists in positive action in combination with restraint, the proper alignment and utilization of potentially destructive energies to useful, benevolent ends. He says at one point in these essays (3 January) that he knows no better general definition of virtue than that it is "a delight in doing good," and his most admirable characters bear this out. The operative word here, though, is "delight." Fielding's meanest inventions, those people we are meant most to detest, those deployed most obviously for the reader's edification and improvement (Blifil, Lord Fellamar, Trulliber, Walpole's dramatic personae, Wild, assorted highwaymen) are each capable of doing some apparent good—on occasion and for their own ends. It is into the genuineness of their motivation that we must inquire as best we can; there we shall find truths of being and answers to certain difficult questions about man. Although Joseph, Tom, Heartfree, and others appear spontaneously and therefore naturally good, we infer that these same energies could have been applied with equal facility to evil ends. It is not clear in Fielding precisely *how* one is good, only *that* one is, Squire Allworthy being perhaps the ultimate example of opaque, even unmotivated, virtue.

In pursuit of an ethical rationale to explain human evil, Fielding, in *The Champion,* tries repeatedly to come at a set of moral dicta that provides a satisfactory basis of judgment. What he appears to be attempting to accomplish in 1739 and 1740 is the unraveling in a nonfictional or semifictional format of classic problems of human behavior and in the process to arrive at some satisfactory answers to questions of good and evil. In a fundamental way, the novels that follow these essays are extensions of this unraveling. They are immensely skillful and crammed full of his wondrous gifts of characterization, plot, and comic narration, but at bottom they project, through the tensions and conventions of prose fiction, much of the same quandary over aberrant human behavior encountered in these early *Champions.*

In a 4 March essay, for instance, Fielding laments the devilish attraction of reputation, calling it a common harlot and one of the chief threats to man's virtue.[12] Indeed, a good deal can be learned about his views on human nature by observing different characters' attraction or indifference to reputation. Authority may confer an ill-defined if real power upon particular men, but the seeking after authority (and its by-product, reputation) is a contradiction in terms, for it appears to be acquired naturally or not at all. Tom could be, one suspects, an excellent Army officer fighting in the '45 on whichever side he chose. He is bold, fair minded, generous, brave, honest, but he is overwhelmingly apolitical, disinterested except in rare moments of gloom in any problems larger than his own frangible love affair with Sophia. Like others of Fielding's good men and women, he contains the essential elements of virtue outlined variously in *The Champion.*[13] Contrariwise, he and his fellow laudables avoid the stigmata of evil through generosity, selflessness, and a sense of public obligation. Fielding's good people often possess, too, a reluctance to assert themselves in a brazen or pushy way, a condition separating them from, among other castes, politicians, whose self-aggrandizing clawing after fame Fielding so contemns.

The subjects of vice and virtue and their centrality to the lives of men are further illustrated in an earlier *Champion* where Fielding, sounding like a Christian apologist, attacks deists, atheists, and assorted philosophical rabble. In this instance he is again prolonging an offensive already begun against Mandeville and Hobbes. What should be noted here is his conviction that if men will only use their common sense and follow the moral instructions of the wisest commentators, they will see that virtue does indeed reward her adherents handsomely. The problem, he argues, is that writers both for and against conventional Christian morality have misled mankind by suggesting that virtue is a spare and barren regimen devoid of any real pleasures, when, in fact, the very opposite is the case for the true believer. A close examination of the nature of man, Fielding suggests, will reveal that he needs and is happy with a virtuous life; the problem lies in convincing him of it:

. . . if we strip virtue and vice of all their outward ornaments and appearances, and view them both naked, and in their pure, native simplicity, we shall, I trust, find virtue to have in her every thing that is truly valuable, to be a constant mistress, a faithful friend, and a pleasant companion; while vice will appear a tawdry, painted harlot, within, all foul and impure, enticing only at a distance, the possession of her certainly attended with uneasiness, pain, disease, poverty, and dishonour (24 January)

Furthermore, he repudiates the familiar notion of virtue as "morose," "rigid," or as a "cruel mistress" who seeks to deny her followers any worldly happiness, claiming for her instead a far more permanent level of satisfaction than any offered by her evil counterpart. Finally, the added practical fillip gained with a virtuous life is pure Fielding: vice will make you nervous, virtue will calm you. This quaint enticement is linked to his calls for restraint in eating, drinking, and copulating where moderation allows the body and mind to last longer, remain stronger, and ache less. Vice will flatter, deceive, mislead, consume, and wear us out too early, leaving us to long for the tranquil (and protracted) satisfactions of a moral life.

It is an interesting approach, actually, one that he employs often in the fiction and essays to render morality more competitive in the battle for men's souls. Repeatedly, his good men and women manage to preserve their virtuous selves without sacrificing physical courage or beauty or intellectual worth or femininity. It seems clear that Fielding is intent throughout *The Champion* on combating the familiar proscriptive tendencies of a forbidding Christian morality while at the same time endorsing the happy permanence of a virtuous life: "This is that virtue which wanton wits have strove to ridicule, and wicked sophisters have argued to be so contrary to our worldly interest; whereas, her commands are most easy, and her burthens light; she commands us no more than to be happy, and forbids us nothing but destruction. In short, her ways are ways of pleasantness, and all her paths are peace" (24 January).

What commands could be easier to follow? Yet, with one eye always on our foibles, Fielding, two months later, is warning his audience about the curious sin of excessive virtue. In the 15 March *Champion* devoted to hyperactivity of all sorts, we are cautioned that "many more vices and follies arrive in the world through excess than neglect" and later in the same essay that "men often become ridiculous or odious by over-acting even a laudable part: for Virtue itself, by growing too exuberant, and (if I may be allowed a metaphor) by running to seed changes its very nature, and becomes a most pernicious weed of a most beautiful flower." To drive home the point he cites examples of overly modest (Steele's "outrageously virtuous") women and others who possess characteristics and interests that, in moderation, are most attractive, but gall when overblown—civility, complacence, friendship, love, religion, law, literature.

The effect of establishing these perimeters around behavior leads Fielding toward an oddly balanced view of human nature in *The Champion,* a view that seems to say: "I can't define moral behavior, precisely, but I know it when I see it." And so, he thinks, should we if we are paying attention. For example, the morality of certain characters (Adams, Partridge, Booth, Tom) strongly suggests an elementary version of situational ethics, a fact that greatly bothered eighteenth- and nineteenth-century critics.[14] But the reason for the characters' ethical fluidity is that the instructional-didactic canvas of the novels is painted in the broadest possible strokes, and even though at one level evil is usually punished and good usually rewarded, what we actually see damned or defended are men. Over and over we confront human beings caught in the crossfire of real-life stresses and then watch as they live up or fail to live up to a generalized code of right—unselfish—behavior toward their fellow-man. In this sense, Fielding's ethics are almost pre- or a-Christian, for the devil is not obtrusively proffering his cankered apple at each temptation.[15] What we have in the novels, instead, is the enjoining of behavior that is susceptible of the widest social application, never mind how well it fits a strictly Christian mold. What we have, in brief, is Fielding's concept of good nature.

This partially homegrown condition of virtue has long been a favorite subject of Fielding-watchers of all stripes.[16] It makes its first appearance as part of his organized ethical vocabulary in *The Champion* of 27 March where he spells out in some detail his notion of its composition. Citing Locke's observation on the ambivalence of language as the source of men's communicative difficulties,[17] Fielding promises to break down the idea into its components by showing first what good nature is and then what it is not. His first sally contains a fine hornbook definition: "Good Nature is a delight in the happiness of mankind, and a concern at their misery, with a desire, as much as possible, to procure the former, and avert the latter; and this, with a constant regard to desert."

Applied at random among Fielding's novels, this definition will in large measure exclude the evil characters and embrace the good (it will even exclude certain bad parts of good characters). When Tom or Adams or Booth or Allworthy deviates briefly from an ideal course, the anomaly can be linked to a temporary failure in their perception of right behavior (as in Allworthy's blindness to Blifil and Tom's respective merits) and not to any deep-seated corruption.

One aspect of good nature is sometimes overlooked when considering Fielding's nonaggressive heroes and heroines. In the above definition, the final phrase, "and this, with a constant regard to desert," is centrally important to the idea, for Fielding appears always at pains to inject a goodly portion of fiber and resolution into good-natured men. To that end, he says, "Good Nature is not that weakness which, without distinction, affects both the virtuous and the base, and equally laments the punishment of villainy, with the disappointment of merit, for as this admirable quality respects the whole, so it must give up the particular, to the good of the general." In short, the possession of good nature does nothing to prevent men from exercising their critical faculties, nor from exacting tough penalties for the antisocial or unacceptable behavior of associates. Specifically, good nature "is not that cowardice which prevents us from repelling or resenting injury; for it doth not divest us of humanity. . . ." Tom's splendid defense of Molly in the great graveyard battle and Parson Adams's recurrent pugnacity are integral and conscious parts of their make-up.

Fielding's essential pragmatism radiates throughout the 27 March essay, particularly when he touches upon the necessity for maintaining workable standards for human behavior, standards designed to preserve society's equilibria. The stability of this balancing act is contingent upon two considerations: first, the wisdom with which it is initially established, that is, what natural forces within man are allowed to shape societal organization, and, second, the willingness of persons in power (politicians, religious leaders, poets) to exercise the judgment requisite to alter existing conditions for the better. It is in this latter restorative work that good-natured men must be employed if society is to be well governed both religiously and secularly. The responsibility for such governance, Fielding maintains, falls naturally upon those men (good or evil) most willing to discharge it, with the sly and duplicitous always eager for the chance—which is why he calls upon a curious elite corp of good-natured men to save the state. Pusillanimity has no place in their composition; they must avenge their injuries whether personal or systemic, and they must realize that "to bring a real and great criminal to justice, is, perhaps, the best natural office we can perform to society, and the prosecutor, the juryman, the judge, and the hangman himself may do their duty without injuring this character [of good nature]. . . ." Finally, with patented irony, Fielding suggests that the hangman's job may in fact be "the best natured, as well as the highest post of honour in the kingdom."

In order to exercise the authority necessary to govern himself or his milieu, the good-natured man must be able to distinguish the wisest course from among several alternatives; in order to do that he must possess vision combined with discretion—or judgment. Summing up this phase of good nature, Fielding offers a succinct observation: "That as good-nature requires a distinguishing faculty which is another word for judgment, and is perhaps the sole boundary between wisdom and folly, it is impossible for a fool, who hath no distinguishing faculty, to be good-natured." It is on these grounds that Allworthy fails of our highest regard, for although he is no fool, his discriminations in matters of good and evil are deficient (as, at times, is the case with Dr. Harrison, Booth, Adams, Heartfree, Amelia, Sophia, and others). One final descriptive flourish by Fielding apotheosizes good nature for all time:

> This is that amiable quality, which, like the sun, gilds over all our other virtues; this it is, which enables us to pass through all the offices and stations of life with real merit. This only makes the dutiful son, the affectionate brother, the tender husband, the indulgent father, the kind master, the faithful friend, and the firm patriot. This makes us gentle without fear, humble without hopes, and charitable without ostentation, and extends the power, knowledge, strength, and riches of individuals to the good of the whole. It is (as Shakespeare calls it) the milk, or rather the cream of human nature, and whoever is possessed of this perfection should be pitied, not hated for the want of any other. (27 March)

Fielding's formulae for human deportment are not always consistent either in plays, fiction, or these first efforts at journalism. He seems unable to decide whether we are born to be hanged, as is suggested of Tom Jones, or if we earn our damnation by hard work and the sweat of our brow. In either event, good nature and good works, charity, generosity, and spontaneous goodness are the best antibiotics against corruption, and it is in *The Champion* that the preeminence of these virtues first becomes clear both to Fielding and to us. It is there that we first learn in what good nature consists and how deeply it is embedded in his psychology. *The Champion* essays provide Fielding his first opportunity for extended and thoughtful formulations of criteria for right behavior. Throughout the months of his affiliation with it, this paper served as a vehicle for display of an ethical system that saw its fullest application in the novels and in the author's own life. The origins and first tentative elaboration of preoccupations he will recur to again and again in his best work can often be traced here. Also to be discovered are his prescriptions for survival, and if men are to continue living successfully in large complex societies it will be due largely to the generosity of spirit and strength of character typified by Fielding's most admirable fictional creations, because "the good-natured man can never carry his enjoyment too far, this being the only affection of the human mind which can never be sated."

NOTES

[1] For a full discussion of the circumstances leading up to Fielding's involvement with *The Champion*, see F. Homes Dudden, *Henry Fielding, His Life, Works, and Times* (Oxford: Clarendon Press, 1952), I, 234–87; also Wilbur L. Cross, *The History of Henry Fielding* (1918; rpt. New York: Russell and Russell, 1963), I, 205–60.

[2] George R. Levine, *Henry Fielding and the Dry Mock* (The Hague: Mouton & Co., 1967), see especially Ch. ii, pp. 31–62. See also Andrew Wright, *Henry Fielding, Mask and Feast* (Berkeley and Los Angeles: Univ. of California Press, 1966).

[3] Sheldon Sacks, *Fiction and the Shape of Belief* (Berkeley and Los Angeles: Univ. of California Press, 1967), p. 115.

[4] *The Complete Works of Henry Fielding, Esq.,* ed. W. E. Henley (New York: Croscup and Sterling, 1902), XV, 94. All subsequent *Champion* references will be to this volume of the Henley edition.

[5] James A. Work, "Henry Fielding, Christian Censor," in *The Age of Johnson*, ed. Frederick W. Hilles (New Haven: Yale Univ. Press, 1949), pp. 139–48.

[6] Martin C. Battestin, *The Moral Basis of Fielding's Art* (Middletown: Wesleyan Univ. Press, 1959).

[7] Much later in the *Covent-Garden Journal* he will elaborate on his understanding of this dualism and of the resultant potentials for good and evil: "In the worthiest human Minds, there are some small innate Seeds of Malignity, which it is greatly in our Power either to suffocate and suppress, or to forward and improve their Growth, 'till they blossom and bear their poisonous Fruit; for which execreable Purpose, there is no Manure so effectual as those of Scandal, Scurrility, and Abuse." *The Covent Garden Journal*, ed. Gerard Edward Jensen (New Haven: Yale Univ. Press, 1915), I, 232. Similarly, in a December 1739 *Champion* Fielding notes "though I am unwilling to look on human nature as a mere sink of iniquity, I am far from insinuating that it is a state of perfection."

[8] In this connection, it is interesting to note the terms of Fielding's warm letter of praise to Richardson (15 October 1748) regarding the recently published 5th volume of *Clarissa*. In it he recounts his very positive reactions to the novel and, importantly for us, justifies those reactions, revealing in the process a good deal about his own critical instincts. He praises Richardson's skill at involving us deeply in Clarissa's dilemma

through "Terror" and "Compassion" and "Admiration" for the heroine. The fact that she has been tempted profoundly by natural love and passion, that she has succumbed to their blandishments (sufficient at least to elope with Lovelace), that a terrible price is being exacted from her, and that Richardson has succeeded in making us care by making us believe in her agony, these are the criteria, we infer from Fielding's remarks, that invest life and therefore fiction with its sublimest moments. They were missing in *Pamela*—although Fielding diplomatically avoids saying so. The point is that Clarissa's temptation and its aftermath move us so that we come to wish very much for her escape and rehabilitation, perhaps even for the apotheosis that later occurs. Pamela's temptation by comparison, is cold-blooded and lifeless, failing to stir our larger sympathies. The operative difference turns on the need to prove human worth by human actions and to do so in the heat of this world's fires. It is such a criterion that Fielding consistently applies to imaginative literature, for man must be shown, not merely told, ways of confronting evil in the world, something fiction can do much better than mere history.

⁹ The people hate their enemies.

They hate all those whose interests are incompatible with their own.

They hate all such as pursue interests different from their own.

They hate their oppressors.

They hate all the devisers and promoters of laws, restrictive of their liberties.

They hate the inventors of schemes prejudicial to their properties.

They despise those whose abilities are known to be in no wise equal to their offices.

They despise and hate those who have been raised from very low to very high degrees without public merit and services.

They despise men in high station, whose persons are clumsy, whose behaviour is awkward, and whose manners are low and mean.

They hate all subjects in power, who dispose of preferments without any regard to merit or capacity.

Lastly, they hate those from whom they apprehend their destruction, and by who much the more they despise such, by so much the more they hate them.

All the above are aimed directly at Walpole and the violations laid at his feet by members of the Opposition. We must remember that the funding and organizing of *The Champion* was effected by a syndicate of Opposition politicians and booksellers who turned all editorial duties over to Fielding and a companion, James Ralph. Fielding's sense of evil and his emerging ethical system should be seen as developing in the midst of a highly charged political atmosphere into which he threw himself with considerable spirit.

¹⁰ "Whoever shall consider the errors and obscurity, the mistakes and confusion, that are spread in the world by an ill use of words, will find some reason to doubt, whether language, as it has been employed, has constituted more to the improvement or hindrance of knowledge amongst mankind." Fielding pursues this line in the *Covent-Garden Journal* No. 4, which opens thus: " 'One may observe,' says Mr. Locke, 'in all Languages, certain Words, that, if they be examined, will be found, in their first Original, and their appropriated Use, not to stand for any clear and distinct Ideas.' Mr. Lock gives us the Instances 'of Wisdom, Glory, Grace, Words which are frequent enough (says he) in every man's Mouth; but if a great many of those who use them, should be asked what they mean by them, they would be at a Stand, and not know what to answer: A plain Proof, that tho' they have learned those Sounds, and have them ready at their Tongue's End; yet there are no determin'd Ideas laid up in their Minds, which

are to be expressed to others by them.' " Of all professions, Fielding holds, politics excels most fully in this dubious habit.

[11] See Miriam Austin Locke's excellent annotated edition of *The True Patriot* (University, Al.: Univ. of Alabama Press, 1964).

[12] He opens this essay by observing: "There can be nothing so discouraging from the pursuit of reputation as a reflection, which we too often see occasion to make, that it is the prize of the undeserving. Men are apt, and with some seeming justice, to despise a reward which they observe to be promiscuously bestowed on vice and virtue, wisdom and folly."

[13] It must be admitted that in the 4 March number, the idealization of virtue as goddess results in a peculiarly feminine and passive definition that fits Amelia, Sophia, and Fanny better than Tom: "True virtue is of a retired and quiet nature, content with herself, not at all busied in courting the acclamations of the crowd; she is plain and sober in her habit, sure of her innate worth, and therefore neglects to adorn herself with those gaudy colours, which catch the eyes of the giddy multitude." At the same time, the crucial ingredients hinted at here of interior balance, self-possession, kindness, and sense of relative place reappear in laudable characters of both sexes. Similarly, his description of vice zeroes in on the despicable qualities of mankind, for vice is of a "noisy and boisterous disposition, despising herself, and jealous of the contempt of others, always meditating how she may acquire the applause of the world, gay and fluttering in her appearance, certain of her own ill features, and therefore careful by all the tricks of art to impose on and engage the affections of her beholders."

[14] For a look at their discomfort in Fielding's presence, see Frederic T. Blanchard, *Fielding the Novelist* (1926; rpt. New York: Russell & Russell, 1966) and *Henry Fielding, The Critical Heritage*, ed. Ronald Paulson and Thomas Lockwood (New York: Barnes & Noble, 1966).

[15] See Dorothy van Ghent's discussion of *Clarissa* in these terms in *The English Novel: Form and Function* (New York: Rinehart, 1953), pp. 60–83.

[16] Two fairly recent book-length studies of Fielding's sources and subsequent application of good nature are Morris Golden, *Fielding's Moral Psychology* (Amherst: Univ. of Massachusetts Press, 1966) and Martin C. Battestin, *The Moral Basis of Fielding's Art*, earlier referred to. Note also George Sherburn, "Fielding's Social Outlook," *Philological Quarterly*, 35 (1956), 1–23, where he argues that Fielding's "major concern in his fiction is the dramatization of Good Nature."

[17] Locke says, "Those gross and confused conceptions which men ordinarily have, and to which they apply the common words of their language, may serve them well enough in their ordinary discourses and affairs; but this is not sufficient for philosophical inquirers."

SUSAN MILLER 〰️ EIGHTEENTH-
CENTURY
PLAY AND
THE GAME OF
TOM JONES

THE RELUCTANCE OF AN ACADEMIC READER to admit that the experience of a novel can be sheer fun is, or rather should be, astonishing.
If in all literature there is a masterpiece more entertaining than *Tom
Jones*, I have yet to encounter it. Yet even a brief look at what has been
written about Fielding's novel reveals ponderous pontifications about
its heuristic value, or, going back far enough, priggish reactions to its
frivolity, as if literature existed only in terms of Arnold's high seriousness. Or, if the academic reader deems himself superior to old-
fashioned moral evaluation, he is likely to treat the work as a pure
aesthetic object, calling attention, as Ronald S. Crane does, to its
internal coherence and to its formally realized structure (the interdependency of its constitutive elements). Well and good. All of these
responses are legitimate of course, and no tolerant critic is likely to
deny them. But why, the question remains, pretend that an art object
is not first of all valuable as provoking an enjoyable experience?
Coleridge recognized that the immediate object of a work of art was
pleasure, even if he did exhibit nineteenth-century seriousness by
claiming that its ultimate object was, or ought to be, truth. He re-
sponded to the "fresh air and sunlight feeling that pervades all" [1] of
Tom Jones, and so should we. We understand instinctively that reading
Tom Jones is a recreative (re-creative) experience, but too often we are
unaware that recreation is not only a result of the author's fictional
techniques but that it is formative of the novel's heuristic value.

Becoming aware of eighteenth-century attitudes toward the value of
recreation in general and of Fielding's own views of recreation and its
heuristic function provides a compromise between those who demand
aesthetic value and those who require moral earnestness in a work of
art; for fun and frivolity had social value in eighteenth-century England,
and indeed the growth of Tom's character from rowdy boy to man

capable of maintaining approved status in eighteenth-century society was predicated in part upon his activities that can be called "play."

In his study of *Popular Recreations in English Society, 1700–1850,* Robert W. Malcolmson has reminded less systematic historians of eighteenth-century social, political, and economic attitudes toward play. As this careful study reveals, it took both the emergence of religious enthusiasts, who restated and tended to implement Puritanical attitudes toward popular forms of play, and the necessity for a disciplined labor force to implement the shift from agrarian to industrial economy, finally to enforce Puritanical complaints about the popular games, numerous holidays, and the common sports that until 1740 defined English culture. Popular recreations declined along with the gradual decline of traditional society that a rising market economy and changing values and material controls on social relations caused. Traditional popular recreations had been rooted in an agrarian and parochial social system that was characterized by a profound sense of community identity. Once this identity began to be undermined by urban growth, contractual government, and industrial individualism, recreation slowly, inexorably, began also to lose ground, for culture had to be molded to allow for the distance between work and home that was newly defined, imperatively travelled. Congested cities, factory discipline, and free enterprise required that play be modified—ultimately, totally revamped—and this recasting was to take several generations before it resulted in the reified work ethic of the nineteenth-century.[2] This slow but relentless change, Malcolmson makes clear, left us with a work-oriented world view and with little feeling for the nature or importance of popular recreations in Fielding's time.

First, occasions for "vacation" were more numerous. The number of holidays in the yearly calendar during the eighteenth century was substantially greater than the number of public occasions for merriment and relaxation that are now assumed. The twelve-day Christmas season, Plough Monday, Shrove Tuesday, Easter, May Day, and Whitsuntide were annually and extensively celebrated. In addition, there were annual parish feasts, weeklong celebrations in each parish that occurred during the week following that Sunday commemorating the dedication of the parish church. These wakes were secularized festivals that most popularly were held in the late spring and early summer; John Bridges, a barrister, recorded 206 wakes in Northampton alone during the period between 1719 and 1724. Just as religious celebrations provided secular occasions for recreation, so also did commercial enterprises. Fairs held throughout the country—"horse fairs, cattle fairs, sheep or hog fairs, cheese fairs, fairs for hardware, or leather, or general merchandise" (p. 20)—provided additional annual opportunities for public fun. These occasions, coupled with the comparatively loose hours and daily variety of agrarian tasks, suggest that the majority of the population in eighteenth-century England found play more of a socially useful, unexceptional daily activity than we now do (pp. 89–117).

Secondly, Malcolmson makes it clear that the commercial and religious characteristics of public recreations, and the interdependency of participants in rural sports and games, prevented eighteenth-century England from rigidly separating classes while pursuing fun. Since many popular pastimes depended on the sufferance, support, or participation of gentlemen of means, specifically popular recreations neither excluded the upper classes nor necessarily reinforced class distinctions made on both sides. Like the fictional squires of Somersetshire, country gentlemen spent time in London and at home, playing in both settings without modifying, to any large extent, either context. In common with urban people of the upper classes, they participated in city pastimes; at home, they shared and maintained the sports of common country folk (p. 68).

Awareness of the frequency of eighteenth-century organized merriment, and of the normal class mixing that it occasioned through the middle of the century, clarifies its relevance to *Tom Jones*. Malcolmson disagrees with those recreational theorists who insist on the noninstrumental nature of play,[3] and he describes its social functions as largely responsible for the traditional culture and modes of self-definition that were later replaced in enclosured, industrialized, evangelical England. The frequent fairs, festivals, and spatially open games (for example, football matches in which the goal was a mile outside town and the players, 500 to 1,000 on each side, swam the River Derwent or took the ball through the town sewer system) provided, as much play does, outlets for usually unlicensed feelings. Sexual liberty, group and individual resolution of conflict against authority, or social cohesiveness and a sense of community were the products of the frequent recreations of the time. Participants might expect opportunities for actual evaluation of their social status or prestige, for their roles as players were not artificially divorced either from their daily occupations or their neighbors' perceptions (Malcolmson, p. 85). Eighteenth-century play was, then, a fundamental social activity that did not stand apart from social reality. It supported and linked plebian and gentlemanly experience, taking meaning from, and giving meaning to, the whole fabric of society (p. 88).

Recreational activities had an important role in providing individuals with a social context and class mobility. Before the middle of the century, recreation provided most people, as jobs or professions now do for us, the context for defining what a man *might* be. Play offered early and mid eighteenth-century people not only relaxation, but an immediate arena for trying their potentiality both within a group and alone. It is no wonder that industrial workers later rioted to restore the commons to the people. As Sebastian de Grazia points out, "in the old villages there had been cockfighting, badger baiting, whippet racing, coursing, hunting, fishing, and bowling, fighting matches, football, quoits, and dancing in the streets. The worker's troubles had begun when he lost his space,. . . his native ground, his place in the world." [4]

Fielding's attitudes toward the role of play in forming and maintaining a man's place in the world are evident throughout his works, but they may, without a complete understanding of these cultural changes, seem ambiguous. He both easily accepted traditional practices as part of the personal, defining context in which a man and his neighbors lived and saw these practices as inappropriate, almost anachronistic impediments to his, and the public's, freedom. As a magistrate writing about the poor, or about increasing theft, he asserted the post midcentury work ethic as a remedy for the evils of luxury, but as a novelist and playwright concerned to educate both characters and audiences he usually assented to pre-eighteenth-century attitudes toward the value of play in fostering and defining individual character.

In *An Inquiry into the Causes of The Late Increase of Robbers* (1751), he acknowledges the divine character of recreation: "Six days shalt thou labour, was the positive command of God in his own republic. A severity, however, which the divine wisdom was pleased somewhat to relax; and appointed certain times of rest and recreation for His people." [5] Acknowledging that "From constant labour arises a certain dulness and langour of the spirits" (XIII, 26), he nonetheless focuses on unregulated play as the chief cause—among the lower classes—of increasing theft. He differentiates repeatedly between the play suitable to the upper classes and to the lower:

> I would be understood to aim at the retrenchment only, not at the extirpation of diversion; . . . I confine myself only to the lower order of people. Pleasure always hath been, and always will be, the principal business of persons of fashion and fortune. . . .
>
> . . . .
>
> In diversions, as in many other particulars, the upper part of life is distinguished from the lower. Let the great therefore answer for the employment of their time to themselves, or to their spiritual governors. . . .
>
> . . . .
>
> To the upper part of mankind time is an enemy, and (as they themselves often confess) their chief labour is to kill it; where as, with the others, time and money are almost synonymous. (XIII, 27–28)

Writing at the time Malcolmson identifies as the watershed for popular recreations, Fielding discreetly identifies the curtailment of recreation necessary to regulate his society toward a time-equals-money ethic. He simultaneously reveals his belief that pastimes identify and singularize "the great," setting them apart from the poor.

Although Fielding repeatedly expressed the most usual sentiments of his contemporaries on what F. Homes Dudden calls the "common topic" of the evils of excessive luxury,[6] his participation in the movement that eventually curtailed popular recreations and created the work consciousness that resulted should not be mistaken for our modern separation of play from useful pursuits. He was aware of the human necessity for recreation and suspicious of temperaments not moderated in play. In his *Charge to the Grand Jury* (1753), he goes out of his way to make this clear:

> There is a great difference, gentlemen, between a morose and over sanctified spirit which excludes all kind of diversion, and a profligate disposition which hurries us into the most vicious excesses of this kind. "The common law," says Mr. Pulton, in his excellent treatise *de Pace*, fol. 25, b. "allows many recreations, which be not with intent to break or disturb the peace, or to offer violence, force, or hurt to the person of any; but either to try activity, or to increase society, amity, and neighbourly friendship." He there enumerates many sorts of innocent diversions of the rural kind, which for the most part belong to the lower sort of people. For the upper part of mankind, and in this town, there are many lawful amusements, abundantly sufficient for the recreation of any temperate and sober mind. (XIII, 214)

As Malcolmson does, Fielding recognizes the uses of play—its role in creating a complete individual and its ability to create social bonds while it tests, or examines ("tries"), activity.

The position Fielding took in these legal writings and the positive attitude toward play that is embodied in *Tom Jones* were in the mainstream of pre-eighteenth-century theories of the educational nature and functions of fun. Educational theorists specifically incorporated playfulness into their notions of the most efficacious teaching methods and theories of the development of personality long before twentieth-century psychologists recognized, as they have, what the Caplans call *The Power of Play*.[7] As Richard Altick documents in *The English Common Reader,* pre-eighteenth-century educators, not concerned about the social theory of degree or determined to limit the education of the lower classes in ways that would make them docile workers satisfied with the separation of the classes, had what later theorists would call "liberal" attitudes toward the role of play and diversion in education. Before the middle of the eighteenth century and new industrial expediency, it was not yet necessary either to curtail, or to make unpleasant, public education. Accepting the human growth accomplished in play and diversion was natural, for example, for Ben

Jonson, who says in the *Discoveries* that "change is a kind of refreshing in studies, and infuseth knowledge by way of recreation. Thence the Schoole it selfe is call'd a Play, or Game: and all Letters are so best taught to Schoolers." [8] John Milton, in *Of Education,* consistently sought to stimulate the pleasure and, therefore, the good will of students. Charles Hoole proposed a "petty school" in 1660 that would teach reading so that its pupils would "gain such a habit and delight in reading as to make it their chief recreation. . . and . . . be a means to sweeten their. . . sour natures, that they may live comfortably towards themselves, and amiably converse with other persons." [9] Locke, whose *Thoughts Concerning Education* repeatedly acknowledged the principle that children learn easily when they act on their desires rather than under the pressure of either coercion or a moral work ethic, also defined recreation as the best source for discovering and implementing the individual child's uniqueness:

> This farther Advantage may be made by a free liberty permitted them in their *Recreations,* That it will discover their Natural Tempers, shew their Inclinations, and Aptitudes; and thereby direct wise Parents in the choice, both of the Course of Life, and Imployment they shall design them for, and of fit Remedies in the mean time to be applied to whatever bent of Nature, they may observe most likely to mislead any of their Children. [10]

Locke's summary of the uses of play in the natural growth of the individual and of the ways in which parents (and, by extension, society) may guide a child by watching him in his recreation conveniently expresses Fielding's use of play within *Tom Jones.* Writing about that rustic upper class Malcolmson identifies as open still to class mixing in a world that incorporated public recreations more frequently than our own, Fielding could appropriate play as a metaphoric as well as representational method of describing Tom's growth from the status of an illicit foundling to that of a responsible member of the play-oriented upper class to which he was, in fact, born. The play within, and the playfulness of, *Tom Jones* were created by an author whose society and available psychological theory still unselfconsciously accepted the individual and collective uses of recreation.

Consequently, if *Tom Jones*'s reliance on play for both content and form is identifed, Tom no longer seems "mis-educated," or only innately good rather than learning as his story progresses. [11] The plot, characters, setting, and narration of the novel all employ characteristics of actual or metaphoric games. Johan Huizinga, in *Homo Ludens: A Study of the Play Element in Culture,* characterizes play as a voluntary, superfluous activity, an actualization of freedom. It exists outside ordinary or real life in a temporary, self-contained world of its own. It is disinterested; while the presence of play in all cultures suggests that humans need

play, play does not serve material or biological ends. It is also temporally and spatially limited, having an arbitrary beginning and end. It is
capable of repetition that becomes cultural memory and tradition. Its
space is also arbitrarily and formally marked off from the real world, so
that play is, finally, an order of its own as well as an order-creating
activity.[12]

The story of *Tom Jones* (distinguished, artificially, from its narrative
pattern and its narration) is an archetypal quest tale, predictable in both
its hero's progress and its outcome. Tom is a foundling who must realize
his destiny by undertaking adventures, by receiving inspiration from his
love of a goddess (Sophia), by being tempted, by making peace with his
father(s), and finally by mastering the worlds of family and society. His
status as a foundling divorced initially from any social class and necessarily in search of identity, establishes both his own need to win and the
reader's participation in a detective fiction, gamelike contest for information. Although the comic tone of the novel's first events indicates
that Tom will inevitably be found to belong in Allworthy's household,
these events also demand unravelling a mystery. The question asked
after Tom is discovered in Allworthy's bed, "Who did it?," provides a
detective story beginning whose clues and complications demand careful scrutiny. Tom seeks not only identity—competing, as he does this,
with Blifil, who frequently acts as a spoil sport (see Huizinga, pp.
11–12)—but also aims to win Sophia, who is the prize of wisdom.[13] The
characters who populate the fictional world that contains Tom's story
are, then, essentially functional, a label that may transcend the frequently expressed critical dissatisfaction with their level of reality.[14]
Tom's role as an archetypal hero surrounds him with others who allude
to various familiar types who are appropriate to Fielding's comic-
historic-epic; they either maintain a one-dimensional flatness that Fielding may introduce repetitively (Squire Western is perhaps the best
example of this), or they display themselves in relationship to the
exigencies of any particular fictional moment, acting as players within
Tom's adventure.

Even a brief catalogue of the characters who populate Tom's world
reinforces this point. Squire Allworthy, the master of Paradise Hall,
fulfills all of the functions of a godlike father and authority figure whose
rules must be obeyed and who umpires the action at the same time.
Sophia not only represents the wisdom Tom needs to achieve, but also
embodies every trait of the sought after, virginal heroine. She is the
prize for which Tom competes within the play world whose rules
Fielding controls, as well as the object of her father's hunt. Blifil is the
classical rival and villain, made most distasteful because, in a story
whose actions point toward a successful solution to the mysterious and
unrealized fulfillment of the hero's destiny, his chief weapon is misrep-

resentation and lying. By concealment and duplicity he in effect attempts to shatter the fictive world that aims to discover the truth about Tom. Partridge, the hero's faithful companion, transcends that role by also representing the surrogate father Tom seeks. Just as Black George and Tom hunt partridge in Tom's youth, so also does the human Partridge (whose name is first Little Benjamin) twice become the quarry sought by the intent of the story. He is first caught by his wife and Allworthy, and later, by Tom. Similarly, the women in the book whom Tom dallies with on the way to Sophia—Molly, Mrs. Waters, and Lady Bellaston—represent progressively sophisticated, yet repetitive, figures of the seductress. They are all distractions from Tom's goal.

As this quest progresses, Tom's activities are largely defined by his participation in common contemporary games and playful pastimes. While he is still in the rural, spatially open childhood setting of Allworthy's estate, he begins to define himself (as Fielding suggested above that "the great" will) in terms of games and play. He poaches with Black George, Allworthy's gamekeeper,[15] engages in boyhood and adolescent fights, competes with Blifil by tree climbing to restore Sophia's pet bird, and courts Sophia during his confinement after a hunt shared with Squire Western. On the road to London, Tom repeatedly engages in playful events: storytelling, hide and seek (in the Keystone cops adventure at Upton), and a puppet show all mark Tom's mental as well as physical progress toward London, where urban pastimes—masquerade, play going, and even duelling—become his arenas for action. If it is kept in mind that both Fielding and more recent theorists identify play as an activity in which we freely, without consequence, can test ("try") and explore real life goals, even Tom's sexual adventures during this progress become useful activities that contribute to his ability to live responsibly with Sophia. If these dalliances are play, Tom's final conversion may be seen as less sudden, for it represents a simple commitment to stop playing games and enter real life. An analogy might be drawn between Tom and Shakespeare's Prince Hal, who becomes capable of ruling by playfully "redeeming time."

Fielding thus uses play in its best and worst senses (recreation and luxury) to define Tom's good nature (in opposition to Blifil's "morose and over sanctified spirit"), to demonstrate and develop his physical and moral prowess, and to establish the social context usually denied to a foundling. Tom is educated by playing, winning, and losing, but he is also warned by the excesses that tempt him in London. Merely shifting the focus from Puritanical attitudes toward time wasting to a point of view that accepts the frequency and value of play as readily as did pre-industrial England reveals that Tom's activities need not cause embarrassment or diminish his heroic status.

The setting and narration of the events in *Tom Jones* also exemplify the characteristics of a game. We are struck as we read by the emphatically social nature of the novel's places and events: the inn, the Sunday churchyard, well-travelled roads, magisterial trial scenes, the roadshow or playhouse, Vauxhall, a jail, or private homes that become social settings locate the book's actions in emphatically social, *interacting,* spaces. These places provide the context for educating both Tom, who consistently competes in these settings to identify himself and his good qualities to others, and the reader, who identifies with a variety of audiences, or spectators, of the sport. As Tom plays out his role as protagonist (literally a first player), he is educated about the role that climactic knowledge of his own place in the world casts him into—a man capable of assuming upper-class responsibility in the loosely defined, noble and practical positions of a rustic squire in an increasingly urban land. His qualifications for the work life in fact holds in store are developed at the same time that the public, social nature of the novel's events integrate him into his class and help him to enter a social context. As Locke suggests, Tom's characteristically public recreations discover his "Natural Temper," show his "Inclinations and Aptitudes," and direct those who observe him toward wise understanding and advice.

Although the modern predisposition to accept authoritarian structures as the best means of education—and hard work rather than pointless play as the activity of a trustworthy person—may hide Tom's progress, it is, finally, evident that Tom is re-created by playing and that we too have become more perceptive players because of our reading experience. The delight and fun that characterized the primary responses of the novel's first supporters initially identified Fielding's technical achievement in *Tom Jones,* for he teaches good judgment and heightens his readers' perceptions by fictionally engaging them in the game of distinguishing his levels of presentation while they also pursue the answer to the riddle of Tom's origins and feel suspense about the book's outcome. It is to this purpose that Fielding's didactic techniques work. The structure of the novel, for example, is, like the organization of a fugue, playfully repetitious and contrapuntal. Critics like Frederick Hilles and Charles A. Knight,[16] who diversely identify the balances, situational repetitions, almost allegorical character doubling, and tensions that control telling this story, are marking the interplay of events Fielding manipulates in order to create his readers as players who become alert to the variation within repetition that organizes games. The narration of *Tom Jones* by a controlling, umpirelike judge, referee, and timekeeper, the "Fielding" who is sometimes within and sometimes outside his own fictional world, equally reinforces the reader's need to participate alertly in defining the distance and credibility that should inform his perspective. The reader acquires good judgment by testing his perception of Tom's story against the narrator's presentation and becomes involved in playing with possible interpretations or solutions as complicated as moves in a game of chess.

If reading was itself a relatively new popular recreation in the middle of the eighteenth century, Fielding's book as a typographical object certainly contributed to the pleasure of the sport. Short chapters whose titles frequently draw attention to the reading process ("Containing such grave Matter, that the Reader cannot laugh once through the whole Chapter . . ." [I, vii], "A short Chapter; but which contains sufficient Matter to affect the good-natured Reader" [VI, xi], "A most dreadful Chapter indeed; and which few Readers ought to venture upon in an Evening, especially when alone" [VII, xiv]), references to reading time, and frequent connections between the pages in the book and situations in the fictional world contribute to the sense that reading *Tom Jones* is confronting an opponent, in the structure of a game. The conspicuous artifice of the novel sharpens the reader's apprehension that reading is an active, rather than passive, process; Fielding demands that his readers self-consciously play *Tom Jones,* that they pursue not only a solution to the story's puzzle, but also an awareness of themselves as reading agonists.

Tom Jones is, then, a recreative, re-creative, experience. The fun of reading it is agonistic; both freedom and pursuit (mirrored in Tom's activity and travels and the metaphoric hunt that recurs throughout the novel) combine to define our growth as readers. Neither Tom, understood in the cultural and educational context of his time, nor we as readers participate in dangerous frivolity or luxury, but instead redeem time by freely testing our perceptive powers in a fictional context.

NOTES

[1] *Miscellaneous Criticism,* ed. T. M. Raysor (Cambridge, Mass.: Harvard Univ. Press, 1936), p. 302.

[2] Malcolmson, *Popular Recreations* (Cambridge: Cambridge Univ. Press, 1973), pp. 170–71.

[3] See, for example, Johan Huizinga, *Homo Ludens: A Study of the Play Element in Culture* (Boston: Beacon, 1950), and *Games, Play, Literature,* ed. Jacques Ehrmann (Boston: Beacon, 1968).

[4] *Of Time, Work, and Leisure* (1962; rpt. Garden City, New York: Doubleday, Anchor, 1964), pp. 189–190.

[5] *The Complete Works of Henry Fielding, Esq.,* ed. William Ernest Henley (New York: Croscup & Sterling Company, 1902), XIII, 24.

[6] Dudden cites the warnings of Smollett and Goldsmith as well as Fielding in the *Champion* and the *Enquiry: Henry Fielding: His Life, Works, and Times* (Hamden, Conn.: Archon Books, 1966), II, 771–72, n. 3.

[7] Frank and Theresa Caplan, *The Power of Play* (1973; rpt. Garden City, N.Y.: Anchor Books, 1974), summarize the history of theories of play and supply a useful, fairly complete bibliography.

⁸ *Ben Jonson*, ed. C. H. Herford, Percy and Evelyn Simpson (Oxford: Clarendon Press, 1925–52), VIII, 614.

⁹ Cited in Richard Altick, *The English Common Reader: A Social History of the Mass Reading Public, 1800–1900* (Chicago and London: Univ. of Chicago Press, 1957), p. 33.

¹⁰ James L. Axtell, ed., *The Educational Writings of John Locke* (Cambridge: Cambridge Univ. Press, 1968), p. 212.

¹¹ Both positions are argued, on the basis of investigating educational tracts, by C. R. Kropf, "Educational Theory and Human Nature in Fielding's Works," *PMLA*, 89 (1974), 113–20.

¹² See Huizinga, pp. 7–10, and Erving Goffman, *Frame Analysis: An Essay on the Structure of Experience* (New York: Harper Colophone Books, 1974), pp. 41–44.

¹³ See Martin Battestin, "Fielding's Definition of Wisdom: Some Functions of Ambiguity and Emblem in *Tom Jones*," *ELH*, 35 (1968), 188–217.

¹⁴ Ever since Dr. Johnson distinguished Fielding from Richardson on the basis of Fielding's concern with "manners" and Richardson's with the "heart," the reality of Fielding's characters has been a critical issue. See, for example, Wayne Booth, *The Rhetoric of Fiction* (Chicago and London: Univ. of Chicago Press, 1961), p. 198; Michael Irwin, *Henry Fielding: The Tentative Realist* (Oxford: Clarendon Press, 1968), pp. 104–05; Henry St. C. Lavin, "Rhetoric and Realism in *Tom Jones*," *UR*, 27 (1965), 19–25.

¹⁵ Malcolmson (p. 15) identifies poaching as one of the most common recreations in eighteenth-century England. Fielding (III, i) specifically defines George as a *"preserver of the game."*

¹⁶ Hilles, "Art and Artifice in Tom Jones," in *Imagined Worlds: Essays on Some English Novels and Novelists in Honor of John Butt*, ed. Maynard Mack and Ian Gregor (London: Methuen & Co., 1968), pp. 91–110; Knight, "Multiple Structures and the Unity of 'Tom Jones,' " *Criticism*, 14 (1972), 227–42.

T.C. DUNCAN EAVES ✣ AMELIA AND CLARISSA

In his *History of Henry Fielding* Wilbur L. Cross conjectures that Fielding began *Amelia* immediately after the publication in January 1751 of his *Enquiry into the Causes of the Late Increase of Robbers &c. with Some Proposals for Remedying This Growing Evil* and remarks that it is in some ways "a criminal pamphlet expanded into a novel" and "as much as the 'Enquiry' was written to lay bare the ills of the social state, with less stress, however, upon the means of reform; for the story must speak for itself." He credits the "grave" tone of *Amelia* to the sobering effect of Fielding's "illness and his experience as a police magistrate." "His imagination," Cross says, "was filled with the most serious affairs of life and death"—apparently allusions to the deaths of Fielding's daughter Mary Amelia in December 1749, of his sister Catherine in July 1750, of his sister Ursula in November 1750, and of his sister Beatrice in February 1751.[1] F. Homes Dudden in *Henry Fielding,* as usual, follows Cross and suggests that Fielding may have been "already shaping in his mind the plan of the novel" while he was preparing his *Enquiry,* though "it is improbable. . . that he commenced the actual writing of *Amelia* before he had finished the *Enquiry,* i.e. towards the end of 1750." [2] Cross frankly admits that his conjectural date on which Fielding began his novel "is based upon no positive statement by Fielding or his associates. In the literary ana of the period there is no mention of Fielding's being engaged upon 'Amelia' " (II, 311). And Dudden remarks "there is no positive evidence" for his "hypothesis" (II, 798).

Unaccountably both Cross and Dudden missed a reference to the composition of *Amelia,* though both quote from the paragraph that contains it.[3] In writing to Lady Bradshaigh in late November 1749 Samuel Richardson comments:

So long as the world will receive, Mr. Fielding will write. . . . . The Pamela, which

he abused in his Shamela, taught him how to write to please, tho' his manners are
so different. Before his Joseph Andrews (hints and names taken from that story,
with a lewd and ungenerous engraftment) the poor man wrote without being
read, except when his Pasquins, &c. roused party attention and the legislature at
the same time, according to that of Juvenal, which may be thus translated:
    Would'st thou be read, or would'st thou bread ensure,
    Dare something worthy *Newgate* or the *Tower.*
In the former of which (removed from inns and alehouses) will some of his next
scenes be laid; and perhaps not unusefully; I hope not.[4]

Richardson could have heard of Fielding's plan for *Amelia* (which of
course begins with Captain Booth's arrest and imprisonment) or of the
already written opening part of it from either Andrew Millar, publisher
of *Tom Jones* and friend of both novelists, or from Sarah Fielding, the
one of Fielding's four sisters who seems to have been most intimate
with Richardson. But whoever his informant was, there can be no doubt
that Fielding began work on *Amelia* well over a year before Cross and
Dudden conjectured he did. He could have started planning the novel
even before the publication of *Tom Jones* on 28 February 1749, when
Millar would undoubtedly have been eager for another work by the
same hand. The unusual double name of his daughter baptized on 6
January 1749, Mary Amelia (Cross, II, 225), suggests that already
Fielding had his new heroine in mind and named his daughter for her
and for his wife, just as later, in January 1750, he was to name another
daughter for the heroine of *Tom Jones* (II, 248).[5]

   The instantaneous popularity of *Tom Jones* must have elated Fielding,
and the fact that second and third editions were quickly called for must
have further delighted him (Cross, II, 121–23). As a recently appointed
justice of the peace for Westminster, he was, as Cross says, "rising into
eminence" during 1749. In May of that year he was made chairman of
the Quarter Sessions of the Peace for the city and liberty of Westminster, and in June he delivered his first charge, which was published "by
Order of the Court and the unanimous request of the Grand Jury." In
July he had to contend with a series of riots, which resulted later that
year in the trial, conviction, and hanging of Bosavern Penlez. Fielding
defended his role in this case, which had aroused some public indignation, in a pamphlet, *A True State of Bosavern Penlez,* published in
November (II, 230–31, 234–40). He also, of course, had to attend to
his many other duties as magistrate. All of these activities together with
the content and tone of three surviving letters to the Duke of Bedford,
Lord Hardwicke, and Lord Lyttelton (II, 242–47) indicate that his health
was generally good until December. Fielding was then seriously ill,
according to the *General Advertiser* of 28 December: "Justice Fielding
has no mortification in his foot as has been reported: that gentleman has

indeed been very dangerously ill with a fever, and a fit of the gout, in which he was attended by Dr. Thompson, an eminent physician, and is now so well recovered as to be able to execute his office as usual" (II, 247). Attacks of the gout were nothing new to Fielding: he had suffered from the disease as early as 1742, and, according to Cross, he was "already becoming infirm with the gout" while he was composing *Tom Jones* (I, 351; II, 100). But his earlier financial problems must have seemed to him finally solved through his appointment as a justice of the peace for Westminster, a pension granted him by the Duke of Bedford (II, 242–43), and the knowledge that Millar would undoubtedly pay him generously for any future works of prose fiction he might find time to write in the midst of his busy professional life.[6] Altogether 1749 must have been to Fielding a rare satisfying, hopeful year as far as his prospects for the future were concerned.

Illness, depression, gloom, or even a greater awareness of the sordidness of the world (surely by 1749 he must have been aware of just how sordid the world is) could not, then, have influenced Fielding to become more morally earnest or to change his tone in composing *Amelia*. As George Sherburn says in "Fielding's *Amelia:* An Interpretation," Fielding's "seriousness . . . is intentional," he "had not lost" his facetious "tone: he had simply changed it for another." And he goes on to cite as evidence of Fielding's "consciously serious and 'high-class' intention" his more frequent quotations from the classics (often without translation), his "imitation of the classical epic that marks the structure of the novel," which would "recall at least remotely the masterpiece of Vergil," and his preoccupation "with an organizing theme—held in his day to be a prime essential in epics."[7] But Sherburn does not attempt to answer the question of why Fielding in *Amelia* chose to be more "consciously serious" and less facetious than in his earlier novels.

The answer, I think, lies in Fielding's great admiration of Richardson's *Clarissa,* the first two volumes of which are warmly praised in his *Jacobite's Journal* of 2 January 1748 for their simplicity, manners, deep penetration into nature, and power to raise and alarm the passions so that one is eager to read the rest. In the same periodical of 5 March 1748 these volumes are again praised and also defended from the contradictory attacks against the heroine as being undutiful and too dutiful, too cold and too fond, using her parents too well and too ill. Later, upon reading the fifth volume (in advance of publication), Fielding became ecstatic in a letter to Richardson dated 15 October 1748: "Let the Overflowings of a Heart which you have filled brimfull speak for me." And they do: Clarissa's return to Mrs. Sinclair's lodgings shocks him and raises his "Terrors." "But when I see her enter with the Letter in her Hand, and after some natural Effects of Despair, clasping her Arms about the Knees of the Villain, call him her Dear Lovelace, desirous and yet unable to implore his Protection or rather his Mercy; I then melt into Compassion, and find what is called an Effeminate Relief for my Terror. So I continue to the End of the scene." Lovelace's announcement of the rape leaves him "thunderstruck." Clarissa's "Letter to Lovelace is beyond any thing I have ever read. . . . Here my Terror ends and my Grief begins which the Cause of all my tumultuous Passions soon changes into Raptures of Admiration and Astonishment by a Behaviour the most elevated I can possibly conceive, and what is at the same time most Gentle and most natural. . . . During the Continuance of this Vol. my Compassion is often moved; but I think my Admiration more."[8]

Sherburn has pointed out that Fielding placed on the title page of *Amelia* two lines from Horace and two from Simonides of Amorgos, which should have indicated to the learned reader "that the novel was by its author intended to present a picture of durable matrimony and of the beauty of virtue in woman" (p. 1). Captain Booth and his wife, Amelia, we are told in the opening sentence of the novel, are "a very worthy couple." Fielding continues: "The distresses which they waded through were some of them so exquisite, and the incidents which produced these so extraordinary, that they seemed to require not only the utmost malice, but the utmost invention, which supersition hath ever attributed to Fortune." But he adds that "the miseries in which men of sense sometimes involve themselves" are not the result of Fortune but the quite natural result of their "quitting the directions of Prudence, and following the blind guidance of a predominant passion." "To retrieve the ill consequences of a foolish conduct, and by struggling manfully with distress to subdue it, is one of the noblest efforts of wisdom and virtue." [9] Sherburn sees this as "the theme that the novel attempts to dramatize" (p. 4). It is certainly the theme of the story of Captain Booth (though the reader might question just how "manfully" he struggles), and Sherburn devotes most of his article to proving that Booth, essentially noble, has some faults, the worst of which "is that his moral courage is weak because he believes men act from their natural and not from their rational appetites," and that "it was the psychological and moral task of the novel to rescue Booth from this mental state" (pp. 6–7). He devotes only a single paragraph to Amelia, "doubtless . . . far the worthier of the two; for she is a devout Christian with no doubts or beliefs in a ruling passion. . . . Amelia is not merely the idealization of the *ewig-weibliche;* she is an embodiment of moral courage—precisely what her husband lacks" (pp. 4–5). But Fielding did not entitle his novel *The History of Captain Booth.* He called it *Amelia,* an indication that the "picture of durable matrimony and of the beauty of virtue in woman" is a theme of equal if not of greater importance than that for which Sherburn so convincingly argues. Also by calling his novel simply

Amelia Fielding probably hoped that his readers would compare his heroine favorably with the heroine of Richardson's admired masterpiece, *Clarissa,* and that they would be moved by her distresses as he had been by Clarissa's.

Fielding's double purpose[10] forced him to create in Captain Booth a character that conforms to his idea of the type of admirable character he recommends to novelists in Chapter i of Book X of *Tom Jones* and in Amelia one which he there condemns:

> . . . we must admonish thee, my worthy friend (for, perhaps, thy heart may be better than thy head), not to condemn a character as a bad one because it is not perfectly a good one. If thou dost delight in these models of perfection, there are books enow written to gratify thy taste; but, as we have not, in the course of our conversation, ever happened to meet with any such person, we have not chosen to introduce any such here. To say the truth, I a little question whether mere man ever arrived at this consummate degree of excellence. . . . nor do I, indeed, conceive the good purposes served by inserting characters of such angelic perfection . . . in any work of invention . . . for he [the reader] may be both concerned and ashamed to see a pattern of excellence in his nature, which he may reasonably despair of ever arriving at. . . .
>
> In fact, if there be enough of goodness in a character to engage the admiration and affection of a well-disposed mind, though there should appear some of those little blemishes *quas humana parum cavit natura,* they will raise our compassion rather than our abhorrence. Indeed, nothing can be of more moral use than the imperfections which are seen in examples of this kind; since such form a kind of surprise, more apt to affect and dwell upon our minds than the faults of very vicious and wicked persons.[11]

There may be "enough of goodness" in Booth's character "to engage the admiration and affection of a well-disposed mind" so that his "little blemishes" (his moral weakness, his irresponsibility, his addiction to gambling, his willingness to commit adultery with Miss Matthews, his failure to be open with Amelia, his lack of a firm faith in Christianity, and his naiveté or perhaps blind stupidity) will raise the reader's "compassion" rather than his "abhorrence"—each reader must decide for himself. But his character is scarcely such as to make a marriage endure—that task depends almost solely on the character and efforts of his wife.

In the opening chapter of *Amelia* Fielding remarks, "By examining carefully the several gradations which conduce to bring every model to perfection, we learn truly to know that science in which the model is formed" (I,4). At the end of the novel Booth may, in Fielding's opinion, have become a "model," though there were probably few readers in his day and none in ours who could be convinced that a reading of Isaac Barrow's or anybody's sermons could "perfect" a Billy Booth. But

Amelia throughout the novel is perfect, or almost so. Early in the narration of her story she (according to her husband) has "every perfection of human nature" (I, 85, 98), and perhaps in case the reader may think Booth's opinion biased Fielding too, in rare authorial comment, early assures his readers that she is "the best woman in the world," "the most excellent of women," an "admirable woman" who "never let a day pass without instructing her children in some lesson of religion and morality" (I, 161, 171, 174–75). Almost all characters, both the good and the bad, take occasion to express similar sentiments: "The finest woman in the world," Colonel James calls her (I, 182); Sergeant Atkinson says that she is "one of the best as well as one of the handsomest women in the kingdom . . . and the sweetest-tempered, best-natured lady she is that ever trod on English ground" (II, 90); Mrs. Atkinson describes her as "the worthiest and best of creatures" (II, 96); and that model of goodness and wisdom, Dr. Harrison, remarks that she "hath a sweetness of temper, a generosity of spirit, an openness of heart—in a word, she hath a true Christian disposition. I may call her an Israelite indeed, in whom there is no guile" (II, 146).

One of Fielding's tasks in his novel, then, is to demonstrate by subjecting Amelia to various trials that she does indeed possess "every perfection of human nature" and deserves to be called "the best woman in the world." Her first trial, the coach accident in which "her lovely nose was beat all to pieces" and she lost thereby "the admiration of others," made Booth recognize that "the woman who had been so much adored for the charms of her person deserved a much higher adoration to be paid to her mind; for that she was in the latter respect infinitely more superior to the rest of her sex than she had ever been in the former": "with what astonishment ought we to behold, with what praises to honour, a young lady, who can with patience and resignation submit to the loss of exquisite beauty, in other words to the loss of fortune, power, glory, everything which human nature is apt to court and rejoice in!" (I, 55–56). Her patience, dignity, good humor, and resignation to the dispensations of Providence shown in this first trial prepare the reader for her behavior in her future greater trials, never the result of her own imprudence or folly but of her husband's, though at times they are inflicted upon her (sometimes through him) by the malevolence or callousness of others. Her beauty, of course, must be and is restored by the surgeon since several of her trials are due to her possession of a loveliness that arouses the lust of the wicked. Fortunately, as her first would-be seducer, Mons. Bagillard, discovers, she is "a woman, who, joined to the most exquisite beauty, was mistress of the most impregnable virtue" (I, 136).

To show that Amelia is "the best, the worthiest and the noblest of women," "the best of creatures that ever blest a man" (II, 82; I, 264),

Fielding gives his heroine all sorts of qualities, attitudes, and accomplishments necessary for the ideal wife. She has "innocence" or "simplicity," yet "is the most sensible woman in the world" (I, 60, 272, 282; II, 96–97); she is all "sweetness, softness, innocence, modesty" (I, 60); she has "delicacy" (II, 28); "she hath indeed the best constitution in the world" (I, 77, 145). She has the highest respect for her husband (I, 268) and knows that love and cheerfulness are important duties of a wife. When Booth after his release from prison is overcome with a "deep melancholy" and "tears stand in his eyes," her cheerful and loving remarks cause him to exclaim, "O my Amelia, how much are you my superior in every perfection! how wise, how great, how noble are your sentiments!" (I, 169–70). She never upbraids him, even when he has foolishly lost all his own money and fifty pounds more at cards: "Upbraid you, my dear! . . . would to heaven I could prevent you upbraiding yourself. But do not despair. I will endeavour by some means or other to get you the money." And after pawning "not only her own little trinkets, and those of the children, but the greatest part of her own poor clothes" in order to pay his debt, she "with much cheerfulness" delivered him the money (II, 241, 243). She is ever the constant, consoling wife, who rightly (in spite sometimes of evidence to the contrary) thinks her "understanding" inferior to his: "I shall always submit to your superior judgment" (I, 188; II, 248). She is the ideal dutiful wife, who at the request of her husband declines Mrs. Ellison's (and the noble lord's) invitation to Ranelagh "(I shall never desire to go to any place contrary to Mr. Booth's inclinations")," though, not wanting to be treated like a child, when she is alone with him she does ask for an explanation (I, 278–83). She even consents when he desires her to dine at the Jameses, though she rightly suspects Colonel James's designs on her virtue (II, 116–18). More important, she wisely and charitably understands and forgives Booth's infidelity to the marriage bed during his stay in prison: "I cannot now forgive you the fault you have confessed; and my reason is—because I have forgiven it long ago. . . . I made large allowances for the situation you was then in; and I was the more satisfied, as the letter itself [Miss Matthews' first letter to Amelia], as well as many other circumstances, convinced me the affair was at an end" (II, 272–73).

She has other, somewhat lesser and occasionally unnecessary feelings, attitudes, and accomplishments: she feels for the distresses of Mrs. Bennet (I, 267; II, 38); she pities rather than scorns the fallen Miss Matthews (I, 167); she is not "learned," her reading confined to English plays and poetry, "the divinity of the great and learned Dr. Barrow," and "the histories of the excellent Bishop Burnet" (I, 288); she has "the truest taste and enjoyment of the ridiculous" (I, 128); she has no "blameable curiosity" (I, 233, 269); she is neither jealous nor suspicious (I, 180). When Mrs. Atkinson accuses her of prudery, she vehemently replies, "I do not know what you mean by prudery. . . . I shall never be ashamed of the strictest regard to decency, to reputation, and to that honour in which the dearest of all human creatures hath his share" (II, 208). Amelia detests cards (II, 142)—in fact, "all diversions are" to her "matters of . . . indifference" (I, 280); "no woman could outshine her in a drawing-room," and "none could make the drawing-room itself shine brighter" (II, 259); her dress is frugal but always neat, and as a hostess she is decorous and unaffected (I, 176). She performs "the office of a cook" for her family and is, in fact, "a great mistress" in "cookery," as she is "of every economical office from the highest to the lowest" (I, 265; II, 259); and near the end of the novel, when she thinks that she and Booth have lost all hope of any financial assistance, she firmly assures him that they can live by their own labor: "I am able to labour, and I am sure I am not ashamed of it" (II, 304). Before he breaks the good news of her unexpected inheritance Booth himself tests her: "My angel . . . I am assured that one who can so heroically endure adversity, will bear prosperity with equal greatness of soul; for the mind that cannot be dejected by the former, is not likely to be transported with the latter." Her reply is just what he (and the reader) expects from the Amelia who years before bore with patience, dignity, good humor, and resignation the loss of her lovely nose and the painful surgery that restored it: "If it had pleased Heaven . . . to have tried me, I think, at least I hope, I should have preserved my humility" (II, 305).

Occasionally Fielding teases Booth and sometimes his readers that Amelia may not, after all, possess "every perfection of human nature." At Montpelier she appears to Booth (and to the reader) to be jealous of his friendship with Mons. Bagillard and unreasonable in her vehement insistence that they quit their lodgings and move elsewhere, but Booth later discovers that this insistence was the result of her fear that he would discover Mons. Bagillard's attempts on her "impregnable virtue" and challenge him to a duel (I, 127, 136–37). Again she appears to Booth unreasonable in her refusal to let him go to the West Indies alone (one of the conditions that Colonel James insists upon if Booth is to receive his much needed company) and leave her under the protection of James, who, as Booth tells her, "will not only be a father to my children, but a husband to you": "I will give you my resolution in a word: I will do the duty of a wife, and that is, to attend her husband wherever he goes." Even Dr. Harrison, to whom the dispute is referred, assures her that she is "in the wrong." But the reader knows that Amelia suspects the Colonel's plan to seduce her, though, of course, she cannot tell Booth the real reason for her resolution because of the consequence of such a revelation (II, 124–29). Again her fear of the inevitable duel causes her to lie to Booth concerning the reason for her resentment towards James (II, 140), and when Booth at last thinks he has discovered the truth and accuses her of concealing secrets that he should have known, she pacifies him by suppressing "one or two of the strongest" circumstances of James's conduct and "giving such a turn to the rest" that he "was pretty well pacified" by her "narrative, and said he was glad to find a possibility of the colonel's innocence; but that he greatly commended the prudence of his wife" (II, 198). She again appears unreasonable to Booth in requesting him not to see James if he comes to visit him in prison, but she has opened James's letter to Booth containing a challenge and fears the consequence if the two meet (II, 274, 261). She deceives Booth (and the reader) by letting Mrs. Atkinson go in her place to the masquerade, but her reason for such deceit ("the first deceit I ever practised," she says) is good—she does not want to encounter Colonel James (II, 178–79).

There are perhaps some slight "blemishes" in Amelia's character or conduct. Early in her marriage she may be a little selfish in her desire for Booth to change his commission (as had been planned) and stay at home rather than remain with his regiment, which has been ordered to Gibraltar, but Dr. Harrison quickly convinces her that Booth's duty to king and country and regard for his character as an officer demand that he go (I, 87, 97–98). She may have too much concern for Booth's "honor" or "reputation" after she has read James's challenge, though doubtless this blemish (if indeed it is one) was inserted in order to enable Fielding through Dr. Harrison to preach on the falsity of what the world calls "honour" (II, 278–79). Fielding does suggest that Amelia is vain about her beauty. Dr. Harrison teases her about it, Amelia and Mrs. Atkinson both fix "their eyes on the glass" and smile after Mrs. Atkinson remarks that she believes "the first wish of our whole sex is to be handsome," and Fielding himself comments, "Nay, why should we conceal the secret satisfaction which that lady [Amelia] felt from the compliments paid to her person? since such of my readers as like her best will not be sorry to find that she was a woman" (II, 133, 13; I, 195). But this mild vanity is indeed a small blemish, one that is attended with no evil consequences, and Fielding obviously considered it really no blemish at all.

A more serious charge has been made against Amelia's perfection. It has been argued that she "comes uncomfortably close to doubt and despair," that indeed her "final error is despair" and she loses "her faith in the providential arrangement of the universe." [12] The evidence for this assertion is three scenes in the novel. When Amelia hears that the wise and good Dr. Harrison is the cause of Booth's first arrest for debt, in her surprise and shock, she cries out, "Dr. Harrison!. . .Well, then, there is an end of all goodness in the world. I will never have a good opinion of any human being more." She vents her emotions to Mrs. Atkinson, but shortly she recognizes (even before she learns just why

Dr. Harrison's conduct, according to Fielding, was "truly congruous with all the rules of the most perfect prudence as well as with the most consummate goodness") that her "excesses" have been "unwarrantable" and tells her confidante that she has "been guilty of many transgressions": "First, against that Divine will and pleasure without whose permission, at least, no human accident can happen; in the next place, madam, if anything can aggravate such a fault, I have transgressed the laws of friendship as well as decency, in throwing upon you some part of the load of my grief; and again, I have sinned against common sense, which should teach me, instead of weakly and heavily lamenting my misfortunes, to rouse all my spirits to remove them" (II, 52, 64–65, 70, 111–13). When after telling Dr. Harrison "all she knew, all she had seen and heard, and all that she suspected" of Colonel James she remarks "sure all mankind almost are villians in their hearts," the "almost" saves her. But Dr. Harrison nevertheless takes the occasion to expound on one of Fielding's favorite topics—how the goodness of human nature is debauched by "bad education, bad habits, and bad customs" (II, 131–32).

The closest Amelia comes to despair is after she reads Colonel James's challenge and knows that Booth has left his family and her homely meal to sup with Miss Matthews and cries out to little Billy: "Mention him no more . . . your papa is—indeed he is a wicked man—he cares not for any of us. O Heavens! is this the happiness I promised myself this evening?" This complete loss of faith in her husband's goodness (the result of her quite logically thinking that he all along has been continuing his affair with Miss Matthews) lasts for only a short time. She receives his letter of confession written from the bailiff's, and to her it "was at present rather of the medicinal kind, and served to allay her anguish. Her anger to Booth too began a little to abate, and was softened by her concern for his misfortune." But "doubts" linger: "Upon the whole . . . she passed a miserable and sleepless night, her gentle mind torn and distracted with various and contending passions, distressed with doubts, and wandering in a kind of twilight which presented her only objects of different degrees of horror, and where black despair closed at a small distance the gloomy prospect." The next morning, however, she hears Booth's full confession of "all that had passed between him and Miss Matthews, from their first meeting in the prison to their separation the preceding evening" and "all that he had done and suffered to conceal his transgression from her knowledge," and her faith in him is restored "and tears of love and joy gushed from both their eyes" (II, 261–64, 270–73). Amelia's loss of faith that there are good men in this world (and in the first instance in the providential arrangement of the universe) is always transitory, the result of shock and partial knowledge, and is completely restored when she is better informed of the facts. It can scarcely be considered a serious error, if it is an error at all.

Amelia indeed has almost "every perfection of human nature." But if Fielding wanted to give his readers a new Clarissa and "carefully" examine in her "the several gradations which conduce to bring every model to perfection," he failed. Amelia, like Sir Charles Grandison, is perfect when she first steps onto the stage, whereas Clarissa has serious flaws in her character that her severe trials and final humiliation force her to recognize and eradicate. She does indeed just before her death become a model, but she has been an only too human woman for hundreds of pages before that. Amelia's virtue is tested, it is true, but, again like Sir Charles Grandison, she must always feel and act "just as she ought" (though unlike Pope's Chloe, her feelings and thoughts are always "generous"). Only once, and that when she briefly doubts the faithfulness of Booth, is there any demonstrable conflict within her. We enter her mind no more than we enter Grandison's. In narrating her early life prior to her marriage to Booth, Fielding could have developed in her a conflict between duty to her mother, who (like the Harlowes with Clarissa) tries to force her to marry a man she does not love, and duty to herself and to Booth, but if such a conflict takes place in Amelia's mind and heart, the reader is not made aware of it. Similarly her spiteful and wicked sister, Betty (perhaps suggested by Clarissa's sister, Arabella), might have been made a vivid and irritating character who could have aroused in Amelia the spirit that Clarissa shows at Harlowe Place, but Betty's character is merely sketched, she does not live, and Amelia is too perfect to come in conflict with her. Clarissa is attracted to Lovelace, she even allows her emotions to overcome her reason and falls in love with him, but Amelia is not even tempted by her would-be seducers, Mons. Bagillard, Colonel James, or the noble lord—her heart always belongs to Booth. Moreover, Booth is really never unfaithful to her—his infidelity in prison, like Tom Jones's infidelities to Sophia, is an infidelity of the body rather than of the heart. In a sense, then, Amelia's trials, though distressing to her and at times pathetic to the reader, are external rather than internal and, therefore, never so severe as Clarissa's. Like Tom Jones, she is really not tested: when all seems hopeless Dr. Harrison is there to come to the rescue, and at the conclusion of the story the improbable conversion of Booth and the unexpected discovery of Betty's supreme wickedness and Amelia's gaining, thereby, her rightful inheritance enable the "worthy couple" to remove themselves from sordid London to the less sordid country and to live happy, independent of the Colonel Jameses and noble lords whose favors (always, of course, to be granted only on the condition of some outrageous return) would make existence possible. "My angel," as Booth upon occasion calls Amelia, is indeed a character "of such angelic perfection" as might have made some eighteenth-century readers "both concerned and ashamed to see a pattern of excellence" in human nature which they "may reasonably despair of arriving at." "Such angelic perfection," as Fielding recognized when he wrote *Tom Jones,* perhaps serves no useful purpose. It also makes it difficult for a reader to identify with, and such identification with Amelia is necessary if the novel is to be moving.

That Fielding wanted to move his readers emotionally is certain from many remarks he makes in *Amelia.* In his Dedication he refers to his hope that "the good-natured reader" should have his "heart . . . affected" by the book, and in the first paragraph of the novel he describes the distresses of the "worthy couple" as "exquisite" (I, xv, 3). He (and sometimes his characters) describe scenes as "tender" or "pathetic" (I, 98, 104, 118; II, 114, 242, for example). He at times wants to move his readers by suggestion rather than by development or description of a scene: "The scene that followed [Amelia's weeping over her children and thereby causing them to weep also after Booth's first detention at the bailiff's], during some minutes, is beyond my power of description; I must beg the readers' hearts to suggest it to themselves. . . . to draw out scenes of wretchedness to too great a length is a task very uneasy to the writer, and for which none but readers of a most gloomy complexion will think themselves ever obliged to his labours" (II, 65). When Dr. Harrison finds Amelia "in the highest agonies of grief and despair, with her two little children crying over their wretched mother," Fielding comments, "These are, indeed, to a well-disposed mind, the most tragical sights that human nature can furnish" (II, 113). And when Booth has told Amelia of his debt to Trent, Fielding again refuses to paint the pathetic: "A pathetic scene now ensued between the husband and wife, which would not, perhaps, please many readers to see drawn at too full a length" (II, 242).

But *Amelia* moved few, if any, of Fielding's contemporaries and fails to move all twentieth-century readers. The comment of Mrs. Delany, who "was almost broken-hearted at some Passages [of *Clarissa*], and raised above this World in others" (Eaves and Kimpel, p. 174), probably expresses what most readers feel about *Amelia:* "It has more a moral design than either appears in Joseph Andrews or Tom Jones, but has not so much humour; it neither makes one laugh or cry, though there are some very dismal scenes described, but there is something wanting to make them touching."[13] That the "dismal scenes" are not "touching" seems to me to be the result of their brevity and Fielding's refusal, or perhaps inability, to let the reader enter the minds of his characters and show them struggling with inner conflicts (though occasionally we briefly enter Booth's). At times he (or Miss Matthews, or Booth, or Mrs. Atkinson in their long narrations) seems to be afraid of expanding a scene, of running "into too minute descriptions," for fear his readers will find him boring or tedious (I, 36, 40, 45, 58, 62, 81, 87, 98, 104, 117, 145, 147; II, 4, 11, 242). Or he says some scenes are beyond his power of description (II, 65, 96, 114). Instead he resorts to methods of exciting his readers' emotions that are on the whole unsuccessful. The adjective "poor" (usually with the meaning of "unfortunate") appears almost a hundred times in the course of the novel and, though most often applied to the good characters, Amelia, Booth, their children, Sergeant Atkinson, Booth's sister, Major Bath's sister, Mr. and Mrs. Bennet and their little Charley, is also used to describe the bad, Robinson, Miss Matthews, and even the wicked noble lord. The pages of the novel, like those of Henry Mackenzie's, are bedewed with tears. Early Miss Matthews bursts "into an agony of tears" and then sheds "a large flood" (though Fielding suggests that this second downpour may be the result, not of sorrow or shame, but of rage), and she cannot think of her father "without tears" and is "almost dissolved in tears" when he discovers her affair with Hebbers (I, 26–27, 32, 40).

Booth, as would be expected, is more copious in his weeping: "a torrent of tears" gushes "from his eyes" when he tells of Amelia's accident (I, 56); he cannot mention his sister Nancy's name "without tears" and wipes his eyes, remarking that he "shed a thousand tears" over her "dear lifeless corpse" (I, 70–71); he weeps with Amelia at the prospect of his going to Gibraltar and wipes his eyes when telling of her consent and of his departure from her (I, 97–98, 103); "the tears stand in his eyes" when after his release from prison he sees his children (I, 169); Colonel James's generosity in giving him money brings "tears into" his "eyes," his generosity in visiting him at the bailiff's makes his eyes water, his promise of further generosity brings from him tears, and he again weeps in reporting this promise to Amelia (I, 178; II, 79, 84, 124); Atkinson's generosity causes his tears to burst forth (I, 226); he even weeps at Captain Trent's feigned generosity (II, 200). And of course he weeps at his reconciliation with Amelia (II, 273).

But it is Amelia who weeps most copiously and is, in addition, prone to fainting fits. Tears stream "from her bright eyes" when Booth tells her he has settled his affections on Miss Osborne and when, seeing her grief, he declares that it is she he loves she faints in his arms (I, 62). When he tells her that in spite of their love it would be imprudent for her to marry him, the tears overflow "all her lovely cheeks," and her mother, finding them together, has to support "the poor, trembling, fainting Amelia" from the room (I, 65–66). Mrs. Harris's discovery of the couple after their elopement causes Booth to fear that Amelia will faint, and indeed she does fall "back in her chair with the countenance in which ghosts are painted" (I, 81). Amelia is "drowned in her tears" at the thought of Booth's going to Gibraltar, and when he decides to go and she thinks of the miles that will separate them she bursts into tears, drops "more tears than words," clings around his neck, and "the blood entirely" forsakes "her lovely cheeks" and she becomes "a lifeless corpse" in his arms (I, 97, 99, 101). While preparing for his departure she weeps, and when she gives him the casket "a flood of tears" gives her relief (I, 103). She has "violent fits" after reading Betty's letter announcing Mrs. Harris's death and Amelia's disinheritance (I, 123). She weeps over her mother's death and upon her return to England weeps again (I, 146). On seeing Booth in prison she immediately faints away, which causes Booth almost to faint too (I, 166). She bursts "into an agony of tears" after reading Dr. Harrison's upbraiding letter, and the children accompany "their mother's tears" (I, 174). After little Billy is shaken by the foot soldier and is rescued by Booth, Amelia staggers "towards him [Billy] as fast as she could, all pale and breathless, and scarce able to support her tottering limbs," and when they get home she almost faints (I, 192-94). She weeps when Mrs. Ellison lets her read Mrs. Bennet's letter, and when Mrs. Bennet (now Mrs. Atkinson) tells her the story of her misfortunes, she almost faints at the drowning of her mother and does faint at her rape (suggested perhaps by Clarissa's) after drinking little more than half a pint of drugged small punch given her by the noble lord, who Amelia now recognizes has a similar plan for her own undoing (I, 267; II, 6, 38). She bursts into tears when she thinks Booth is jealous of the noble lord (I, 284). She bedews her children with her tears and the children's eyes overflow "as fast as their mother's" when Booth is arrested at the instigation of Dr. Harrison (II, 64). When Mrs. Ellison tells her of the impossibility of her keeping Booth out of prison, she discharges "a shower of tears" and gives "every mark of the most frantic grief" (II, 66). When Mrs. Atkinson tells her of her suspicions regarding James and of James's abuse of Booth, Amelia bursts "into an agony of grief, which exceeds the power of description" (II, 96).

Dr. Harrison finds Amelia "in the highest agonies of grief and despair [after Booth's arrest], with her two little children crying over their wretched mother" (II, 113). She bursts "into tears" when Dr. Harrison argues that she should let her husband go to the West Indies alone (II, 129). The tears "burst in a torrent from her eyes" when she sees Booth after her quarrel with Mrs. Atkinson (II, 210). After Booth assures her he will never gamble again and she replies, "Keep that resolution . . . my dear, and I hope we shall yet recover the past," she casts her eyes on her children and "the tears burst from her eyes" (II, 242). She weeps "with compassion" when Atkinson, thinking that he is dying, reveals to her his long adoration of her (II, 252, 258). She vents "a large shower of tears" (and so do both of her children) when she thinks Booth has been faithless to her and to them, and she and Booth weep with "tears of love and joy" after their reconciliation (II, 262, 273). Finally, she cries "profusely" with joy over her children when she learns of her inheritance (II, 307). Amelia also shows further signs of a tender, sensitive heart: she sighs, trembles, and often drops on her knees. And there are other characters (especially Sergeant and Mrs. Atkinson) who are addicted to the expression through tears and sighs and fainting fits of the tender emotions.

But having the characters in a novel weep and faint and sigh and fall into agonies does not necessarily move the reader. The characters and their experiences must do this. An author, as Dr. Johnson said of Shakespeare and Richardson, must be "able to affect his readers as he himself is affected, and to interest them in the successes and disappointments, the joys and sorrows of his characters" (Eaves and Kimpel, p. 338). The scenes in *Amelia* are related too objectively, too briefly, and usually without sufficient intensity to enchain the reader's attention and move his emotions. There is perhaps too much plot, and the narratives of Miss Matthews and Mrs. Atkinson are too long and too detailed—we need to know about them, but we do not need to know as much as they tell us. One is reminded of the stories of Wilson and of the Old Man of the Hill. Though Fielding does withdraw somewhat from his story, he occasionally comments, and his comments (unlike those in *Tom Jones*) too often seem to be intrusions that tend to destroy the emotions he desires to arouse in his readers. And there are other intrusions, passages and occasionally whole chapters of the novel, that though often interesting in themselves and perhaps at times important for Fielding's exposé "of some of the most glaring evils, as well public as private, which at present infest the country" (I, xv) keep the reader from concentrating on the distresses of his "worthy couple." [14]

The failure of *Amelia* is then partly the result of Fielding's attempt to do something different from what he had done in *Tom Jones* without wholly discarding the narrative method he had so successfully used in that novel. He desired to emulate Richardson in *Clarissa* and create a model character, but he could not bear for his model to have any faults and created an Amelia who neither changes nor develops and whose sorrows and joys fail to reduce the reader to tears. The result is his least successful novel. It is perhaps ironic that Richardson's desire to counteract what he considered the bad moral effect of Tom Jones and Captain Booth caused him to draw a model character for the hero of his least satisfying novel, *Sir Charles Grandison,* [15] in which he (probably unconsciously) adopts one aspect of the structure of *Tom Jones,* that of inserting into his main story various episodes to illustrate the virtues of his hero. If either Amelia or the Good Man ever had any real faults or inner conflicts, they are overcome or successfully solved before their stories begin, and what minor faults or conflicts remain are never convincingly demonstrated.

NOTES

[1] (New Haven: Yale Univ. Press, 1918), II, 312–13, 310–11, 248. Fielding also buried a son, Henry, in August 1750 (see T. C. Duncan Eaves and Ben D. Kimpel, "Henry Fielding's Son by His First Wife," *N&Q,* 213 [1968], 212).

[2] (Oxford: Clarendon Press, 1952), II, 798.

[3] Cross, I, 305, II, 142; Dudden, I, 319, 388, II, 724.

[4] *The Correspondence of Samuel Richardson,* ed. Anna Lætitia Barbauld (London: Richard Phillips, 1804), IV, 285–86.

[5] It is possible, of course, that Fielding renamed the heroine of *Amelia* for his daughter, perhaps sentimentally after her death in December 1749. But an extensive reading of London parish registers during the first half of the eighteenth century reveals very, very few people with more than one given name.

[6] Fielding had been handsomely paid for the copyright of *Tom Jones.* See Cross, II, 108, 118–20.

[7] *ELH,* 3 (1936), 2–4.

[8] Quoted by T. C. Duncan Eaves and Ben D. Kimpel, *Samuel Richardson: A Biography* (Oxford: Clarendon Press, 1971), pp. 294–95.

[9] Everyman Library Edition (London: J. M. Dent & Sons; New York: E. P. Dutton & Co. [1930]), I, 3. All references to *Amelia* given in the text are to this edition.

[10] There are, of course, many subsidiary themes, most of them designed "to expose some of the most glaring evils, as well public as private, which at present infest the country" (*Amelia,* I, xv).

[11] Modern Library Edition (New York: Random House, 1950), pp. 447–48. In writing this passage Fielding may have had in mind the Pamela of Richardson's continuation of his first novel.

[12] Allan Wendt, "The Naked Virtue of Amelia," *ELH,* 27 (1960), 136–38.

[13] *The Autobiography and Correspondence of Mary Granville, Mrs. Delany,* 1st series (London: Richard Bentley, 1861), III, 79.

[14] For example, Bk. VIII, Ch. v ("Comments upon authors"), Ch. x ("In which are many profound secrets of philosophy"); Bk. IX, Ch. iii ("A conversation between Dr. Harrison and others"), Ch. viii ("In which two strangers make their appearance"); Bk. XI, Ch. ii ("Matters political").

[15] Of course the continuation of *Pamela* is less satisfying than *Grandison,* but Richardson was forced to write it.

AUBREY L. WILLIAMS ❦ WHAT POPE DID TO DONNE

EXAMINATIONS OF THE WAYS that Pope "Versifyed" two of Donne's *Satyres* have emphasized his reformation of Donne's "numbers" or argued that his repatterning of verse sequences and his stylistic changes create a "difference in tone" and a "change in the speaker's stance." Thus Ian Jack, twenty-five years ago, stated that it "is sufficient to notice that Pope followed Donne in subject and in the general development of his argument, much as he did with Horace," and then he added that the two poets "differ less than might have been supposed" in their diction and imagery and that "it is above all in the 'numbers' that the difference between the satiric idioms of the two men lies." [1] Much more recently Addison C. Bross has added to our sense of the way Pope altered Donne's sequential patterns for dramatic or expository purposes and also of the way his "revisions of Donne's 'numbers' do ultimately constitute a crucial alteration in the attitude or dramatic stance of Donne's satiric persona." [2]

Suggestive and helpful as these two studies have been, it is not quite sufficient to say that Pope generally "followed Donne in subject." In their concentration on the style or form, or even the tone, of the works in question, the critics have failed to note the ways in which Pope's modifications involve changes in the actual subject matter of Donne's poems, especially in his reworking of *Satyre II,* which not only represents Pope's latest effort to recast Donne, but also, since it exists in two stages (an early draft of 1713 and a much modified version published in 1735),[3] enables us to trace accurately the process by which he narrowed the compass and gave a new twist to the Donnean original. And as Pope's contractions are traced, it becomes clear that he provided his altered subject matter with a dominant, but totally appropriate, pattern of imagery.

The more contracted scope of Pope's *Second Satire* is announced in his opening changes. Donne had begun by declaring that

> there's one state
> In all ill things so excellently best
> That hate towards them, breeds pity toward the rest,

clearly stressing (though in paradoxical fashion) no single overruling vice or sin but rather a superlative degree or "state" of odiousness in all "ill things," implying a scale of odiousness in each kind or category of sin. Pope, by contrast, emphasizes one single "Giant-Vice" itself rather than a degree or state in all vices, and his opening lines not only give a oxymoronic twist to Donne's paradoxical phrasing but also initiate the image pattern that will serve his new purposes:

> Yet here, as ev'n in Hell, there must be still
> One Giant-Vice, so excellently ill,
> That all besides one pities, not abhors;
> As who knows Sapho, smiles at other whores.

Donne's "excellently best" becomes Pope's "excellently ill," and the reference to Sappho's "whoredom" introduces the image pattern that will form his reticle and catch his theme—the venality of man and the trade by which it can be most aptly illustrated.

Donne, it is true, has three references to whoredom: a rather glancing one in line 20, a heavily redundant phrase in line 64, "imbrothel'd strumpets prostitute," a blunt analogy to "carted whores" in line 73; and no doubt these guided Pope to his own more systematic and pervasive development of the image. Neither the Donne poem nor the early Pope version of 1713, however, carries any references to whoredom in its opening lines. Indeed, Pope's early version scarcely differs in its opening from Donne's: he does introduce his oxymoron, but he also retains the idea of "One supreme State" in "all Evils" rather than change the emphasis to "One Giant-Vice." In the early version, however, he did use the word "abhorrd," which is not in Donne and which may have led him to the rhyme word he most wanted.

In the two ensuing paragraphs Pope roughly follows Donne in subject, but he gives more specific stress (amidst their common, and exaggerated, notice of the bourgeois tendency to blame the country's ills on the "crying sin" of poetry) to such matters as "th' *Excise* and *Army*," two tax burdens that would be particularly onerous to a profit-minded mercantile class. Furthermore, in the passage that parallels Donne's sardonic comment on the power of money to move the heart when verse itself proves impotent,

One would move Love by rythmes; but witchcrafts charms
Bring not now their old fears, nor their old harms.
Rams, and slings now are silly battery,
Pistolets are the best Artillery,

Pope's lines are markedly changed for a more dramatic stress on an
overpowering greed:

One sings the Fair; but Songs no longer move,
No Rat is rhym'd to death, nor Maid to love:
In Love's, in Nature's spite, the siege they hold,
And scorn the Flesh, the Dev'l, and all but Gold.

Venery and venality are not only once more brought together, but the
paragraph drives to a resounding finish on "Gold"—less witty and
"conceited," no doubt, than Donne's "Pistolets" (a small pistol, and a
small gold coin), but also more downright and more scornful. Indeed, as
the manuscript version of 1713 shows, Pope apparently decided, most
deliberately, to eschew the kind of conceit into which "pistolets" could
be fitted, for at that time he penned this rather timid adjustment of his
original:

One wou'd move Love; by Rhymes; but Verses charms
Like those of Witchcraft now can work no harms:
The Fair are furnish'd of Defensive Arms:

Against the Witty, Gallant, Brave and Bold,
In Nature's spight, the Stubborn Siege they hold
And scorns[sic] all Arms, all Battery—but Gold.

In the later version the two triplets are replaced by two couplets, and
the attempt to retain, in tamer form, Donne's military imagery is
practically abandoned, for all that is left of his conceit is the one word
"siege."

Perhaps the most telling illustration of Pope's more contracted
theme is found, however, in his lines that parallel Donne's introduction
of his main satiric butt, Coscus, whose "insolence"

only, breeds my just offence,
Whom time, (which rots all, and makes botches pox,
And plodding on, must make a calf an ox)
Hath made a Lawyer.

In his earlier version Pope retained the name Coscus and also Donne's
primary emphasis on his insolence:

> 'Tis *Coscus* only breeds my just Offence,
> *Coscus* renown'd for matchless Insolence.

But how different, and more pointed, is his later version, from which the very name of Coscus has been removed:

> One, one man only breeds my just offence;
> Whom Crimes gave wealth, and wealth gave impudence.

In Donne's introduction of his Coscus there is no hint of criminality or of riches gained by crime, though some twenty-five lines later he does attack "men which chuse/ Law practice for meer gain" and also tells his "bold soul" to "repute" them "Worse than imbrothel'd strumpets prostitute"—the powerful, but isolated, phrase that perhaps prompted Pope to his more sustained imagery of whoredom.

The most noteworthy and meaningful change in this portion of the poem, however, is the way Pope alters the diction and imagery by which Donne portrays Coscus's solicitation of women, given here at length to illustrate again Pope's more direct collocation of venality and venery. Jollier in his new lawyership than "new benefic'd Ministers," Donne's Coscus throws

> Like nets, or lime-twigs, whereso'er he goes
> His title of Barrister on every wench,
> And wooes in language of the Pleas and Bench.

Then occur ten lines of Coscus's "conceited" wooing that have no parallel in Pope at all:

> A motion, Lady: Speak Coscus. I have been
> In love ever since *tricesimo* of the Queen:
> Continual claims I've made, Injunctions got
> To stay my rival's suit, that he should not
> Proceed; spare me: in Hillary term I went,
> You said, if I return'd next size in Lent,
> I should be in Remitter of your grace;
> In th' interim my letters should take place
> Of Affidavits. Words, words, which would tear
> The tender labyrinth of a Maids soft ear. . . .

Of all these lines, Pope picks up only the last, and to it joins a line original with him, one that substitutes, for the whole bundle of Coscus's legalistic jargon, the blunt diction of commercial credit. Recognizing, surely, Donne's pun on "ear" (i.e., the vagina), he once more couples venality with venery:

Pierce the soft labyrinth of a Lady's ear
With rhymes of this *per Cent.* and that *per Year.*

Immediately after his sketch of Coscus as seducer, Donne sets down his scorn of those who practice law for "meer gain," and from this point to the end of the poem his lines offer examples of Coscus's shady deals and unscrupulous manipulations of legal technicalities. To go with such practices, Donne also offers a crowd of images, often in crabbed and obscure diction and syntax, several of which are dropped altogether by Pope. The major change in Pope's version, however, is his construction of a new "character" to replace Donne's catalogue of fraudulent and vicious maneuvers engaged in by Coscus. And though Pope used the name of Coscus when his poem was first published, he later in the same year substituted the name "Peter," obviously based on the person of Peter Walter, a notorious money scrivener of his time. While Pope describes Walter, in a note to line 125 of his *Epistle to Bathurst,* as "a dextrous attorney," there seems little question that the man was infamous in the age chiefly as a money scrivener and for the success he had as an unconscionable loan shark and manipulator of others' funds.

As John Butt notes in his biographical sketch of Walter, a money scrivener is "one who received money to place out at interest, and one who supplied those who wanted to raise money on security" (p. 390). But such a dictionary definition (from the OED) pales beside the traits commonly attributed to the profession in character sketches of the seventeenth century. One such "character" of "A Crafty Scrivener" tells that "*Hee* is the safest man from danger in the pedigree of rapines; for first, the Gallant lives by sale and Countrey Tenants; the Citizen by the Gallant; the Scrivener and the Devill upon both, or all."[4] In another "character," by Samuel Butler, the scrivener "has a table of use upon use in his memory, and can tell readily what a penny let out in the *Conqueror's* time would amount to this present year."[5] And another, of particular relevance to passages in both Donne and Pope, asserts that the scrivener "has blanckes ready to insert names, and in drawing of writings hee will leave out some materiall clause, that so it may occasion a suite in law."[6]

In actual life Peter Walter not only acquired considerable property and enormous wealth but also became a member of Parliament for Bridgeport—and became also the original of Fielding's Peter Pounce. His aptness as a character symbolic of tricky venal practice, furthermore, is illustrated by the fact that Pope in several other poems scarcely needs to explain his laughter "at Peers that put their Trust in Peter" (*Sat. II.* i. 40), or his admonishment to Swift,

What's *Property?* dear Swift! you see it alter,
From you to me, from me to Peter Walter, (*Sat. II.* i. 168)

or his ironic comment that a poet, after all, is a harmless creature:

To cheat a Friend, or Ward, he leaves to Peter;
The good man heaps up nothing but mere metre. (*Ep. II.* i. 197–98)

With the introduction of his "Peter," Pope not only breaks completely from Donne in a passage of nearly twenty lines, but also constructs his own "character," some of whose details would have been familiar stuff to an age brought up on the character-book genre. He begins his portrait of Peter, moreover, with another allusion to whores, the streetwalkers of the theater district:

Curs'd be the Wretch, so venal and so vain;
Paltry and proud, as drabs in Drury-lane.
'Tis such a bounty as was never known,
If Peter deigns to help you to your *own;*
What thanks, what praise, if Peter but supplies!
And what a solemn face if he denies!
Grave, as when Pris'ners shake the head, and swear
'Twas only Suretyship that brought 'em there.
His Office keeps your Parchment-Fates entire,
He starves with cold to save them from the Fire;
For you he walks the streets thro' rain or dust,
For not in Chariots Peter puts his trust;
For you he sweats and labours at the Laws,
Takes God to witness he affects your Cause,
And lyes to every Lord in every thing,
Like a King's Favourite—or like a King.

Having established Peter as the mercenary individual, Pope moves to the larger *class* of venal operators. His shift is the more pronounced at this junction because of his change from the singular pronoun to the plural, from "he" to "they" or "them," whereas Donne uses the singular "he" almost without exception in his account of Coscus's practices. Pope had followed Donne's use of the singular in the 1713 version, but the changes of 1735 suggest once more how deliberately his adjustments were being made. In introducing his class of men, moreover, he begins with a highly ironic allusion, not found in Donne, to Christ's parable of the talents, and one that may have had the special force implied by this comment in a seventeenth-century "character" of "An Vsurer": "Hee grounds the lawfulness of his vsury from the Parable, wherein the servant was not approv'd of, that had not improv'd his talent" (Saltonstall, p. 37). Here is Pope's denunciation:

> These are the talents that adorn them all,
> From wicked Waters ev'n to godly ———
> Not more of Simony beneath black Gowns,
> Nor more of Bastardy in heirs to Crowns.

Dismissing Donne's imagery of the hapless but "thrifty wench" who saves "kitching stuff" and who barrels the "droppings, and the snuffe/ Of wasting candles" in hopes of buying, in some thirty years, some "Wedding chear," Pope replaces it with money language:

> In shillings and in pence at first they deal,
> And steal so little, few perceive they steal;
> Till like the Sea, they compass all the land,
> From Scots to Wight, from Mount to Dover strand.
> And when rank Widows purchase luscious nights,
> Or when a Duke to Jansen punts at White's,
> Or City heir in mortgage melts away,
> Satan himself feels far less joy than they.
> Piecemeal they win this Acre first, then that,
> Glean on, and gather up the whole Estate:
> Then strongly fencing ill-got wealth by law,
> Indentures, Cov'nants, Articles they draw. . . .

As the two poems draw to a close, there are two notable differences. In the first place, Pope expands Donne's ten closing lines to twenty, and secondily he introduces his image of the "Vestal Fire" emulated in the kitchens of bygone country estates. The expansion in the lines seems to give Pope's close a more grave and measured pace to go along with the ancient pieties and hospitable customs he wishes to celebrate. By contrast Donne's concluding lines seem cramped, hurried, abrupt. And in the allusion to "Vestal Fire" Pope provides a suitable, concluding counterpart to the imagery of whoredom with which he had begun his poem. The allusion seems even more calculated, in addition, since Donne mentions a household fire only in the most vague and scant fashion (the woods of the Donne manor are not used to build, "nor burnt within doore"), and since Pope in 1713 had set down "usal Fire," not "Vestal Fire."

Critical comment on Donne's *Satyre II* reflects considerable uncertainty as to the poem's central theme, and if the various titles given it in early manuscripts are considered, the uncertainty is several centuries old. As the recent editor of the *Satyres* points out, the poem has variously been called "Law Satyre," "Satyre I," "Satyre II," and "Satyre I: Agaynst Poets and Lawyers."[7] In the same editor's opinion, "the second and fourth Satires" (the two Pope chose to "versify") can only be said to "fall apart badly" (p. xxiv). Attempts to demonstrate *Satyre II's* unity are still being made,[8] and it would be presumptuous, and irrelevant, to suggest that they will be anything but successful. At the same time, the history of confusion about the poem's precise aim or subject may indicate that Pope's incentive to its alteration should not be considered merely a concern to give it new "numbers" or a higher stylistic gloss. In view of the considerable alterations he made in its substance, he, more likely, like some of the most recent critics, viewed it as in conflict with itself, as divided in its assaults upon poets and lawyers, and so decided to contract its theme to one overriding vice—the "One Giant-Vice" of venality that seemed to dominate his age and to have corrupted the generality of his nation.

Pope lived in an age, after all, when corruption and the buying and selling of public office had become systematized at the highest level and when the prime minister himself supposedly had coined the statement, "Every man has his price." His adjustment of Donne's sights and the finer bead he took on his target should not be surprising in light of such poems as *Epistle to Bathurst,* where "secret Gold saps on from knave to knave" and where even gold itself has been improved upon by

> paper-credit! last and best supply!
> That lends Corruption lighter wings to fly!
> Gold imp'd by thee, can compass hardest things,
> Can pocket States, can fetch or carry Kings;
> A single leaf shall waft an Army o'er,
> Or ship off Senates to a distant Shore;
> A Leaf, like Sibyl's, scatter to and fro
> Our Fates and Fortunes, as the winds shall blow:
> Pregnant with thousands flits the Scrap unseen,
> And silent sells a King, or buys a Queen.

NOTES

[1] "Pope and 'The Weighty Bullion of Dr. Donne's Satires,'" *PMLA,* 66 (1951), 1009–22, rpt. in *Essential Articles for the Study of Alexander Pope,* ed. Maynard Mack (Hamden, Conn.: Archon Books, rev. ed., 1968), pp. 420–38.

[2] "Alexander Pope's Revisions of John Donne's *Satyres,*" *Xavier University Studies,* 5 (Dec. 1966), 133–52.

[3] *Imitations of Horace,* in *The Twickenham Edition of the Poems of Alexander Pope,* ed.

John Butt (New York: Oxford Univ. Press, 1946), iv, 129–45. My citations of Donne's *Satyre* are from the text provided on the facing pages of this volume.

[4] John Stephens the younger, *Essays and Characters, Ironicall and Instructive* (London, 1615), p. 342.

[5] See *Characters and Passages from Note-Books*, ed. A. R. Waller (Cambridge: University Press, 1908), p. 256.

[6] Wye Saltonstall, *Picturae Loquentes*, ed. C. H. Wilkinson, rpt. from edns. of 1631 and 1635 (Oxford: Basil Blackwell, 1946), p. 70.

[7] W. Milgate, *John Donne: The Satires, Epigrams and Verse Letters* (Oxford: Clarendon Press, 1967), p. 128.

[8] By Marvin Thomas Hester, for example, in his University of Florida doctoral dissertation, *Studies in John Donne's Satyres*, 1972.

CALHOUN WINTON 🕮 JOHN WILKES
AND "AN ESSAY
ON WOMAN"

SURELY ONE OF THE HIGH POINTS of the *Life of Johnson* is the episode at
Dilly's in May 1776 where the biographer has maneuvered his revered
subject into accepting an invitation to dinner, knowing as Johnson
himself does not that John Wilkes will also be a guest.[1] Boswell has set
both the social and literary scenes with extraordinary care. He had to.
As he recalls, "I was persuaded that if I had come upon him with a direct
proposal, 'Sir, will you dine in company with Jack Wilkes?' he would
have flown into a passion, and would probably have answered, 'Dine
with Jack Wilkes, Sir! I'd as soon dine with Jack Ketch.' " In the event,
although Boswell has some difficulty negotiating Mrs. Williams's permission for Johnson to dine out, the meeting between Christian Tory
and libertine Whig is amicable enough. The whole sequence is a masterpiece of unobtrusive Boswellian stage-managing. Both on their best
social behavior, Johnson and Wilkes make common cause in ragging
Boswell about his Scottish ancestry:

> When I claimed a superiority for Scotland over England in one respect, that no
> man can be arrested there for a debt merely because another swears it against him
> . . . and that a seizure of the person . . . can take place only, if his creditor
> should swear that he is about to fly from the country. . . . WILKES. "That, I
> should think, may be safely sworn of all the Scotch nation." JOHNSON. (to Mr.
> Wilkes) "You must know, Sir, I lately took my friend Boswell and shewed him
> genuine civilised life in an English provincial town. I turned him loose at
> Lichfield, my native city, that he might see for once real civility: for you know he
> lives among savages in Scotland, and among rakes in London." WILKES. "Except
> when he is with grave, sober, decent people like you and me." JOHNSON.
> (Smiling) "And we ashamed of him." (p. 77)

The delicious point of the encounter, as Boswell, Johnson, and Wilkes of course all knew, is that Johnson and Wilkes were bitter political foes and that Johnson disapproved of Wilkes precisely for being one of those rakes among whom Boswell lived. The question at issue here is the basis of Johnson's attitude, and that of other observers, towards Wilkes. He objected to Wilkes's morals (by which I mean to include, as Johnson would, his ethical philosophy) and his politics, but which came first? To what extent, that is, were the views of Wilkes's contemporaries and of later commentators about his politics colored by his reputation as a freethinker and a rake? There is evidence that they have been highly colored indeed, to the present day, and that his lurid reputation can be traced in large part to the so-called publication of "An Essay on Woman" and the ensuing hullabaloo. Since that 15 November 1763, when the "Essay" was read in the House of Lords, whatever else one may say about John Wilkes is qualified by a reference to his rakish character. Roland Stromberg, for example, in his widely used *A History of Western Civilization* characterizes him as "a wayward playboy." F. A. Pottle is perhaps more sympathetic, summing him up as a "profligate, a sceptic, a cynic, an opportunist, but never a hypocrite." A recent anonymous reviewer in the *Times Literary Supplement,* however, rejects him unceremoniously as a "blasphemer and pornographer."[2]

Any politician's private life is likely to attract the scrutiny of the curious public—and of the opposition: Walpole and Maria Skerrett, for instance, or Wellington, Harriette Woodward, and "Publish and be damned"; Lord Randolph Churchill and syphilis or John Profumo, Christine Keeler, and Mandy Rice-Davies. This is the froth that has titillated the public since David cast glances at Bathsheba. Politicians, the public is delighted to discover anew, like girls, or sometimes boys. The case of John Wilkes is, however, outstanding for the vehemence with which he was denounced at the time and for the interesting fact that the climactic event as far as the critics of his moral life have been concerned, the so-called "publication" of "An Essay on Woman," took place precisely at the high tide of his political success, when, as George Rudé has shown, the cry of "Wilkes and Liberty" was echoing all over the English-speaking world.[3]

The outcry against the "Essay" is remarkable. Certainly the government orchestrated its case against Wilkes as the source of the infamous "Essay" with care, if it did not in fact engineer the whole episode. Sir Fletcher Norton, the Solicitor General, solemnly charged in his Information to the court

that John Wilkes . . . most wickedly devising in tending [*sic*] and endeavouring to vitiate and corrupt the minds and morals of his said Majesty's subjects and to introduce and diffuse amongst the people of this Realm a general debauchery and depravity of manners and a total contempt of Religion Modesty and virtue and

also most impiously and prophanely presuming and intending to blaspheme
Almighty God and to ridicule our Blessed Saviour and the Christian Religion on
the first day of July [1763] . . . most wickedly and maliciously printed and
published and caused to be printed and published a certain malignant obscene
and impious libel or composition intitled An Essay on Woman.[4]

What was this fiendish document with which Wilkes set out to corrupt
the morals of an entire people, reprints of which even today are kept
carefully locked in library safes while *Fanny Hill* reclines unprotected
on the open shelves? What were the true facts of its composition and
printing, and of what did its contents consist? The British Library of the
British Museum, indeed, does not acknowledge the existence of their
copy (of a reprint). Guessing that the collection includes a copy one
must first learn by some means the correct shelfmark and then request
access to the hideous instrument by means of a letter to the Keeper of
Printed Books explaining in detail one's reasons for seeing it.[5] Because
of the natural secretiveness of libraries, then, but also because the
uproar attendant to Wilkes's denunciation was so great, and finally
because Wilkes himself muddied the waters after the poem's "publication" in order, presumably , to throw off his pursuers, some answers
must be tentative, but here follows the gist, based on a reconsideration
of manuscript and printed sources.

During the middle years of the decade 1750–60 Wilkes and his
friend Thomas Potter, M.P., son of the Archbishop of Canterbury, had
been engaged in some kind of desultory literary collaboration. Potter's
ambitions were sexual rather than literary or political, judging from his
surviving correspondence.[6] As a member of Parliament his major
constructive action seems to have been a bill he introduced in 1753
proposing the first national census, a bill that alarmed politicians of
every stripe, who united in righteous indignation to crush it as "profane
and subversive of liberty." [7] Besides retailing scabrous stories about
their contemporaries, the Wilkes-Potter literary collaboration appears
to have included writing several poems with titles derived from works
by Alexander Pope. Wilkes had acquired Bishop Warburton's 1751
edition of Pope, and Potter, not incidentally, was apparently sleeping
with Warburton's wife.[8] The poems involved in the 1763 "publication"
controversy were "An Essay on Woman" and three short poems, the
"Universal Prayer," "Veni Creator," and the "Dying Lover to his Prick,"
the last of course an imitation of Pope's "Dying Christian to His Soul"
(itself an imitation of the Emperor Hadrian's poem).

Potter died in 1759, and about 1762 Wilkes decided to have a few
copies of a collection of these four poems printed for circulation among
his friends. The question of authorship can perhaps never be entirely
resolved. After the controversy heated up in 1763 Wilkes was at pains

to minimize his part in the composition of the poems, and he may have destroyed the manuscript, which his printer deposed was in Wilkes's hand. His most recent biographers as well as George Rudé have followed Wilkes's own suggestion that the poems were principally Potter's compositions whereas the notes and commentary (humorously ascribed on the titlepage to Bishop Warburton) were the work of Wilkes. The evidence, in my opinion, indicates that Wilkes's hand was the dominant one in the poems themselves.

In the first place, Potter displayed few literary inclinations, again judging from his correspondence, whereas Wilkes fancied himself a man of letters and dabbled in poetry all his adult life.[9] Moreover, there are references to persons and events in the poem that postdate Potter's death: an image of the Earl of Bute as prime minister, for example. Wilkes, of course, could have inserted these references in the poem after its composition. There is additionally, however, the direct testimony of Michael Curry, Wilkes's printer. In a deposition to a government lawyer, Philip Carteret Webb, made about four months after he had printed the poems, Curry stated that the "Copy of this Essay on Woman I am positive was in Mr. Wilkes's own Hand Writing & from some singular Circumstances am positive it was his Composing." [10] Unfortunately Curry nowhere enlarges on what those circumstances were. It could be and has been argued that Curry is here making a self-serving statement, but matters of fact in his narrative that can be verified are generally accurate. Finally, the quotation from one of Potter's letters on which the biographer Raymond Postgate and those following him rely as proof of Potter's hand in the poems' composition appears to me rather to argue for Wilkes as author, especially when read in context. Potter, travelling in Devonshire with Mrs. Warburton, had written Wilkes on 31 July 1755, "Who your Mrs M. is with whom you rather wish me to copulate I am at a Loss to guess. I could reverse the Letter & attempt the Essay on Woman without even the Hope of having a Commentator." [11] This does not signify, as I read it, that Potter is about to write the "Essay" as Postgate assumes, but that he could reverse the letter M to W (for Warburton) and try her virtue (attempt the Essay on Woman) without even the hope of having a commentator (Wilkes not being present).

For these reasons I believe that Wilkes was principally responsible for both the poetry and commentary of the collection. Be the question of authorship as it may, it is certain that by the autumn of 1762 Wilkes had caused a titlepage to be engraved for the collection *"An Essay on Woman" by Pego Borewell Esq. with the notes of Rogerus Cunaeus, Vigerus Mutoniatus* [12] *And a Commentary of the Rev. Dr. Warburton Inscribed to Miss Fanny Murray* (a well-known prostitute).[13] The titlepage included an engraving of a phallus over a representation of a ten-inch scale (this

was to cause Wilkes plenty of trouble) and a Latin inscription identifying the archetype of the phallus as that belonging to the Most Reverend
George Stone, Archbishop of Armagh and Anglican Primate of Ire-
land. This begins a joke about Stone's alleged sodomitical practices that
runs through the annotation or such of it as has survived. At this time
(1762) Wilkes referred to the work as "my Essay" in a letter to his
printer and ordered that proofs be struck of the titlepage and two other
plates with which the work was to be embellished.[14] Apparently—and
most unfortunately—these have not survived. Wilkes and his friend
and collaborator Charles Churchill were then in the midst of a controversy with Hogarth of which Hogarth's famous caricature of the
crosseyed Wilkes was a product. One would like to be able to judge the
standards of Wilkes's own graphic sense.[15] No part of the letterpress
was printed in 1762.

In April 1763 Wilkes was arrested and imprisoned in the Tower for
publishing *North Briton* No. 45, "a seditious and treasonable paper,"
released on a writ of habeas corpus on 6 May, discharged by Chief
Justice Pratt on the grounds of parliamentary immunity, and escorted to
his home in triumph by a mob of thousands shouting "Wilkes and
Liberty." This was a cry, it will be recalled, that was picked up in the
American colonies, where pro-Wilkes fervor resulted in the naming of
Wilkes-Barre, Pennsylvania, and Wilkesboro, North Carolina, and the
grant of £1,500 sterling by the Commons House of Assembly of South
Carolina towards the payment of his legal fees.[16] It was a famous
constitutional imbroglio, with George III himself behind the scenes
personally urging the government on and with Wilkes one step ahead
of the hounds, but only one step.

Wilkes suspected that the government agents who ransacked his
house had seen the collection of poems. They had made away with a
good many other letters and documents, but apparently he was mistaken
in this particular.[17] Presumably to counter some sort of "publication"
on the part of the government, he placed an advertisement in *The Public
Advertiser* for 10 May announcing the impending publication of "An
Essay on Woman" by Philip Carteret Webb and Lovell Stanhope, the
lawyers who had engineered the raid on his house.[18] At this point—and
here the biographers have not been helpful in accounting for an apparently incredible action—Wilkes decided to set up a small printing
establishment in that very house on which he would reprint *The North
Briton* and print for the first time the "Essay on Woman" collection.
Why Wilkes should have chosen to order the printing done under his
own roof has never been satisfactorily explained; it was almost as if he
were daring the government to catch him.[19] The decision proved to be
a disastrous misjudgment for Wilkes.

The copytext, according to Michael Curry, the printing foreman, was a leatherbound octavo volume of Pope's *Essay* with the Wilkes-Potter poems written in Wilkes's hand on the facing pages.[20] Wilkes directed Curry to begin work on twelve copies of the collection in red letter. After the prefatory matter, ninety-four lines of the "Essay," and six pages of the shorter poems had been printed, Wilkes ordered work stopped and departed for a visit to France, leaving behind the incriminating twelve fragments and also a thirteenth that Curry had thoughtfully printed for his own use, as well as a set of proofs in black letter with Wilkes's corrections on them. This printing, incidentally, is what the government later successfully argued constituted "publication."

By October Curry's red letter fragment and the corrected proofs had been supplied through various intermediaries to the government. These intermediaries included the Earl of March's chaplain, the improbable Reverend John Kidgell, himself author of a salacious novel, *The Card*.[21] The details of the transaction—whether, that is, it was by mere chance that Kidgell happened to see the poems, which he then in a spasm of indignation arranged to have delivered to the government officialdom (this was his and the official version) or whether, as seems more likely, the whole operation had been set in motion months earlier on the initiative of one of Wilkes's former friends now in high position specifically to entrap him—these details are perhaps forever lost in the thicket of charges, countercharges, denials, and perjury that were to come.[22] What is certain is that on 15 November 1763 the government attacked Wilkes in both Houses of Parliament, successfully moving the resolution in Commons that the *North Briton* No. 45 was a "false, scandalous, and seditious libel" and in the Lords that the "Essay on Woman" was a "most scandalous, obscene, and impious libel"[23] on Bishop Warburton and therefore a breach of privilege. Lord Sandwich, who had been in earlier years with Wilkes one of the riotous Monks of Medmenham Abbey, read the fragment of the "Essay" and its accompanying commentary line by line, pausing from time to time to express his horror, while Bishop Warburton and the other peers of the realm listened in varying attitudes of interest, irritation, and amusement. "The Bishop of Gloucester [Warburton]," Horace Walpole reported to Sir Horace Mann, "has been measuring out ground in Smithfield for [Wilkes's] execution, and in his speech begged the devil's pardon for comparing him to Wilkes." Even Pitt for the Opposition in Commons deserted his old bottle companion and proclaimed Wilkes "the blasphemer of his God and the libeller of his king."[24]

The poems themselves though usually referred to as parodies are actually imitations, in the eighteenth-century sense of the term.[25] The general structure of Pope's original is employed, but the scene is transferred from the philosopher-poet's study or garden to the sexual athlete's bedroom, as it were, with results of varying comic effectiveness. The principal satiric victim is Warburton rather than Pope or woman, and there are other satiric references to the former chief minister, the Earl of Bute, and, as noted above, Archbishop Stone.

Since all that was printed of the "Essay on Woman," and with the exception of a single couplet from the Fourth Epistle apparently all that remains,[26] represents no more than an eighth of the complete poem, no final judgment on its merit is possible. The tone is good humored throughout, if at times somewhat sophomoric, except where Warburton and the Earl of Bute are concerned. In a prefatory Advertisement, for example, the Editor gravely discusses Cibber's assertion that Pope had also written an "Essay on Woman." "The truth I take to be this: Mr. Pope might indeed, and in all probability he actually, and frequently did handle this subject in a cursory way, but I dare say he never *went deep* into it." Beyond this, Pope does not figure much in the work; Warburton is the quarry.

In this century we may be inclined to overlook just how ponderous and self-serving Warburton's editing of Pope was. The volume containing the *Essay on Man* on the octavo 1751 edition, for example, has as a preface a long "Essay on Satire . . . Inscribed to Mr. Warburton" by John "Estimate" Brown that is grossly flattering to Warburton. Brown's attitude seems to be that Pope the poet existed for Warburton the commentator's benefit. In this regard Thomas Edwards, the literary critic, observed to a friend after reading Warburton's commentary on the *Essay,* "Poor Pope, though he has the upper hand in the title page, makes but a very mean figure in the body of the work." [27] An unfavorable opinion of Warburton as a critic seems to have been something of a commonplace in Wilkes's circle. His friend John Armstrong, writing to thank Wilkes for the gift of some cheese, observes that he values his opinion so highly that if Wilkes had "made me a present of Beet Root or Bread Sauce or W——n's critical productions I believe I should directly begin to find them very good things." [28] Warburton was a fierce and unforgiving literary controversialist, but his annotation of Pope's *Essay* does strike vacuous notes that invite satire. Consider his comment on the opening lines: "The Opening of this poem, in fifteen lines, is taken up in giving an account of the Subject; which, agreeably to the title, is an Essay on Man. . . ." [29]

Wilkes adapts the famous opening to his purposes. The original

Awake, my ST. JOHN! leave all meaner things
To low ambition, and the pride of Kings

becomes the poet's apostrophe to the prostitute Fanny Murray (with the usual secondary meaning of "fanny"):

Awake, my Fanny, leave all meaner things,
This morn shall prove what rapture swiving brings.

The use of the Middle English gerund "swiving" from Old English "swifan," to copulate, is interesting. My colleague Donald Siebert has reminded me that the Earl of Rochester employed the same verb in his poems. Is this, then, a conscious echo of Rochester in a poem not unlike some that he wrote? At any rate, the passage attracts a wonderfully inane footnote ascribed to "Dr. Warburton" and sounding for all the world like Dr. Chasuble in *The Importance of Being Earnest:*

> Philosophers agree that the two great duties Nature has Enjoined all her children, are *to preserve the Individual, and to propagate the Species.* We ought therefore to be studious, that our daily food be such as will not only please our Palate at the time, but will afterwards turn to good account, and perhaps more to the Gratification of the Woman than the Man. This shews, that it is not only lawful, but expedient for Clergymen to eat Crawfish, Soup, Lampreys, &c. not to indulge their own inordinate appetites, but as Provocatives to the *fuller discharge* of what is due to the dear Partners of our Beds, according to the Modus of Benevolence prescribed by St. Paul.

The poet displays considerable tact in adapting the familiar metaphors of Pope to his design. "The Lamb thy riot dooms to bleed today,/ Had he thy Reason, would he skip and play?" becomes "Thy lust the Virgin dooms to bleed today,/Had she thy reason would she skip and play?" That is an easy solution but not a bad one.

A more substantial example is his treatment of Pope's famous metaphor of analogical theology. Pope:

> Say First, of God above, or Man below,
> What can we reason, but from what we know?
> Of Man what see we, but his station here,
> From which to reason, or to which refer?
> Thro' worlds unnumber'd tho' the God be known,
> 'Tis ours to trace him only in our own. (I. 17–22)

Wilkes inverts the analogy with woman, or woman's hidden charms, constituting the unknowable instead of God:

> Say first of Woman's latent Charms below,
> What can we reason but from what we know?
> A Face, a Neck, a Breast are all, appear,
> From which to reason, or to which refer.
> In ev'ry Part we heavenly Beauty own,
> But we can trace it only in what's shewn.

Possessing some comic subtlety is his imitation of the Great Chain of Being motif. Pope:

> Of Systems possible, if 'tis confest
> That Wisdom infinite must form the best,
> Where all must full or not coherent be,
> And all that rises, rise in due degree;
> Then, in the scale of reas'ning life, 'tis plain,
> There must be, somewhere, such a rank as Man. (I. 42–48)

In his adaptation Wilkes weaves an insulting reference to his archfoe, King George's beloved Earl of Bute, until April 1763 leader of the government:

> Of Pego's possible, if 'tis confess'd
> That Wisdom infinite must form some best,
> Where all must rise, or not coherent be
> And all that rise must rise in due Degree;
> Then in the scale of various Pricks, 'tis plain,
> God-like erect, BUTE stands the foremost Man. (I. 43–48)

Here Wilkes also contrives to remind his readers of the rumor, vastly elaborated in political caricatures of the day, that Bute owed his worldly success to an affair with the King's mother, the Dowager Princess of Wales.[30]

Judged on their own terms, the three short poems and the fragmentary "Essay on Woman" are not without merit in the genre of obscene imitations. The indignation displayed by the Earl of Sandwich was of course counterfeit, he having no doubt heard them read at Medmenham Abbey or elsewhere. Sandwich was popularly referred to afterwards as Jemmy Twitcher (of *The Beggar's Opera*) for having "peached" on his former friend Wilkes. In all likelihood Bishop Warburton was genuinely angry.

A question remains that must be addressed in today's world. What was the attitude towards woman or women expressed or implied in the "Essay"? Wilkes later contended that it "idolised the sex," a statement that has evoked much scornful laughter.[31] There is something to be said for Wilkes's contention, however. Women are represented as having, or at least being capable of having, greater sexual knowledge than men. Notice how Wilkes adapts Pope's metaphor of the gradations of intelligence. Pope:

> Heaven from all creatures hides the book of Fate,
> All but the page prescribed, their present state;

From brutes what men, from men what spirits know:
Or who could suffer Being here below? (I. 76–80)

In the version by Wilkes an ascending order of knowledge is implied, parallel to the brutes-men-spirits sequence of Pope, with women being the superior:

Heaven from all Creatures hides the Book of Fate,
All but the Page prescrib'd, the present State:
From Boys what Girls, from Girls what Women know,
Or what could suffer being here below? (I. 77–80)

In a sense Wilkes does "idolise the sex." Women are treated, in the modern jargon, as "sex objects"; the poet is a male chauvinist right enough, but the manner is that of *Playboy* or, perhaps more precisely for students of American popular culture, of *Esquire* in the days of the Petty girls: women are desirable and desiring, idols of a sort.

After the House of Lords wound up its denunciation of Wilkes the government brought him to trial, and he fled to France to avoid prosecution, carrying the "Essay" manuscript with him. The furor went on for some years, with fake "Essays" even more obscene than the original being purveyed to the curious. Eventually Wilkes returned, was tried, and sentenced by Lord Mansfield to twenty-two months imprisonment for his part in the publication. Although his parliamentary constituency did not abandon him, Wilkes had been established in the public mind as a libertine who wrote dirty poems. The copy of the 1871 reprint that I consulted in the library of a great university was brought out to me by a curator, after some lengthy, seemingly rather panicked whisperings in his office. With it was an instruction on bright orange paper reading THIS BOOK MUST NEVER BE LEFT OPEN ON THE DESK and directing me to return it to a member of the library staff rather than to a (presumably more impressionable) undergraduate assistant. Wilkes was a libertarian radical, but the government won its case at the bar of public opinion: to posterity John Wilkes has been a corruptor of morals.

NOTES

[1] *Boswell's Life of Johnson,* ed. G. Birkbeck Hill, rev. L. F. Powell, III (Oxford: Clarendon Press, 1934), pp. 65–79. For a full discussion see Sven Eric Molin, "Boswell's Account of the Johnson-Wilkes Meeting," *Studies in English Literature,* 3 (1963), 307–22.

[2] Rev. *The Infamous Essay on Woman,* ed. Adrian Hamilton (London: Andre Deutsch, 1972), *TLS,* 15 December 1972, p. 1532; Pottle, *Boswell's London Journal 1762–1763*

(London: William Heinemann, 1950), p. 35; Stromberg, *A History of Western Civilization*, rev. ed. (Homewood, Ill.: Dorsay Press, 1969), p. 426.

[3] *Wilkes and Liberty* (Oxford: Clarendon Press, 1962), pp. 17–36.

[4] British Library, Additional MS. 57, 733, fols. 2–3.

[5] Librarians have argued that books such as the "Essay" attract the attention of mutilators and must receive unusual care. This theory should be put to the test by the recent publication of Adrian Hamilton's edition, which includes a paperbound "Reader's edition," an exact duplicate of the hardbound text, intended for the open shelves. Both volumes have been locked in the Rare Book Collection of my own university library, however. All references to the text of the "Essay" in this paper are derived from this edition unless otherwise noted. Hamilton's editing is careful and accurate, but the work is rather lightly annotated for scholarly use.

[6] There are a number of letters from and about Potter among the Wilkes manuscripts in the British Library. Some notion of his sense of levity may perhaps be derived from a letter of 31 July 1755 to Wilkes in which he boasts of having had intercourse in public with a cow: "You see I glory in what I have done. I avow it without being *cow'd.*" Additional MS. 30, 880B, fol. 3.

[7] *Dictionary of National Biography*, s.v. Thomas Potter.

[8] Wilkes's copy of Warburton's *Pope*, with his manuscript notes, is now in the British Library, shelfmark G 12850–58. For Potter see the letter from Exeter of 31 July 1755: "I shall then carry home Mrs W. to Prior Park & lodge her in the Arms of her Spouse . . . ." In my opinion the case for Wilkes's authorship of the poems made by Eric R. Watson has never been refuted; see his series of articles, "John Wilkes and 'The Essay on Woman,' *N&Q*, Ser. 11, 9 (Jan.–Jun. 1914). 121–23, 143–45, 162–64, 183–85, 203–05, 222–23.

[9] This is not to say that Wilkes entertained any exalted notions of his poetic powers; see *The Correspondence of John Wilkes and Charles Churchill*, ed. Edward H. Weatherly (New York: Columbia Univ. Press, 1954), passim.

[10] British Library, Additional MS. 22, 132, fol. 271^r. This appears to be an earlier draft of the more elegantly phrased deposition in Guildhall MSS. 214/2, p. 49.

[11] British Library, Additional MS. 30, 880B, fol. 3^v.

[12] An unusual Latin word, employed by Martial, signifying "richly endowed with phallus."

[13] As described in Guildhall MSS. 214/2, p. 6, by the government, which at the time had one of the original thirteen copies. None appears to have survived.

[14] Wilkes's letters to his printer concerning the titlepage, later seized in a raid on his house, are in Guildhall MSS. 214/1.

[15] *The Correspondence of John Wilkes and Charles Churchill*, pp. 15–16, 59.

[16] Rudé, *Wilkes and Liberty*, pp. 23–28; Jack P. Greene, *The Nature of Colony Constitutions* (Columbia, S. C.: Univ. of South Carolina Press, 1970), pp. 5–38: "In this sense, the Wilkes Fund Controversy was the bridge to revolution in South Carolina" (p. 38).

[17] Guildhall MSS. 214/ 1–3, the collection of documents assembled by the government for its case against Wilkes, would presumably have included some indication if the poems had been found among the other materials.

[18] Reproduced in facsimile in Adrian Hamilton, *The Infamous Essay on Woman*, p. 97.

[19] This is the suggestion of the anonymous reviewer of Hamilton's volume in *TLS*.

[20] Guildhall MSS. 214/2, pp. 49–50.

[21] See *Dictionary of National Biography*, s.v. John Kidgell.

[22] Rudé, *Wilkes and Liberty*, p. 32, after considering the evidence concludes that "it seems reasonably certain . . . that Curry was bribed and probably intimidated."

[23] Rudé, p. 33; *Lords Journals*, 15 November 1763, p. 415.

[24] *The Yale Edition of Horace Walpole's Correspondence*, XXII: *Horace Walpole's Correspondence with Sir Horace Mann, 1762–68*, ed. W. S. Lewis, Warren H. Smith, and George L. Lam (New Haven: Yale Univ. Press, 1960), p. 185. Pitt as quoted in Rudé, *Wilkes and Liberty*, p. 33.

[25] See Howard D. Weinbrot, *The Formal Strain: Studies in Augustan Imitation and Satire* (Chicago: Univ. of Chicago Press, 1969). Wilkes is employing Cowley's mode of "paraphrase and consistent modernization of an announced model" (p. 49), though Pope's *Essay*, in itself a classic by 1763, has of course replaced the customary Latin or Greek model.

[26] Eric Watson, "John Wilkes and 'The Essay on Woman,' " quotes from a letter of Wilkes to his physician, Dr. Brocklesby, under date of 19 December 1763 the following couplet: "Ask of the learned the way? The learned are blind./ That way a Warburton could never find." This corresponds to *Essay on Man*, IV, 19–20, and perhaps indicates that Wilkes had the manuscript with him in France. Since none of Curry's thirteen copies in red letter, nor the corrected proofs, nor the manuscript has survived, the best text is that, like Hamilton's and the 1871 London reprint, based on the so-called Dyce copy in the Victoria and Albert Museum. Eric Watson sets forth the criteria by which one of the genuine copies could be identified if it appeared. Wilkes's manuscript, in his own hand, should be easily identifiable.

[27] Oxford University, Bodleian Library, MS. Bodley 1011, p. 24, Edwards to Philip Yorke, 27 Nov. 1747.

[28] British Library, Additional MS. 30, 867, fol. 42, 17 January 1750.

[29] Octavo edition (London: J. and P. Knapton, 1751), sig. A2^r.

[30] See Herbert M. Atherton, "George Townshend, Caricaturist," *Eighteenth-Century Studies*, 4 (1971), 437–46.

[31] In the letter to Dr. Brocklesby.

ULYSSES:
Take but degree away, untune that string
And hark, what discord follows.

—Shakespeare,
Troilus and Cressida

REBECCA ARMSTRONG ❧ THE GREAT CHAIN
OF BEING
IN DRYDEN'S
ALL FOR LOVE

SINCE ITS INCEPTION, Dryden's *All For Love* has eluded the grasp of scholars attempting to impose upon the play a single comprehensive scheme capable of reconciling a number of seemingly disparate elements. One of the most formidable tasks, the assimilation of the vast amount of inorganic imagery,[1] has been tackled by Earl Miner, whose view of the play in terms of ebb and flow imagery accounts in part for the peripatetic structure and the references to nature.[2] The diversity of the natural imagery has also prompted Derek Hughes's study of the play as a series of cosmic cycles and conflicts.[3] A second major problem in dealing with the play, the incongruity between the sanction of passionate love in the conclusion and the censure of it in the preface and early part of the play, has been cited as evidence that *All For Love* lacks any thematic unity.[4] However, the theories concerning the imagery are evidently part of a larger vision of the play and are assimilable with the thematic conclusion if the play is viewed as conflict between order and disorder. Because the concept of order was inextricably linked in Dryden's and Shakespeare's day to a larger notion, it seems cogent that in *All For Love* the Great Chain of Being serves as a framework that unifies the natural imagery, structure, and thematic conclusion of the play.

Although perhaps the Great Chain of Being is generally associated with the Elizabethans, Dryden was a contemporary of Milton, and this concept did continue as part of the intellectual atmosphere of the Restoration. Even if Dryden is placed in the context of eighteenth-century thought, the influence of the great chain is still evident. Arthur Lovejoy in *The Great Chain of Being* affirms that

> there has been no period in which writers of all sorts . . . talked so much about the Chain of Being, or accepted more implicitly the general scheme of ideas

connected with it, or more boldly drew from their latent implications, or apparent implications.[5]

It is axiomatic that Dryden and his audience were thoroughly exposed to the great chain and, further, to its predominating constituent—order.

The Great Chain of Being was essentially, of course, an attempt to view existence as an ordered structure with correspondences between the sublunary and supralunary worlds. According to E.M. Tillyard's study, *The Elizabethan World Picture*, all nature was divided into classes that were graduated from the lowest inanimate class up to man, the angels, and finally God. Each class was designated a link in the chain and even within the links the members were ordered, with primates in the superior position. Since God set the elements (earth, air, fire, and water) in opposition after the Fall, any breach in the order or law of nature in the postlapsarian world would result in a corresponding disorder in the universe. Sin produced discord in the elements, which in turn mirrored in the universe the transgression of order on earth (see Tillyard, pp. 1–93). An awareness of the hostile elements, their relation to sin, and the importance of one's position in the universe are evident in *All For Love*.

Universal disorder in *All For Love*, seen primarily in cosmic disturbances, is certainly related to the immense amount of elemental imagery in the play. This imagery is composed of references to the four scientific elements (earth, air, fire, and water) and their characteristics (hot, cold, moist, and dry). Hughes has observed that the events of the play are couched in images that reflect Lucretius' concept of "natural cycle and violent upheaval caused by eternal conflict of earth, air, fire and water" (p. 541). This hostility between the elements can also be explained as the universal reflection of a lapse in the order of the sublunary world. The most obvious reason for the war of the elements is the unlawful love of Antony and Cleopatra. Antony seems aware of this when he attributes the loss of good fortune to his "careless days" and "luxurious nights"; [6] and Octavia, representing the lawful or natural law of marriage, accuses Cleopatra of possessing charms that "make sin pleasing" (III.443). The sinful love, then, would be sufficient to bring about the frequent elemental disturbances in the universe.

The awareness of the principle of ordered links in the great chain is evident in the concern of the characters with their position in the universe. Antony equates himself with the lion (III.55, V.297), the eagle (II.138), and the oak (I.235), and although this may be partly conventional these are all primates of their classes and therefore fitting for the position of Antony as emperor. When Ventidius labels Antony "next to Nature's God" (I.182) and later "My Emperor; the man I love next heaven" (I.252), he is careful to subjugate Antony to his proper position. Antony himself, as a superior primate, is equal only to Caesar as he asserts when he calls Caesar "my equal" (III.208) and then asks Octavia:

> Shall I set
> A man, my equal, in the place of Jove,
> As he could give me being? (III.278–80)

The problem arises when Antony allows himself to be called a god by Ventidius (I.437) and Alexas (II.59). Furthermore, in recalling his power at its height, when "eastern monarchs . . . forgot the sun,/To worship my uprising" (III.143–44), he assigns himself a place higher than Allah and commits the sin of pride against the order and gradation of existence in the Great Chain of Being. As Lovejoy puts it, "to covet the attributes or imitate the characteristic activities of beings above one in the cosmic order is as immoral as to sink to a lower level of it" (p. 200). Thus, the cosmic agitation throughout the play can be seen as a direct result of Antony's unnatural love and, perhaps, even his attempt to rise above his delegated place.

Although the philosophy of the great chain is apparent in both the structure and conclusion of the play, the most obvious application of the principle occurs in the references to nature. Throughout *All For Love,* there is an ambivalence in the use of images of nature, both in the references to elemental disturbances and to time. For the most part, nature is represented in terms of cosmic disturbances that correspond to the levels of conflict within the play. At the same time, however, it is also associated with order. Serapion's vision at the beginning of the play establishes disorder on several levels:

> Our fruitful Nile
> Flowed ere the wonted season, with a torrent
> So unexpected, and so wondrous fierce,
> That the wild deluge overtook the haste
> Ev'n of the hinds that watched it: men and beasts
> Were borne above the tops of trees, that grew
> On th' utmost margin of the water-mark.
> Then, with so swift an ebb the flood drove backward;
> It slipt from underneath the scaly herd:
> . . . .
> A whirlwind rose, that, with a violent blast,
> Shook all the dome: the doors around me clapt,
> The iron wicket, that defends the vault,
> Where the long race of Ptolemies is laid,
> Burst open, and disclosed the mighty dead.

From out each monument, in order placed,
An armed ghost start up: The boy-king last
Reared his inglorious head. A peal of groans
Then followed, and a lamentable voice
Cried "Egypt is no more!" (I.2–28)

First, disorder on a universal scale is observed in the flooding of the Nile unexpectedly in disregard of its normal cycle (Hughes, p. 545). Second, the Nile itself, which is associated with Egypt, implies disaster and disorder on a national scale, which is reinforced by the prediction of Egypt's annihilation in line 28. Third, the Ptolemies "in order placed" suggest an ordered historical past that contrasts with the present disorder. And last, Cleopatra, who is embodied in the Nile, is linked with its disorder and excessiveness.[7] Thus, Serapion's prophetic speech implies correspondences between disorder in nature and the levels of conflict or disorder in existence, and in this respect it reflects the philosophy of the Great Chain of Being.

Although the natural chaos envisaged by Serapion only ambiguously refers to inner conflict in the mention of "men and beasts" caught up in disorder, it provides an imagistic link between natural, national, and inner disorder. Serapion's whirlwind image, which is echoed in Alexas's words that "the Roman camp/Hangs o'er us black and threat'ning like a storm" (I.43), links the universal disorder of Serapion's speech to the national clash between Rome and Egypt. Later, Ventidius's observation that "the tempest tears him [Antony] up by th' roots" (I.214) implies an inner disorder resulting from his disgrace at Actium. The correspondence between the mental storms and the cosmic ones not only reflects the philosophy of the Great Chain of Being, the continued storm image reinforces the relationship of disorder on the universal, national, and personal levels.

In the application of Serapion's speech to Cleopatra, the Nile is linked to both disorder and excess. The alliteration of lines 2–4 emphasizes "fruitful," "flowed," and "fierce," images of fertility, liquidity, and excitement, respectively, while the use of "torrent" and "wondrous" along with the rising and falling of the Nile also reinforce the idea of excessive sexual passion. The association of Cleopatra with disorder and unnatural passion is verified in her description of her "transcendent passion" (II.20), with its suggestion of rising, and her confession to Antony: "In spite of all the dams my love broke o'er" (IV.519). Thus, her excessive love identifies her with what is unnatural and disordered in the universe.

Cleopatra's passion is not only related to the chaotic universe, she is also related to the cause of disorder through elemental imagery. She is not only equated with the moon (IV.322–26) but also has powers over the planets:

> Her eyes have pow'r beyond Thessalian charms
> To draw the moon from heav'n. . . . Then she's so charming,
> Age buds at sight of her, and swells to youth. (IV.234–39)

Furthermore, her smile is equated with lightning that can turn night to day, and even the celebration she proclaims is a "wild extravagance" (III.448). Cleopatra, then, is associated with the ability to interrupt the order of the universe (Hughes, p. 551); she is both the essence and the occasion of disorder. When Antony says that "loosened nature" may "Leap from its hinges! Sink the props of heav'n,/ And fall the skies to crush the nether world" (II.424–26), he is further associating their excessive love with the disorder in the universe that may accompany it. Elemental imagery not only links the levels of conflict in the play but through it Cleopatra is strongly identified with disorder.

Although temporal imagery in *All For Love* is usually associated with transcience, and thus disorder, it often relates to a larger order. The childhood motif, so frequent in the play, has been viewed as a "natural cycle" by Hughes (p. 544). Childhood is certainly associated with change as in Dolabella's "men are but children of a larger growth" speech (IV.43–58) and Antony's comparison of his fortuitous youth to his present situation (I.295), and in this respect it does reflect a kind of disorder. However, since it is a natural cycle, the mutability it evinces is only part of a greater order. There is a hint of this in Alexas's description of Antony's birthday as

> the day . . . when all heaven
> Labored for him when each propituous star
> Stood wakeful in his orb, to watch that hour
> And shed his better influence. (I.157–60)

The implication is that Antony's birthday, a symbol of aging and flux, is also a component of an ordered revolution of the planets. This disorder as part of order is also observable in the references to time.

Although the passing of time is seen by Hughes as an indication of instability (p. 544), it is, in fact, often related to order. When Serapion states that

> The queen of nations, from her ancient seat,
> Is sunk for ever in the dark abyss;
> Time has unrolled her glories to the last,
> And now closed up the volume, (V.72–75)

he is affirming the principle that disorder ("the dark abyss") caused by time or flux is part of the order of the universe. The unrolling, like the Ptolemies in Serapion's first speech, describes time as an orderly progression. This idea is reinforced by Antony's use of temporal imagery in Act II:

> Witness, ye days and nights, and all your hours,
> That danced away with down upon your feet
> As all your bus'ness were to count my passion! (282–84)

The sense of flux combined with the regularity of "count" indicates the disorder/order relationship. Even the use of the seasons, which are often related to decay (III.21–28), are part of the orderly progression of nature. Temporal images, then, in *All For Love,* are often used in conjunction with the natural cycle to indicate the belief that there is order even in transcience or disorder.

Not only do characters ascribe order to disordered nature, some identification with ordered nature also exists in the play. In Act I, Antony becomes one with nature:

> I'm now turned wild, a commoner of nature,
> Of all forsaken, and forsaking all;
> Live in a shady forest's sylvan scene;
> I lean my head upon the mossy bark,
> And look just of a piece as I grew from it:
> My uncombed locks, matted like mistletoe,
> Hang o'er my hoary face; a murm'ring brook
> Runs at my foot. . . .
> . . . .
> The herd come jumping by me,
> And, fearless, quench their thirst, while I look on,
> And take me for their fellow citizen. (I.232–43)

Although it may be granted that this is partially escapist primitivism (Hughes, p. 546), it is significant that Antony identifies himself so strongly with nature, becoming the very tree itself. It indicates something of a desire for harmony in nature, and significantly music plays while he imagines the scene. Although Antony is described in terms of earthquakes by Dolabella (IV.161–64) and meteors (I.206–09), he is also a Roman "bred in the rules of soft humanity" (II.231) and along with Ventidius is associated with military discipline and order as in the procession in Act II: "*Enter* Lictors *with fasces, one bearing the eagle: then enter* Antony *with* Ventidius, *followed by other Commanders.*" The desire for ordered existence indicates something of Antony's inner conflict to which the only solution is death.

There is also an imagistic link between peaceful, harmonious nature and death. When Antony describes death to Cleopatra,

> and so in dying,
> While hand in hand we walk in groves below,
> Whole troops of lovers' ghosts shall flock about us, (V.394–96)

he pictures it as a peaceful sylvan retreat. Cleopatra sees death as a journey "through long barren wilds" (IV.100), and Serapion's benediction in Act V also implies a satisfaction in death divorced from the discord of the universe, or "the storms of fate" (517). Both Antony and Cleopatra picture death as an ordered natural environment free from disorder.

The disorder/order motif as imaged in nature is somewhat ambivalent. Elemental imagery associates the conflicts on various levels with chaos in the universe and identifies Cleopatra with disorder in the form of change. Change, however, as related to temporal imagery is often seen as part of the cosmic order by the characters, and Antony closely identifies himself with ordered nature. The chaotic universe can be related to the breach in the Great Chain of Being, and the order seen in nature indicates a desire to return to the order of the past.

This desire for order can also be discerned in the attitude of the characters toward fate and in the structure of the play. In the numerous references to fate in *All For Love,* there is a tendency to see the outcome of events as the result of manipulation by an external force (Hughes, p. 555). Cleopatra blames fate for the consequences of her flirtation with Dolabella in this way: "fate took th' occasion;/And thus one minute's feigning has destroyed/My whole life's truth" (IV.520–22). Alexas does the same thing when he must decide how to save himself: "Fate comes too fast upon my soul" (V.255). In both cases the characters themselves are responsible for their actions but insist upon seeing it as the workings of fate. Even Serapion, in relating the betrayal of the Egyptians in Antony's final defeat, blames "false fortune" (V.85) for the disaster. Fate functions not only as justification for behavior but also as assurance that a design or plan exists in the universe.

There is also a proclivity to see fate working against nature as in Cleopatra's comparison of herself to a dove:

> Fond without art, and kind without deceit;
> But Fortune, that has made a mistress of me,
> Has thrust me out to the wide world, unfurnished
> Of falsehood to be happy. (IV.93–96)

This desire to see order in existence is repeated in Antony's statement that "fate mistook him [Caesar];/for Nature meant him for an usurer (V.213–15) and in his description of Dolabella:

> Sure that face
> Was meant for honesty, but heav'n mismatched it,
> And furnished treason out with nature's pomp. (IV. 444–46)

These examples indicate a need to delegate the responsibility for undesirable actions to a higher power. The thought of an external force guiding the actions of the sublunary world is evidence of order in a disordered existence.

This need for order in the midst of instability is also found in the structure of the play with Antony as the pivotal character. The play begins with gross cosmic disorder, the macrocosm of Antony's disordered state of mind that is implied in the stage directions in Act I: *"Enter Antony, walking with a disturbed motion before he speaks."* His desire for order imaged in the identification with the natural scene is realized when he decides to rejoin his troops and fight. This movement toward emotional order and decision is duplicated in Act II when Antony enters in a ritualistic parade of military order, is disconcerted by Alexas's rehearsal of Cleopatra's message, and after a period of disorder is reunited with Cleopatra. In Act III, the temporary order established in the dramatic meeting of the Roman and Egyptian trains is dissolved by Antony's state of turmoil over the appearance of Octavia, the symbol of lawful and familial order.[8] Act IV, which continues the vacillation between order and disorder, begins with a temporary order for Antony that is quickly destroyed by the feigning of Dolabella, Cleopatra, and Alexas, and the final act moves toward order from the satisfaction of Ventidius and Antony in contemplation of death to the disorder ushered in by Alexas's counterfeiting of Cleopatra's death, and the order restored to both Cleopatra and Antony in the death/coronation scene. With the exception of Act IV, the pattern of the play consists of Antony choosing the alternative that will bring the most immediate order to his emotional life.

Structurally, the emphasis is on the alternation of order and disorder. In the opening of each act, the predominance of one of these moods is followed by an opposing one, thereby falsifying the initial expectations for the act. Emotional order is often accompanied by ritual as in Act II, the Roman march, Act III, the joining of Egyptian and Roman trains, and the final ritual of marriage. The rituals not only symbolize order dramatically and visually but also seem to represent a need for the appearance of order, no matter how temporary, in the lives of the characters. Disorder in the plot is also related to the counterfeiting of emotions or posing. Antony's emotional instability in Act II partially brought on by Alexas ironically pretending to be Cleopatra (II.155–60). The complete disaster of Act IV results from Dolabella pretending to be Antony, Cleopatra feigning love for Dolabella, and Alexas's falsehood to Antony. Thus, in accordance with the Great Chain of Being, attempting to be someone or something other than oneself produces disorder. What is unnatural or an effort to rise above one's position in the natural order of things, in the case of Alexas and Dolabella, results in disaster. If Cleopatra is identified with disorder and Antony to some extent with Roman order, then the conflict in the play can be seen as a choice between what is lawful or ordered and what is disordered and unnatural. The demands of these opposites are solvable only in terms of the final order—death.

Aside from the temporary order in ritual, and a tendency to view fate as proof of order in the universe, there seems only a predominance of disorder in the plot. It is, however, in the outcome that we see the real vision of the play. Death is an important element not only in the denouement but also throughout the play, which is pervaded by death-wish (especially on the part of Cleopatra). Although both Cleopatra and Antony embrace death eagerly, Antony finds a sense of release in giving up the world:

> 'Tis time the world
> Should have a lord, and know whom to obey.
> We two have kept its homage in suspense,
> And bent the globe, on whose each side we trod,
> Till it was dented inwards. (V.280–84)

There is a sense, here, of restoration of national order as well as personal release. This idea of liberty in death is espoused by Antony in defending his indifference to dying in battle to Ventidius:

> 'Tis but a scorn of life and just desire
> To free myself from bondage. (V.266–67)

Cleopatra's welcome speech to the aspic and her affirmation

> 'Tis sweet to die, when they would force life on me
> To rush into the dark abode of Death,
> And seize him first; if he be like my lord,
> He is not frightful, sure (V.442–45)

glorifies death and emphasizes it as desirable. There is, in the combination marriage/coronation ceremony that combines death and triumph, a stasis in the figures of Antony and Cleopatra that defies death. When the Priest, on seeing their figures, cries "what havoc death has made!" (V.499), it is almost ironic since death has brought the order desired but denied in life. Death, then, is viewed as a final permanent order for Antony and Cleopatra.

In the terminal speech of the play, the structure and imagery fuse to emphasize Dryden's double vision. Serapion's final words emphasize the glorification, almost deification, in death:

> See how the lovers sit in state together,
> As they were giving laws to half mankind.
> Secure from human chance, long ages out
> While all the storms of fate fly o'er your tomb;
>> And fame to late posterity shall tell,
>> No lovers lived so great, or died so well. (V.515–19)

The use of "laws" and "lovers" implies a canonization of Antony and Cleopatra as saints of the religion of love, even though their authority extends to only half mankind. There is a coming together in this passage of the natural elemental and temporal images with the structural emphasis on death and the restoration of order. Serapion's final blessing opposes the order of death and the security in the long temporal sleep with the natural imagery of disorder in "storms." At the same time, however, there is in death the obliteration of the cause of disorder in the universe. Serapion's reference to "storms of fate" and "human chance" implies not only disorder as opposed to the achievement of order in death but, in addition, in the context of previous references, is a reminder that time and change are also part of a greater order of the universe. Thus, in terms of the Great Chain of Being, the final death does establish order for the lovers, but it also reestablishes the order in the chain of existence. Dryden satisfies the demands of the great chain by punishing the pair with death, while elevating their final status with a permanent order untouched by time or change. It is a tribute to Dryden's genius that the restoration of this double order, while stressing the value of love, also conforms to the demands of moral order in the universe.

In light of the importance of the philosophy of the Great Chain of Being in seventeenth- and eighteenth-century thought and John Dryden's "love of order," [9] it is not surprising to find the concept of order as part of the guiding vision of *All For Love*. The entire play, in fact, can be viewed in terms of the Great Chain of Being. First, the disorder in man mirrored by nature indicates a breach in the natural order brought on by the unnatural passion of Antony and Cleopatra—the catalyst of disorder. Second, the ambivalence of the natural imagery serves to oppose order and disorder in the universe. Cosmic discord, expressed in elemental imagery, emphasizes the levels of conflict in the play and the correspondence between nature and man's behavior that is so essential to the great chain. References to time and fate as manifestations of a universal design stress the necessity of seeing order even in transience and disorder. Third, the structure that portrays a disordered existence resulting from pretense or a breaking of the chain, and relieved temporarily by the appearance of order in ritual, emphasizes the final restoration of order in death. Finally, the dual nature of this final order is shown by the converging of the natural imagery with the structural emphasis of the play. In the treatment of death as the final restitution of order, Dryden is able to satisfy the dictates of the Great Chain of Being while allowing the world to be well lost. The Great Chain of Being serves as a framework that unifies the natural imagery, structure, and thematic conclusion of *All For Love*.

NOTES

[1] Otto Reinert, "Passion and Pity in *All For Love:* A Reconsideration," in *The Hidden Sense and Other Essays,* ed. Maren-Sofie Røstvig et al. (Oslo and New York: Humanities Press, 1963), p. 163.

[2] Earl Miner, "Drama of the Will: *All For Love,*" in *Dryden's Poetry* (Bloomington: Indiana Univ. Press, 1971), pp. 36–73.

[3] Derek Hughes, "The Significance of *All For Love,*" *ELH,* 37 (1970), 540–60.

[4] Everett H. Emerson, Harold E. Davis, and Ira Johnson, "Intention and Achievement in *All For Love,*" *CE,* 17 (1955); rpt. in Bruce King, ed., *Twentieth Century Interpretations of All For Love* (Englewood Cliffs, N. J.: Prentice-Hall, 1968), p. 60.

[5] Arthur O. Lovejoy, *The Great Chain of Being: A Study of the History of an Idea* (Cambridge, Mass.: Harvard Univ. Press, 1966), p. 183.

[6] John Dryden, *All For Love; or The World Well Lost,* in *British Dramatists From Dryden to Sheridan*, ed. George H. Nettleton, Arthur E. Case, and George W. Stone, Jr. (New York: Houghton Mifflin Co., 1969), I.307. All subsequent citations are to this edition.

[7] Eugene M. Waith, *"All for Love," The Herculean Hero in Marlowe, Chapman, Shakespeare and Dryden* (New York: Columbia Univ. Press, 1962); rpt. in Earl Miner, ed., *Restoration Dramatists,* Twentieth Century Views (Englewood Cliffs, N. J.: Prentice-Hall, 1966), p. 55.

[8] Howard D. Weinbrot, "Alexas in *All For Love:* His Geneology and Function," *Studies in Philology,* 64 (1967), 653.

[9] Bonamy Dobrée, *John Dryden* (Oxford: Clarendon Press, 1950), p. 82.

DAVID K. JEFFREY   ✑   THE EPISTOLARY
FORMAT OF
PAMELA AND
HUMPHRY CLINKER

SAMUEL RICHARDSON WOULD DOUBTLESS DISAPPROVE the mating of
his first heroine with Smollett's last protagonist, but they are not, in some
ways, such a strange pair. Pamela in 1740 is the heroine of the first great
epistolary novel, while Humphry in 1771 is the titular hero of the last.
Both begin as servants, both moralize throughout their novels, and both
find themselves elevated socially at each novel's conclusion—Pamela by
marriage to her former master and would-be seducer, Squire B.; Humphry by being legitimated. On the other hand, Pamela's initially violent
reactions each time B. lays heavy, ineffectual hands upon her contrasts
with Humphry's crude, initial (dare I say) appearance, his bare posterior
inadvertently exposed. Literacy separates the two even further; Pamela
writes two hefty volumes about her trials and triumphs, while Humphry
pens not a word, leaving that three-volume task to members of the group
he serves.

Although contemplation of this pairing amuses, the parallels are
clearer between Pamela and Lydia Melford (a member of the group
Humphry serves), especially in regard to their writing and the meaning of the epistolary format. Lydia is in fact one of Pamela's many
daughters.[1] In character, both are young and fair, delicate and virginal
creatures, much given to faints. Smollett does invert Richardson's plot,
however, for the upper-class Lydia loves a man believed beneath her
socially—an actor—although he too is legitimated at the novel's denouement. Lydia is not as prolific a writer as Pamela; few characters are.
Lydia writes only eleven of the eighty-two letters in *Humphry Clinker;*
her uncle, Matt Bramble, and her brother, Jery, write over two-thirds of
the novel, while her aunt, Tabitha, writes six letters and Tabitha's
maid-servant, Win Jenkins, "pursues her anal fixation" [2] through ten
hilarious missives. Pamela writes all but four of the thirty-two letters
and the entire one and one-half volume journal that constitute her
novel.

Why anyone would want to fill two or three volumes with fictional letters puzzles the modern reader. Certainly, the other forms available to Richardson—the romance, the picaresque, the pseudomemoir— seem either far less technically crude or far faster paced. Why then settle on an epistolary format? The answer is not only that letter writing was the habit of Richardson's lifetime but that, as he explains in the Preface to *Clarissa,* the epistolary format has advantages the other forms lack: "Letters . . . written while the hearts of the writers must be supposed to be wholly engaged in their subjects . . . abound not only with critical situations, but with what may be called *instantaneous* Descriptions and Reflections. . . ." *"Much more* lively and affecting," he continues, quoting one of his characters, "must be the Style of those who write in the height of a *present* distress; the mind tortured by the pangs of uncertainty . . . than the dry, narrative, unanimated Style of a person relating difficulties and dangers surmounted, can be; the relater perfectly at ease; and if himself unmoved by his own Story, not likely greatly to affect the Reader." [3] In the Preface to *Pamela* Richardson hints at this same view, calling the format "probable," "natural," "lively," and "mov[ing]." [4] There is in Smollett no similar biographical predilection for the format, but, perhaps, he settles on it at last for the reasons Richardson states. Certainly, Smollett's four earlier novels are less successful than *Humphry Clinker* precisely because of the disparity between lively and affecting events and the dispassionate or ironic narrator who comments on them.[5] But the epistolary format, as Richardson suggests in the prefaces, resolves such disparities by locating its writer somewhere between stream of consciousness and emotion recollected in tranquillity, thus providing at once a temporal closeness to the raw experience of reality and a consciousness which reacts to that reality.

As a consequence of this positioning, the writer of letters is both isolated and unreliable. In the act of writing, he separates himself from the present and cannot fully experience it; he can recreate only the past. Because the past he recounts precedes so immediately his recording of it and because that past so movingly affects him, his record of it cannot be wholly accurate.

I

Richardson pictures his heroine at odds with both familial and social units, and her isolation from such units the epistolary format effectively mirrors. Pamela's emotional isolation from her family is suggested by her parents' response to her first letter. Although Pamela's letter contains not the slightest indication that B. has other than an honorable interest in her or that Pamela feels anything other than gratitude to him for such interest, her parents respond to it by expressing fear that their fifteen-year-old daughter will act in a "dishonest or wicked" way; "we fear," they write, "—you should be *too* grateful—and reward him with that Jewel, your Virtue, which no Riches, nor Favour, nor any thing in this Life, can make up to you" (p. 27). As a result of this extraordinary injunction, Pamela tries for most of the first volume to repress her attraction to B. Only after B.'s open admission of love for her does Pamela give way to the emotions of her own heart; only after her marriage and midway into the second volume can she write guiltlessly of her love, no longer fearful of her parents' reactions.[6] Pamela's first letter also calls attention to her uneasy social position; through the good offices of Lady B., the squire's mother, Pamela has achieved "Qualifications above [her] Degree" (p.25), so that finding another suitable job would be difficult. But, if she is a little more than servant, she is less than B.'s kind, and she strives throughout most of the novel's first volume to escape both him and the concurrent moral and social dilemma his pursuit of her raises. Even after their marriage, she must attempt to make herself acceptable to those of B.'s class who either view her as a curiosity or openly scorn her. Not until she establishes a secure place in his social class does she lay down her pen.[7] Pamela's isolation is also suggested geographically. In the first volume she is abducted from Bedfordshire (where friendly fellow servants aid and comfort her) to Lincolnshire (a wilderness in which, friendless, she endures temptations for some forty days and nights), and her switch from the letter format in Bedfordshire to the journal format in Lincolnshire mirrors her developing isolation, an isolation that works in Pamela's favor, for it forces her to make her own decisions rather than to act as her parents enjoin her. Near the end of the novel, she returns triumphantly to Bedfordshire and stops writing in order to "apply [her]self to the Duties of the Family" (p. 387). She has established her place, both as daughter and wife, within familial and social units.

Smollett's writers face similar difficulties—as they begin their journey from Wales through England and Scotland, they are isolated not only, as a group, from societies new to them but also, as individuals, from each other. Jery struggles to dominate his sister, Lydia, and views his uncle and aunt as "a family of originals" (p. 8). Matt's constipation comically reflects his emotional isolation; his bowels are as constricted as his heart. He even requests his correspondent to "lock up all my drawers, and keep the keys" (p. 6). Jery's isolation from Lydia is more literal. After some years of separation, he has "found her a fine, tall girl of seventeen . . . but remarkably simple, and quite ignorant of the world" (p. 8). In his first letter he parades his duty to the family and to her, such duty consisting, he believes, in stifl[ing her] correspondence" with the man she loves, Wilson the actor. Lydia delineates this injunction in two paired letters—the first to her school mistress, whom she thinks of as a surrogate mother (p. 9), the second to a schoolmate, Letty. As a result of that injunction, she has "promised to break off all correspondence" with Wilson "and, if possible," she adds to Letty, "to forget him: but, alas! I begin to perceive that will not be in my power" (p. 10). This injunction figures importantly in the overall structure of the novel, for the novel will not end until all its letter writers achieve harmony within a familial unit. Matt tames Tabitha during a quarrel near the end of the first volume; Matt and Jery become friendly in the second, finding common ground in their sympathy for Martin, the rakish highwayman they encounter near the beginning of the volume,[9] and in their mutual wonderment at Lismahago, the quixotic figure they encounter on the highway near that volume's end. They are not reconciled with Lydia until the last several pages of the volume, Matt when she calls him "father" in her hysterical relief that he has not drowned (p. 315), Jery soon after that, when, as Lydia phrases it, "the slighted Wilson is metamorphosed into George Dennison, only son and heir of a gentleman"—a gentleman who is also, too coincidentally, Matt's childhood friend (p. 336). The opening letters of the novel, then, introduce separate, because egocentric, consciousnesses, and the novel traces their developing union. As in *Pamela,* the geography of the novel suggests their progress. The characters journey through the urban centers of southern England (where their relationship is as constrained as Matt's bowels) to the north through Scotland (where Matt's pains ascend to his ear and where he and Jery both wax enthusiastic, but where Lydia sickens and writes nothing) to a midpoint between these geographical extremes, Dennison's rural estate, where Matt and Jery find new and even more compatible friends and where all three women—Lydia, Tabitha, and Win—fulfill themselves in marriage.

Thus to isolate a character calls attention to the existential dilemma in which he finds himself—or rather, in which she finds herself. For neither Richardson nor Smollett focuses much attention in these two novels on the existential choices of their heroes. Neither of Smollett's heroes are required to make such choices. Matt Bramble and his nephew, Jery Melford, record the mores of the places they visit but seldom mention their growing affection for each other. They do not, in any case, consciously choose to be affectionate. Squire B., on the other hand, is required to make some such choice, and critics have objected that Richardson has provided no other window into B.'s consciousness than Pamela's letters, which only record the reasons B. gives to her for his choice of her. Perhaps B.'s remarks about unequal marriages suggest reasons for the inequitable pressures only the heroines are forced to withstand. B. says, "A Man ennobles the Woman he takes, be she *who* she will; and adopts her into his own rank, be it *what* it will: But a Woman, tho' ever so noble born, debases herself by a mean Marriage, and descends from her own Rank, to his she stoops to " (p. 349). And he continues in this vein for six paragraphs. Here B. does not so much flaunt his own male chauvinism as he recognizes such chauvinism as the received social condition of his time. In such a society his roles are a given, defined by his birth into a particular class. Virtually nothing he could do would change this given, and thus his choices are essentially uninteresting and unimportant. A woman, however, is not socially defined. No matter her class, she can "debase herself" by "mean" behavior. Her place in society is thus more fluid and uneasy. Her choices are therefore vital, because she is self-defined.

II

A closer examination of the two heroines reveals important differences as well as similarities in the choices that affect their self-definition. Parental figures enjoin both girls at the very outset of the novels, and these injunctions force the heroines to affect roles, roles that are negative and potentially destructive; until they are free from these injunctions, the girls cannot act positively, as autonomous selves, for the injunctions involve them in what transactional analysts call "losing scripts." [10] Pamela's parents conclude the injunction of their first letter thus: ". . . we had rather see you all cover'd with Rags, and even follow you to the Church-yard, than have it said, a Child of Ours preferr'd worldly Conveniences to her Virtue" (p. 28). Here, as elsewhere, Pamela's parents equate dishonor and death; thus, when B. later tells her father that Pamela "is in a way to be happy," her father replies, believing her defiled, "What! then is she dying?" (p. 248). Pamela accepts this equation for the first half of the novel, first threatening suicide (p. 126) and then nearly committing it (pp. 151–54) when she believes she cannot avoid dishonor. Her parents' script provides Pamela with only two roles, "Poor But Honest" and "The Ruined Maid." The former she must embrace, the latter avoid at any cost, even death. Throughout most of the first volume, Pamela's behavior alternates between these two roles: she describes at length either her longing to escape from B. and her preparations for servitude at home (pp. 52, 60) or alternately, and rather warmly, her resistance to B.'s advances (pp. 64–68) and her near suicide. But the trials she undergoes while alone at Lincolnshire free her from her parents' script, and when B. releases her, admitting his love, she acts contrary to her parents' injunction. Her return to B. is an assertion of her own selfhood; she has realized her desires in a winner's role, that of Cinderella.

The consequences of Lydia's choices are less fully explored, although they are similar to Pamela's. Like Pamela, Lydia begins the novel with a loser's role, one assigned her by Jery, Matt, and Tabitha. Her correspondence with Wilson precipitates her brother's attempts to duel with him, and after the lovers are separated, as Matt writes, "the poor creature was so frightened and fluttered, by our threats and expostulations, that she fell sick the fourth day after our arrival at Clifton, and continued so ill for a whole week, that her life wa despaired of " (p. 14). Enjoining her against the role of "Ruined Maid," they have instead scripted her as "Sleeping Beauty." They believe time will erase Wilson from her memory and provide her with a mate of more suitable class. Lydia accepts this role, but she hopes that "time and the chapter of accidents, or rather . . . that Providence . . . will not fail, sooner or later, to reward those that walk in the paths of honour and virtue" (p. 11). Lydia has less appeal as a character than Pamela does because Lydia never rebels against her passive role. Instead, she accepts the pain that role causes her and faints and falls ill repeatedly. Happily for her, but unhappily for the novel, "accident" does convert her loser's role into a winner's. Her lover stumbles through the Brambles that surround her and is "metamorphosed"—from Wilson the Frog into The Prince of Dennison.

So, acceptance of their losing roles leads both girls to sickness and nearly to death. Thus Lydia languishes. And thus Pamela pitifully: "And now my dearest Father and Mother, expect to see soon your poor Daughter, with a humble and dutiful Mind, return'd to you: And don't fear but I know how to be happy with you as ever: For I will lie in the Loft, as I used to do; and pray let the little Bed be got ready . . . and fear not that I shall be a Burden to you, if My Health continues. . . ." (p. 45). Still, one of the roles presented to the heroines has less appeal, because less potential, than the other, as Richardson has Pamela intuit. Pamela, of course, never does return to her parents. Life in a hovel is no life for her; "if my Health continues," indeed. And Lydia's contrasting acceptance of the role chosen for her causes her many illnesses and also, intriguingly, the three-month cessation of correspondence with Letty, while Lydia journeys to and travels in Scotland, her farthest remove from Wilson. In short, acceptance of the role parental figures assign them can lead only to the stultification and stagnation of their personalities. On the other hand, flirtation with ruin—that is, with the role against which the parental figures enjoin them—provides both excitement and the greater potentiality. Pamela's flirtation with this latter role enables her to mature and, in fact, to define her own life, while Lydia's choice of the former role thwarts her maturation and, in some measure, her self-definition.

What does this mean? How do the heroines define themselves? They do so not by projecting their personalities onto an existential reality, but by projecting themselves onto paper.[11] They are, after all, doubly isolated from reality. As they write, they isolate themselves temporally, and the two authors also isolate their heroines spatially. Only Lydia of Smollett's five writers seems to correspond covertly (pp. 27, 58, 134), and Pamela, of course, retires to her writing closet at every opportunity; she even busies herself with scribbling fifteen minutes before the hymeneal night's consummation devoutly to be wished (p. 295). Peculiarly separated from the realities of time and space, the heroines' letters contrast with reality and with the scripted roles, both of which threaten the heroines' destructions.

Just as the roles her parents script would destroy Pamela, so too, of course, would B. He does not at first think of Pamela as fully human; she exists for him simply as an object for his sexual pleasure. Nor does he respond to Pamela's threats, expostulations, faints, or prayers; nothing the girl does moves him. It is her journal, her "ready . . . Talent at [her] Pen" (p. 231), that destroys his "Resolution" (p. 213) to forget her and so "mov[es]" him (p. 208) that he proposes marriage. In her journal he discovers that what he had earlier thought "artful Wiles" (p. 160) and "little villainous Plots" (p. 161) either to escape or to ensnare him were in fact "pretty Tricks and Artifices, to escape the Snares [he] had laid for her, yet all . . . innocent, lovely, and uniformly beautiful" (p. 255). Similarly, B.'s sister, Lady Davers, is somewhat reconciled to Pamela by B., but the "Sight of your Papers," she tells Pamela, "I dare say, will crown the Work, will disarm my Pride, banish my Resentment . . . , and justify my Brother's Conduct" (p. 375), will in fact "make me love you" (p. 374). Lydia's epistles do not serve quite so dramatic a purpose, but they do render her happier than either the role she accepts or her travels with her family. For in her letters she can openly admit the real "condition of [her] poor heart" (p. 93); indeed, only in her letters does she dare to mention Wilson, who figures prominently in them all. Thus, Lydia does not write only of the reality she has experienced during her travels or the torment and sickness caused by her role; she projects in her letters the reality for which she hopes. When these hopes seem to her most unlikely to be realized, the three-month hiatus in her correspondence occurs. Seemingly deprived of the reality she desires, she ceases to exist as a personality. Her epistolary death is the inverse of Pamela's proliferative epistolary life. Richardson has a good deal of fun with this idea of Pamela's papers having life. After catching a carp, for example, Pamela retires to her garden, there to "plant Life," as she says (p. 120). What she plants, of course, is a letter to Parson Williams. Just prior to this episode, she conceals her entire packet of papers "in [her] Under-coat, next [her] Linen" "for they grow large!" (p. 120). Using the same phrase, Pamela calls attention to her epistolary pregnancy once more (p. 198.), just before B. jocularly threatens to strip her of the clothes that conceal her papers; she retires to her bedroom and complains that she "must all undress" before she can deliver the bundle (p. 204). This delivery, by the way, she "stomach[es]. . . very heavily" (p. 206).

In their letters, then, the heroines conceive of a life reality would abort, and each conceives of that life as an artist of his material. Each heroine distances herself from her own raw experience by writing letters, and each projects a more orderly version of that experience in her letters. For each girl, reality is painfully chaotic, and each can give it shape only in her letters. Each girl is rootless, tossed from Bedfordshire to Lincolnshire, around and back, carried throughout England and Scotland. Pamela's loss of and Lydia's need for a mother figure, which each mentions at the beginning of her first letter, stresses this rootlessness. Each heroine, therefore, projects a structure onto her disjointed experiences, and each is aware of doing so.

Pamela's inclusion in her letters of her poems and of her alteration of the 137th Psalm to fit her own circumstances calls attention to her conscious artistry, as does her constant worry about her little store of pen, paper, and ink—the utensils of her art. But she also calls attention to the artistry of her letters, which she writes as a "Diversion" from her troubles (p. 106). From the outset she compares herself and B. to various characters in books she has read—romances (p. 49), the Bible (p. 180), and *Aesop's Fables* (pp. 77, 162). Pamela writes also of the "Inditing" of letters (p. 37), of the "Scene[s]" in them (p. 155), of the "Part[s]" (p. 173) played by the other "Character[s]" (p. 181), of her own "Part" (p. 225), and of her style or "Language" (p. 257). She even suggests that her "Story surely would furnish out a surprizing kind of Novel, if it was to be well told" (pp. 212–13). B., at least, believes it; after reading part of her journal, he pleads with her thus to be shown the rest: "I long to see the Particulars of your Plot, and your Disappointment, where your Papers leave off. For you have so beautiful a manner, that it is partly that, and partly my Love for you, that has made me desirous of reading all you write. . . . And as I have furnished you with the Subject, I have a Title to see the fruits of your Pen.—Besides, . . . there is such a pretty Air of Romance, as you relate them, in your Plots, and my Plots, that I shall be better directed in what manner to wind up the Catastrophe of the pretty Novel" (p. 201). For Lydia, too, the artistry of her own letters provides the primary solace and order of her life. Thus she entrusts the "chapter of accidents"—in the Book of Life?—to reunite her with Wilson, and thus her "method of writing" to Letty affords her "some ease and satisfaction in the midst of [her] disquiet" (p. 307). But when Matt nearly drowns and Humphry is legitimated and Wilson stands revealed as Dennison, poor Lydia's "ideas are thrown into confusion and perplexity" so that she fears she will not be able to impart "either method or coherence" to her letter. She soon does so by settling into "a regular detail" of those events, that is, into a minute narrative of them (p. 334). Like Pamela, she creates order where she does not find it.

The epistolary format, then, enables Pamela and Lydia to structure an artistic version of reality that is less painful to them because given order by them, and both heroines are aware they are using their letters for that purpose. In the face of chaotic realities, they trust their art to provide permanence and stability in their lives. Richardson's remarks about the epistolary format suggest the validity of this interpretation: "Much more lively and affecting . . . must be the *Style* of those who write in the height of a present distress; the mind tortured by the pangs of uncertainty . . . than the dry, narrative, unanimated *Style* of a person relating difficulties and dangers surmounted, can be; the relater perfectly at ease; and if himself unmoved by his own *Story,* not likely greatly to affect the Reader" (my italics). Richardson's remarks do not stress only the psychic torment of his creations; his remarks also indicate his use of those creations as creators, artists aware of their own "Story," aware of their own "Style."

In sum, the epistolary format of *Pamela* and *Humphry Clinker* isolates the heroines from reality and thus enables them to construct their own portraits of themselves. The heroines are aware of the artistry such portraiture involves, and they use their art to structure not only their characters but also the plots of their lives. Essentially, Pamela and Lydia use the format as another of the century's great writers used his journal, and one of James Boswell's plaintive entries may serve as an appropriate epigraph for both Richardson's and Smollett's novels. Boswell wrote: "I am fallen sadly behind in my journal. I should live no more than I can record, as one should not have more corn growing than one can get in. There is a waste of good if it be not preserved. And yet perhaps if it serve the purpose of immediate felicity, that is enough." [12]

This essay was partially supported by a grant from the Auburn University Research Grant-in-Aid Program, and I am pleased to acknowledge my gratitude for this financial assistance.

NOTES

[1] Robert F. Utter and Gwendolyn B. Needham, *Pamela's Daughters* (New York: Macmillan Co., 1936), esp. p. 13.

[2] Sheridan Baker, *"Humphry Clinker* as Comic Romance," in *Essays on the Eighteenth-Century Novel,* ed. Robert Donald Spector (Bloomington: Indian Univ. Press, 1965), p. 163.

[3] Samuel Richardson, "Author's Preface (1759)," *Clarissa,* ed. George Sherburn (Cambridge: Riverside Press, 1962), p. xx.

[4] Samuel Richardson, "Preface by the Editor," *Pamela,* ed. T.C. Duncan Eaves and Ben D. Kimpel (Boston: Houghton Mifflin Co., 1971), p. 3. Subsequent references are to this edition and will be cited in the text.

[5] See Tuvia Bloch, "Smollett's Quest for Form," *MP,* 65 (1967), 103–13.

[6] Cf. Robert Alan Donovan, "The Problem of Pamela," in *The Shaping Vision* (Ithaca: Cornell Univ. Press, 1966), pp. 47–67.

[7] Cf. John A. Dussinger, "What Pamela Knew: An Interpretation," *JEGP,* 69 (1970), 377–93; Stuart Wilson, "Pamela: An Interpretation," *PMLA,* 88 (1973), 79–91.

[8] Tobias Smollett, *Humphry Clinker,* ed. Lewis M. Knapp (London: Oxford Univ. Press, 1972), p. 5. Subsequent references are to this edition and will be cited in the text.

[9] Interestingly, a rake named Martin also appears in the latter half of Richardson's novel.

[10] See, for example, Eric Berne, *Transactional Analysis in Psychotherapy* (New York: Grove Press, 1961) and *What Do You Say After You Say Hello?* (New York: Grove Press, 1972). The latter work Berne devotes to extensive analysis of various life plans, or scripts, finding in such classic fairy tales as Little Red Riding Hood, Cinderella, and Sleeping Beauty patterns of human behavior.

[11] David Goldknopf, "The Epistolary Format in *Clarissa,*" in *The Life of the Novel* (Chicago: Univ. of Chicago Press, 1973), pp. 59–78.

[12] James Boswell, *The Ominous Years, 1774–1776,* ed. Charles Ryskamp and Frederick A. Pottle (New York: McGraw-Hill Book Co., 1963), p. 265.

ROBERT W. HALLI, JR. ✒ "THIS TORRENT
OF DOMESTIC
MISERY"
GEORGE LILLO'S
THE LONDON MERCHANT

GEORGE LILLO'S *The London Merchant* (1731) is recognized as the first wholly middle class tragedy to appear on the English stage, though this genre had had advocates for some time. Richard Steele had noted in 1710 that aristocratic tragedies "do not fail of striking us with terrors," but they "pass through our imagination as incidents, in which our fortunes are too humble" to be bothered. "Instead of such high passages," Steele continued, "I was thinking it would be of great use, if any body could hit it, to lay before the world such adventures as befal persons not exalted above the common level. This, methought, would better prevail upon the ordinary race of men; who are so prepossessed with outward appearances, that they mistake Fortune for Nature, and believe nothing can relate to them, that does not happen to such as live and look like themselves." [1]

Lillo tried to "hit it" and saw *The London Merchant* as a new species of tragedy for which his dedication, to a businessman, offered the poetics:

> If tragic poetry be, as Mr. Dryden has somewhere said, the most excellent and most useful kind of writing, the more extensively useful the moral of any tragedy is, the more excellent that piece must be of its kind.
>
> . . . .
>
> What I would infer is this, I think, evident truth: that tragedy is so far from losing its dignity by being accommodated to the circumstances of the generality of mankind that it is more truly august in proportion to the extent of its influence and the numbers that are properly affected by it, as it is more truly great to be the instrument of good to many who stand in need of our assistance than to a very small part of that number. (Dedication. 5–8, 18–25) [2]

Lillo highly valued tragedy's didactic role and believed it should be a democratic literary form, to be judged by the extent of its influence for good rather than by the artistry of its representation of aristocratic catastrophes. In spite of the author's hopes, however, Robert Gale Noyes points out that "Lillo's attempt to write middle class tragedy in prose stands virtually alone as an experiment in the first half of the century. The unities persisted and the Augustan school continued to propagate the model of *All for Love* and *Cato*." [3] Although he adhered to Steele's advice, "to refine the age, / To chasten wit, and moralize the stage,"[4] very few of his contemporaries chose to follow Lillo's example in tragedy. The moral lesson of *The London Merchant* is portrayed against a background of mercantilism and unfolded in terms of sentiment. These three concepts—mercantilism, sentiment, and morality—dominate the play.

I

The contemporary debate over the values of mercantilism is represented by only one side in the play: the merchant is a good for all humanity. The opposite view was held by the liberals of the day and by the nobles and landed gentry who viewed the rise of the merchant class as an assault on their power. As John Loftis has noted, this was among the "social assumptions" of much Restoration drama, particularly the comedy, whose writers hated the dissenters as latter-day Puritans and hated the merchant class that had supported Cromwell. The neoclassic conception of the drama was that it should be an imitation of "the ideal order of society," which was seen as "an hierarchical and rigid structure." [5] As the belief in the social aspects of the Great Chain of Being declined, and as the mercantile community rose in importance, it was to be expected that the neoclassical critical conceptions would be challenged.

There were significant voices on Lillo's side of the question, however, such as that of Daniel Defoe, perhaps the most persistent advocate of the superiority of middle class values. Robinson Crusoe's father praises the middle station of life,

> which he had found by long Experience was the best State in the World, the most suited to human Happiness, not exposed to the Miseries and Hardships, the Labour and Sufferings of the mechanick part of Mankind, and not embarrass'd with the Pride, Luxury, Ambition and Envy of the upper Part of Mankind. He told me, I might judge of the Happiness of this State, by this one thing, *viz*. That this was the State of Life which all other People envied, that Kings have frequently lamented the miserable Consequences of being born to great things, and wish'd they had been placed in the Middle of the two Extremes, between the

Mean and the Great; that the wise Man gave his Testimony to this as the just Standard of true Felicity, when he prayed to have neither Poverty or Riches.[6]

With regards to mercantilism, Defoe always advocated free trade and free enterprise no matter how much his other socio-political views might change from pamphlet to pamphlet. Joseph Addison also praised the merchants of London in *Spectator* No. 69: "I am wonderfully delighted to see such a Body of Men thriving in their own private Fortunes, and at the same time promoting the Publick Stock; or in other Words, raising Estates for their own Families, by bringing into their Country whatever is wanting, and carrying out of it whatever is superfluous." [7] It cannot be denied that *The London Merchant* often sounds like a Chamber of Commerce pamphlet: "Honest merchants, as such, may sometimes contribute to the safety of their country as they do at all times to its happiness; that if hereafter you should be tempted to any action that has the appearance of vice or meanness in it, upon reflecting on the dignity of our profession, you may with honest scorn reject whatever is unworthy of it" (I.i.16–22). Mercantilism, in the context of this play, has saved and supported "our royal mistress, pure religion, liberty, and laws" (I.i.2–3). Besides this, profitable trade keeps taxes down, and dunning debtors saves them time because they do not have to come to the merchant to pay their bills. In fact, trade seems to be the greatest invention of all time for the benefit of humanity, as Thorowgood proclaims to Trueman: " 'Twill be well worth your pains to study it as a science, see how it is founded in reason and the nature of things, how it has promoted humanity as it has opened and yet keeps up an intercourse between nations far remote from one another in situation, customs, and religion; promoting arts, industry, peace, and plenty; by mutual benefits diffusing mutual love from pole to pole" (III.i.3–9). While this seems a bit much to attribute to the merchants, it is by no means a singular statement in its age, as Addison had written twenty years before that "there are not more useful Members in a Commonwealth than Merchants. They knit Mankind together in a mutual Intercourse of good Offices, distribute the Gifts of Nature, find Work for the Poor, add Wealth to the Rich, and Magnificence to the Great" (I,296).

Addison's statement implies that the merchants of London are men of sentiment in the Shaftesburian sense of that word. Indeed, as Raymond D. Havens has noted, the increasing wealth and comfort of the rising middle class, the weakening of rigid neoclassicism, and the spread and tolerance of emotional religion gave great impetus to the belief in benevolence and goodness as the natural motives of human action.[8] This emphasis on the "boniform faculty" of the soul of man was a reaction to the views of Hobbes.

In the seventeenth century Thomas Hobbes had argued in *Leviathan* (1651) that man was basically a creature of self-interest. His motivations were essentially selfish, inclining toward whatever would bring him the most personal happiness. Thus he was a being whose morality was dominated by individual reason, and his good became that which he desired. This philosophy was repulsive to the Cambridge Platonists and the Latitudinarian Divines of the period, who saw that Hobbes had gone far toward making morality a purely arbitrary thing, wholly dependent on the personal whims of the self-interested individual. They maintained against the *Leviathan* that the individual's primary motive was not selfish desire but rather the good of all mankind. They taught that man possessed an inward sense that recognized good and took pleasure from the contemplation of it. This belief is amplified and explained in a seminal essay by R. S. Crane: "For most of the divines who were thus helping to set the tone of eighteenth-century humanitarian exhortation, the words 'charity' and 'benevolence' had a double sense, connoting not only the serviceable and philanthropic actions which the good man performs but still more the tender passions and affections which prompt to these actions and constitute their immediate reward." [9]

Though this "boniform faculty" of the soul had an objective reality for the Platonists, those philosophers who followed them, notably the third Earl of Shaftesbury, transformed this inward sense, and it became not much more than feeling. The rigor of the earlier arguments for the essential benevolence of man disappeared; the concept was partially deprived of its spiritual quality and became a standard of values as subjective as Hobbes's. Lois Whitney notes that "this anti-intellectual temper is in accord with his [Shaftesbury's] advice to Michael Ainsworth: 'But be persuaded, in the meantime, that wisdom is more from the *heart,* than from the *head. Feel* goodness, and you will see all-things fair and good.' " [10]

Within *The London Merchant* both poles of this philosophical argument are represented. Millwood is the complete Hobbesian who judges everything on the basis of self-interest. When George Barnwell is troubled in conscience after the murder of his uncle, she reveals her position clearly: "No more of this stuff! What *advantage* have you made of his death? Or what *advantage* may yet be made of it? Did you secure the *keys of his treasure*? Those, no doubt, were about him. What *gold,* what *jewels,* or *what else of value* have you brought me?" (IV.x. 24–28). Barnwell, representing the other pole, is all sentiment: "But if you mean the general love we owe to mankind, I think no one has more of it in his temper than myself. I don't know that person in the world whose happiness I don't wish and wouldn't promote, were it in my power" (I.v.33–37). He knows that reason should govern his emotions, but his reason is not strong enough to resist Millwood's assault on his passions. He is delighted to be able to engage in any emotion, but especially in those of pity and compassion: "Millwood: Perhaps you pity me? Barnwell: I do, I do. Indeed, I do!" (II.ix.55–56). Barnwell is more fearful of Millwood's ingratitude than he is of justice. His basic problem is that his sentiment is untempered by his reason.

Thorowgood, as his name implies, is the correct norm between sentiment and reason—not between sentiment and self-interest as he is never motivated by the latter. One of the major attributes of the true man of sentiment is generosity, and this quality is frequently attributed to Thorowgood throughout the play. His commendation of Lucy and Blunt is in terms of moral goodness rather than justice: "What you have done against Millwood I know proceeded from a just abhorrence of her crimes, free from interest, malice, or revenge" (V.i.35–37). It is interesting that, in accordance with her Hobbesian views, Millwood sees the action entirely in the opposite light: "They disapprove of my conduct and mean to take this opportunity to set up for themselves" (IV.xv.1–2). Thorowgood is always ready to forgive and rejoices in Barnwell's repentance, but he makes clear throughout the play that the good man's actions, though they should be motivated by emotion, must be tempered by reason. This view of morality received its clearest expression in the work of the later Scottish philosophers. David Hume held that while a man's sentiment enabled him to recognize morality it did not enable him to act upon it, and he concluded that "*reason* and *sentiment* concur in all moral determinations and conclusions." [11] Like Hume, Adam Smith held that reason was a necessary addition to sympathy in the virtuous mind and disapproved of Shandeian sentimentalism. He could have been thinking directly of George Barnwell when he wrote that "virtue requires habit and resolution of mind, as well as delicacy of sentiment; and unfortunately the former qualities are sometimes wanting, where the latter is in the greatest perfection." [12]

Barnwell has perfected his "delicacy of sentiment" but has not developed his reason to guide rationally his emotive impulses. Thorowgood correctly diagnoses this: "When we consider the frail condition of humanity it may raise our pity, not our wonder, that youth should go astray when reason, weak at the best when opposed to inclination, scarce formed and wholly unassisted by experience, faintly contends or willingly becomes the slave of sense" (II.iv.17–22). The effects of aroused feelings should always be for the good, and it is the duty of reason to turn them in that direction. Lillo and Thorowgood would not have approved of Mackenzie's stimulating sentiment for its own sake in *The Man of Feeling,* and even the great waves of pity and pathos generated by the final act of *The London Merchant* must be turned to a reasonable, practical, and moral purpose. As Trueman concludes,

In vain
With bleeding hearts and weeping eyes we show
A human gen'rous sense of others' woe,
Unless we mark what drew their ruin on,
And, by avoiding that, prevent our own. (V.xi.11–15)

This moral is perhaps common enough in the age, the play following Pope's dictum of being "What oft was *Thought,* but ne'er so well *Exprest,*" [13] but the language in which it is conveyed is rather interesting. The moral is carried chiefly by images familiar to the mercantile community, about and for which it was written. Barnwell, for instance, admits that "to ease our present anguish by plunging into guilt is to *buy* a moment's pleasure with an age of pain" (I.viii.4–5). He decides to buy guilt, however, and sets sail for sin as a merchant would embark on uncharted seas. To the apprentice, his sin of "breach of trust" seems more serious than that of "guilty love." When Barnwell laments the inability to return to the time before his sins, Trueman caps his speech with one that provides a consolation for the past and the only effective preventative for the future: "Though the continued chain of time has never once been broke, nor ever will, but uninterrupted must keep on its course till, lost in eternity, it ends there where it first begun, yet, as Heaven can repair whatever evils time can bring upon us, he who trusts Heaven ought never to despair. —But business requires our attendance—business, the youth's best preservative from ill, as idleness his worst of snares" (II.ii.87–94). A merchant can never recover a good reputation once it is lost, and the robbery of the uncle would be more grievous than the killing, just as sacrilege is more serious than murder. Barnwell delivers his most directly moralizing lines in these terms also:

By my example learn to shun my fate;
(How wretched is the man who's wise too late!)
Ere innocence and fame and life be lost,
Here *purchase* wisdom *cheaply,* at my *cost.* (IV.xiii.15–18)

Alan S. Downer notes that "the moral is, of course, that crime does not pay, and the word 'pay' is to be taken in its most literal sense." [14]

II

In addition to its language, the form of the play merits examination; *The London Merchant* shows the influence of at least three traditions. First, and most importantly, there is much that is similar to the old morality plays in Lillo's presentation. It is a battle for the mind and soul of Barnwell, who, naturally, stands at the center of the conflict.

Thorowgood, Trueman, and Maria try to influence him towards the good and can easily be allegorized as Successful Apprentice, True Friend, and True Love. On the other side are the vice, Millwood, and her two henchmen, Lucy and Blunt. Millwood could be allegorized as False Love. Since Barnwell has already succumbed to the first temptation before the play opens, and since his progression is like that of the central figure in the later morality plays, from temptation to sin to greater sin to damnation, he is never seen as a truly good figure. Thus Thorowgood and company are needed to tell of his goodness. No member of the business family really *does* much in the play, leaving most of the action to Millwood. The intrigues of the London prostitute correspond to those of the older vice, and her gulling addresses to Barnwell are successful. Millwood assumes the homiletic attributes of the vice, revealing her depraved nature and her plans to trap the young apprentice. The revolt of the lieutenant vices from their chief is also found in the morality tradition. There is, however, a very important difference between the philosophy of this play and that of the moralities, which will be handled a little later.

Second, there seems to be some influence of the tradition of heroic tragedy in *The London Merchant,* as William H. McBurney notes: "In particular, the extravagent friendship of the two apprentices can hardly be explained except in terms of the heroic play. Trueman is the friend whom Barnwell loves 'above all,' and the breach of friendship is his 'first' offense." [15] Clearly, too, the play is based on the old heroic conflict between love and duty, this time portrayed as a choice between a prostitute and a good apprenticeship, which is far down the scale from a choice between Cleopatra and Rome.

Third, *The London Merchant* partially reflects the tradition of the criminal biography that reached its peak in Defoe's *Moll Flanders.* Such material was eagerly received by the lower classes of society, and much in Millwood is reminiscent of Moll. For both, and later for Richardson's Pamela, their virtue was their capital, their dowry, and if deprived of that they lost all. Moll and Millwood lost it and were forced into poverty, and by poverty into crime. Millwood's statement on society, "The judge who condemns the poor man for being a thief had been a thief himself, had he been poor" (IV.xviii.64–66), echoes Moll's desperate prayer: *"Give me not Poverty least I Steal."* [16] Lastly, like the criminal biographies, *The London Merchant* claims to be a revelation of actual events as is indicated by the subtitle, *The History of George Barnwell.*

George Lillo did not call *The London Merchant* a morality play, a heroic play, or a criminal play, but a tragedy. Whether it fits this last appellation has been the subject of much critical dispute, particularly since the romantic period. Many faults have been found in the play, particularly by those critics who see it as a logical extension of the morality, or internal conflict, play tradition into the eighteenth century. Cleanth Brooks and Robert B. Heilman make a very suggestive statement about the nature of the play by criticizing it in these terms: "We feel, therefore, that Lillo should have organized his play like *Everyman* or *Dr. Faustus,* for Barnwell's own struggle is the central issue, and therefore his role should have received the emphasis which would be conferred by fuller development. Instead, Lillo makes Barnwell share our attention with too many other people, none of them essential to our understanding of Barnwell. That is, he uses a form more suitable to depicting the *state of a society* than the *struggles of an individual.* Why does he fall into this error?" [17]

The answer is simply that the conflict of *The London Merchant* is directly opposite in kind to that of *Everyman* and *Dr. Faustus.* The inner souls of the title characters of the latter two plays are the battlegrounds for conflicts that take place between separate forces within their natures. *Everyman* is essentially an allegorization of the forces within man's soul, and Mephistophilis very much represents a portion of Faustus's mental anatomy. In sum, these are microcosmic plays with the main action taking place within a character. *The London Merchant,* on the other hand, is a macrocosmic morality play in which characters distinctly outside the central figure fight, or talk, for dominance of Barnwell. It is an objective rather than a subjective play. To understand the relation of these plays to himself, a reader must look within himself when concerned with *Everyman* and *Dr. Faustus,* and he must look out at the society in which he lives when concerned with *The London Merchant.*

Though the reader is told that there is great internal conflict, for it is not dramatically realized, there is no doubt that the emphasis in the play is on Millwood, the only character who really acts. There would be nothing dramatically ineffective in a true conflict between Millwood and Barnwell, but such is not presented in the play. Either in order to strengthen the moral lesson to youth, or because of the dramatist's inability to create a strong Barnwell, Millwood's conquest of the young apprentice is all too easy. While she must have been a beautiful and commanding stage presence, still her snares seem perfectly obvious to the modern reader. The scene of her rendezvous with Barnwell seems almost farcical today, with the gorgeous whore bearing down on the young man who can only retreat and stammer, "I fear I am too bold" (I.v.7). He is not, but he is literally incredibly naive, as is revealed in his first aside: "Her disorder is so great she don't perceive she has laid her hand on mine. Heaven! How she trembles! What can this mean?" (I.v.18–20). Immediately a conflict of love and duty arises as Millwood attempts to detain Barnwell from going about his master's business. His soft sentiments are touched by Millwood's false protestations and the result is inevitable: "Oh, Heavens! She loves me, worthless as I am. Her looks, her words, her flowing tears confess it. And can I leave her then? Oh, never, never!" (I.v. 79–81).

For all intents and purposes, this scene begins and ends the decisive conflict of the play. Barnwell has been won over to sin, and, though he makes some feeble motions back towards goodness later, his destiny is never in doubt, as he says to Millwood: "You are my fate, my Heaven or my Hell" (II.xiii.18). He goes on to commit theft and murder, crimes greater than his "guilty love," but these are only the snowballing results of his previous decision.

These two major characters of *The London Merchant* have been cast in perfectly opposite molds. Barnwell is a naive and innocent young man; Millwood is an experienced and hardened prostitute. Barnwell is another Man of Feeling, believing in the general benevolence of all mankind; Millwood is a Hobbesian, living by a code of selfish reason and firmly convinced of the general depravity of mankind. Barnwell is soft as mush; Millwood as hard as diamond. While only pathetic repentance surrounds Barnwell's death, something of tragic dignity surrounds Millwood's.

One reason why we sympathize with Millwood is that she does not demand sympathy. She is visibly human, yet she maintains a dramatic distance between herself and the audience. Her coolness in handling the blustering Thorowgood is admirable, and her use of her "wit and form" can tempt a saint. Her morality is closer than any other character's to that which Lillo was born to in the Dutch Reformed Church. Millwood never yields in her Calvinistic conception of predestination; even as Barnwell beseeches her to pray for mercy, she replies that "though mercy may be boundless, yet 'tis free. And I was doomed before the world began to endless pains, and thou to joys eternal" (V.xii.45–47). She forsees what this doom means and still espouses a Promethean rejection of a benevolent God: "Heaven, Thou hast done thy worst. Or if Thou hast in store some untried plague, somewhat that's worse than shame, despair, and death—unpitied death, confirmed despair, and soul-confounding shame—something that men and angels can't describe and only fiends who bear it can conceive—now, pour it now on this devoted head that I may feel the worst Thou canst inflict and bid defiance to Thy utmost power!" (V.xii.15–22). Her exit is in a tone of dignified, tragic, almost Shakespearean despair: "Encompassed with horror, whither must I go? I would not live—nor die! That I could cease to be—or ne'er had been!" (V.xii.64–65).

Perhaps Millwood's greatest lines, and the greatest in the play, are those in which she brings her total scorn to bear on the men that have ruined her, condemned her, and now will kill her:

Men of all degrees and all professions I have known, yet found no difference
but in their several capacities. All were alike wicked to the utmost of their power.

. . . .

I hate you all! I know you, and expect no mercy—nay, I ask for none. I have
done nothing that I am sorry for. I followed my inclinations, and that the best of
you does every day. All actions are alike natural and indifferent to man and beast
who devour or are devoured as they meet with others weaker or stronger than
themselves. (IV.xviii.22–24,40–45)

Like Barnwell she adds a didactic twist to her fate, but the turn is away
from encouraging morality:

Oh, may, from hence, each violated maid,
By flatt'ring, faithless, barb'rous man betray'd,
When robb'd of innocence and virgin fame,
From your destruction raise a nobler name:
To right their sex's wrongs devote their mind,
And future Millwoods prove, to plague mankind! (IV.xviii.73–78)

In all this bitterness surrounding Millwood, one accusation that
Thorowgood hurls at her would, if true, completely defeat the play as
tragedy: "I charge you as the cause, the sole cause of all his guilt and all
his suffering" (IV.xvi.46–47). This statement deprives Barnwell of all
responsibility for his actions and indicates that he has made no tragic
choices. Although Thorowgood frequently and obviously speaks for
the author, this accusation is probably made more in his character as
angered London merchant than in his function as Lillo's mouthpiece,
since, even in his first encounter with Millwood, Barnwell has to make a
choice between his duty and what he considers love. There is another
and more dangerous threat to Barnwell's individual responsibility for
his sins in the final act, when he seems to lean toward the philosophy of
predestination held by Millwood in his line: "I was born to murder all
who love me" (V.v.9). At a later time, however, Barnwell comes to the
realization that his downfall has been the result of choices made by a
free will: "I now am—what I've made myself" (V.viii.2). Although
Barnwell may have been predestined for this end, he arrived at it
through his own actions based on free will. God saw what would happen
but did not directly cause it. George Bush Rodman well sums up
another piece of evidence in favor of the youth's free will: "That Lillo
did not intend to present Barnwell as being a character who is in no way
to blame for the catastrophe which overwhelms him, is indicated by his
having Barnwell repeatedly confess his own weakness and make clear
his realization that he is sinning grievously." [18] This was probably the
viewpoint of the early audiences of *The London Merchant,* for the master

businessmen would not have sent their apprentices to see a play in which Barnwell was merely a victim of forces beyond his control. The contexts of his repentances, however, suggest much about his character and lead into another area of examination. Raymond D. Havens points out that "since Barnwell repents as volubly before committing each of his sins as afterwards, there is no assurance that if freed from the gallows he would not relapse into his former courses. He is an amiable, spineless youth whom Lillo judges not by his actions but by how he feels about them" (p. 184).

Whatever goodness Barnwell possesses is portrayed only in his speeches and in those of the Thorowgood household. Throughout the whole play Barnwell never acts the good man. The inevitable result is that Lillo tries to talk an effect rather than dramatize it, and this creates the pathos that surrounds Barnwell.

Lillo did realize that pity and terror are essential to tragedy; what he did not realize was that in a successful tragedy they must be simultaneous responses to an individual character. We may feel admiration for Millwood's defiance of God and man, but we feel little pity for her, and she even says she wants none. On the other hand, the terror we feel on viewing Barnwell's actions stems not so much from that character himself as from Millwood's manipulations of him. He is a puppet, and we feel terror in the motives of the puppeteer. We do not have the fusion of these reactions to drama that is necessary for good tragedy, and the emotions of pity and compassion are allowed to dominate to such an extent that *The London Merchant* becomes overly pathetic.

Nothing is wrong with a dramatist's arousing pity in his audience if pity is a legitimate response to the dramatic action presented. Rodman notes, however, that

> it is not Lillo's attempt to arouse the pity of the audience that makes *The London Merchant* sentimental; for tragedy by its very nature requires that the audience be made to feel pity; rather, it is the lack of correspondence between the feeling of pity that Lillo tries to create and the character who is intended to arouse this feeling that makes *The London Merchant* sentimental. The audience is expected to be profoundly moved by the fall of a young man who is weak rather than good or evil, who lacks the magnitude of spirit which characterizes great tragic figures, who is, in these respects, a Richard the Second of the 'prentice world, without Richard's magic gift of poetry. (p. 59)

To use Eliot's phrase, there is no objective correlative on the stage for the feeling Lillo wishes to generate in his audience. Lillo perhaps realized this, and so, with the exception of the fifth act, he never really tries to excite pity for Barnwell by action where speech will do. The pathos surrounding the murder of the uncle is almost unbearable. He delivers twenty-four prose lines on the nature of death, during which the masked Barnwell sneaks onstage and sometimes raises and sometimes lowers his pistol in the best Fletcherian tradition. After dropping his pistol and thus alarming the old man, who draws his sword to defend himself, Barnwell stabs his uncle with a convenient poniard. Having received his death wound, the benevolent old man first blesses his nephew, then prays for God's forgiveness for his masked murderer, and lastly prays for his own soul. These garrulous speeches are capped, however, by Barnwell's maudlin oration of sorrow and repentance that sobs on through twenty-seven prose lines and three heroic couplets. George Henry Nettleton correctly diagnoses the problem this causes: "So much, indeed, is sympathy enlisted for Barnwell as a man more sinned against than sinning that little compassion is felt for the murdered uncle, who is introduced only as a lamb led to the slaughter." [19]

The final act of the play must stand as some sort of landmark in the tradition of sentimental drama. It is, in effect, a long pathetic epilogue, since all the relevant dramatic action has already been completed. It is also, perhaps, the wettest act in all of English drama, but the tears come too easily, and the modern audience's reaction is more likely to be annoyance at the emotional excess of the characters than pity and compassion for Barnwell. The friends' groveling and embracing on the floor of the prison seems more a cheap sentimental gimmick than a relevant dramatic action. The maudlin embrace of Barnwell and Maria is illuminating, however, as it finally reveals why she is in the play at all, since her role has been generally nonfunctional up to this time. There is too much sentimentality, pathos, and happiness in this act for it to be dramatically effective. Havens's assessment is accurate: "Barnwell thoroughly enjoys his repentance, as his friends do their forgiveness. We are treated to an emotional orgy in which, as at an Irish wake, the seriousness of the occasion is quite forgotten" (p. 184). In fact, Act V totally changes the focus of the play from the moral, if pathetic, strain of the first four acts to one of undue sentimentality, and dramatically this is a disaster.

In spite of these present conclusions, however, *The London Merchant* was immensely successful on its first presentation and remained popular, if popularity is to be judged by frequency of performance, for a hundred years or more. In a contemporary review, the *Gentleman's Magazine* praised the play:

> 'Tis a Tragedy of a new kind; but while it yields a rational Pleasure, its Novelty will be no Objection. It's the finest Lesson to Youth, and what is calculated for their use, is made their Entertainment.
>
> To the foregoing Remarks . . . we beg leave to add one or two of an observing Lady, "That the Distress of great Personages has of late, fail'd of raising those

Passions that us'd to accompany the Representation of exalted Characters. Besides, such is the artful Contrivance of this Play; so delicate is the Texture of its Composition, that none, but a common Prostitute, can find Fault with it." [20]

If fault could not be found in the play, another quality could be found in a badly performed presentation of it. Robert G. Noyes quotes from *The Adventures of Sylvia Hughes,* a novel of 1761: "The Play being ended, I ask'd Mr. Hughes how he lik'd it? 'A Farce you should have said, Madam,' says he; 'and indeed a very droll one it is. When I was at London, I saw this very Play perform'd, but I really was not Half so much diverted as I have been now; for, at the Representation there, I could not avoid Weeping; whereas here, I have been excited to Mirth'" (p. 165).

The play was taken quite seriously by the initial audiences, however, for reasons pointed out by Herbert Carson:

> The English middle class with its semi-Puritan morality and its less-than-refined taste . . . showed little interest in the amorous exploits of young Lords and other semi-nobles. Fresh from their counting boards, these merchants of London saw no humor in the careless dissipation of money. An older outlook made them frown on the excesses of youth, whose spirits they saw as an element to be curbed by the wisdom of age. These merchants liked the pathetic and sentimental, reveling in the luxury of pity denied them in business affairs, but rejecting the rigor and austerity demanded by tragedy.[21]

A more important reason for its continued performance, primarily on holiday nights, was that the merchants of London felt *The London Merchant* was a fine moral lesson for their apprentices, whether or not the play had dramatic value. Ernest Bernbaum claims that "the frequent performance of *George Barnwell* was encouraged by influential citizens, not because they themselves enjoyed it, but because they thought young people should." [22]

Indeed, F. C. Wemyss included the play in *The Modern Standard Drama* in 1849 because it was an "excellent moral lesson to youth," and he even related a tale of how an apprentice was saved from a life of depravity by viewing *The London Merchant.*[23] A little more than ten years later, however, another apprentice had a somewhat different reaction, a reaction shared by most modern critics. After sitting through an horrific reading of the play, Dickens's Pip sums up: "I thought it a little too much that he should complain of being cut short in his flower after all, as if he had not been running to seed, leaf after leaf, ever since his course began." [24]

NOTES

[1] Richard Steele, *Tatler* No. 172, in *The Tatler* (London: Sharpe, 1804), III, 307.

[2] George Lillo, *The London Merchant,* ed. William H. McBurney (Lincoln, Nebr.: Univ. of Nebraska Press, 1965), p. 3. All further citations of Lillo are from this text, and all italics found in such citations are my own and are not found in the original text.

[3] Robert Gale Noyes, *The Neglected Muse* (Providence, R.I.: Brown Univ. Press, 1958), p. 10.

[4] Richard Steel, *The Conscious Lovers,* ed. Shirley Strum Kenny (Lincoln, Nebr.: Univ. of Nebraska Press, 1968), p. 8.

[5] John Loftis, *The Politics of Drama in Augustan England* (Oxford: Clarendon Press, 1963), pp. 155–56, 160.

[6] Daniel Defoe, *Robinson Crusoe,* ed. J. Donald Crowley (London: Oxford Univ. Press, 1972), p. 4.

[7] Joseph Addison, *Spectator* No. 69, in *The Spectator,* ed. Donald F. Bond (Oxford: Clarendon Press, 1965), I, 294.

[8] Raymond D. Havens, "The Sentimentalism of *The London Merchant,*" *ELH,* 12 (1945), 186.

[9] R. S. Crane, "Suggestions Toward a Genealogy of the 'Man of Feeling,' " *ELH,* 1 (1934), 214.

[10] Lois Whitney, *Primitivism and the Idea of Progress* (Baltimore: Johns Hopkins Press, 1934), p. 32.

[11] David Hume, *An Enquiry Concerning the Principles of Morals,* in *Hume's Enquiries,* ed. L. A. Selby-Bigge (Oxford: Oxford Univ. Press, 1902), p. 172.

[12] Adam Smith, "Of Systems of Moral Philosophy," in *The Works of Adam Smith* (London: Cadell and Davies, 1811), I, 576.

[13] Alexander Pope, "An Essay on Criticism," in *The Poems of Alexander Pope,* ed. John Butt (New Haven: Yale Univ. Press, 1963), p. 153 (l. 298).

[14] Alan S. Downer, *The British Drama* (New York: Appleton, 1950), p. 265.

[15] William H. McBurney, "Introduction," *The London Merchant,* p. xviii.

[16] Daniel Defoe, *Moll Flanders,* ed. G. A. Starr (London: Oxford Univ. Press, 1971), p. 191.

[17] Cleanth Brooks and Robert B. Heilman, *Understanding Drama* (New York: Henry Holt, 1948), p. 181.

[18] George Bush Rodman, "Sentimentalism in Lillo's *The London Merchant,*" *ELH,* 12 (1945), 48.

[19] George Henry Nettleton, *English Drama of the Restoration and Eighteenth Century* (New York: Macmillan Co., 1914), p. 205.

[20] *The Gentleman's Magazine,* 1 (1731), 340.

[21] Herbert L. Carson, "The Play That Would Not Die: George Lillo's *The London Merchant,*" *Quarterly Journal of Speech,* 49 (1963), 287.

[22] Ernest Bernbaum, *The Drama of Sensibility* (Boston: Ginn, 1915), p. 158.

[23] F. C. Wemyss, "Introduction," *The Modern Standard Drama,* ed. F. C. Wemyss (New York: Taylor, 1849), XI, iii–iv.

[24] Charles Dickens, *Great Expectations* (London: Oxford Univ. Press, 1953), pp. 109–10.

> The force, therefore, of the production, like the
> delineation of external incident, while the
> character of the agents, like the figures in many
> landscapes, are entirely subordinate to the
> scenes in which they are placed; and are only
> distinguished by such outlines as make them
> seem appropriate to the rocks and trees which
> have been the artist's principal objects.
> —Walter Scott

MALCOLM WARE ✍ **THE TELESCOPE**
REVERSED
ANN RADCLIFFE AND
NATURAL SCENERY

CATHERINE MORELAND AT THE BEGINNING of *Northanger Abbey* shows almost no promise of becoming a true, typical Gothic heroine; among her other obvious deficiencies, she is short, not an orphan, not mysteriously attracted to some local youth named, almost certainly, either Theodore or Valancourt, and not at all proficient at writing sonnets. Furthermore, Jane Austen tells us, she shows little ability with the artist's pen and a distressing lack of taste for the picturesque. She can, to be sure, draw after a fashion. But she draws such unlikely things as "horses, trees, hens, and chickens." [1] Soon, however, Catherine comes under the spell of Gothic fiction, and of necessity acquires new tastes and assumes the distinct pose of the Gothic heroine. In this attempt, one of the first taste Catherine tries to refine is one that characterizes most of the heroines in the fiction Miss Austen is satirizing—an apparently insatiable appetite for the picturesque in nature and the ability to view and evaluate the picturesque in much the same way as a painting. Catherine, with no taste for the picturesque, on a walking tour with the Tilneys, finds herself at a distinct disadvantage:

> They were viewing the country with the eyes of persons accustomed to drawing, and deciding on its capability of being formed into pictures, with all the eagerness of real taste. Here Catherine was quite lost. She knew nothing of drawing—nothing of taste. . . . (p. 132)

Catherine is aware of her deficiency and to Henry Tilney

> . . . declared that she would give anything in the world to be able to draw; and a lecture on the picturesque immediately followed, in which his instructions were so clear that she soon began to see beauty in everything admired by him; and her attention was so earnest, that she became perfectly satisfied of her having a great deal of natural taste. He talked of foregrounds, distances, and second distances;

side-screens and perspectives; lights and shades; and Catherine was so hopeful a
scholar, that when they gained the top of Beechen Cliff, she voluntarily rejected
the whole city of Bath, as unworthy to make part of a landscape. (p. 132)

A taste for the picturesque, or perhaps more precisely an ability to
appreciate the grouping of elements in natural scenery that produces an
orderly and pleasing composition inviting pictorial reproduction, was
an important part of the makeup of a sensitive character in a Gothic
novel. In Mrs. Radcliffe's novels this taste is indulged repeatedly in long
descriptive passages, and the frequency, length, and sameness of these
passages caused some unfavorable comment from many of her contemporaries. Two of her early critics, however, reacted differently and
found these extended descriptive passages integral parts of her craft.
The first of these critics was Nathan Drake, a successful medical doctor
who abandoned his career in order to devote his time to writing essays
on literary topics and, incidentally, to try his own hand, with considerable promise but with no real diligence, at writing Gothic tales. In one
of his essays, "On Objects of Terror," included in *Literary Hours*
(1820), Drake states that Mrs. Radcliffe's use of lengthy description
works successfully to soften the effect of the terror often inherent in
her situation:

> To obviate this result, it is necessary either to interpose picturesque description,
> or sublime and pathetic sentiment; or by the uncertain and suspended fate of an
> interesting personage, that the mind shall receive such a degree of artificial
> pleasure as may mitigate and subdue what, if naked of decoration and skillful
> accompaniment, would shock and appal every feeling heart.[2]

Later, Drake continues:

> No efforts of genius . . . are so truly great as those which, approaching the brink
> of horror, have yet, by the art of the poet or painter, by adjunctive and pictur-
> esque embellishment . . . been rendered powerful in creating the most delight-
> ful and fascinating sensations. (I, 271)

Finally Drake says in a passage giving the highest possible praise to Mrs.
Radcliffe:

> In the productions of Mrs. Radcliffe, the Shakespeare of romance writers, and
> who to the wild landscapes of Salvator Rosa has added the softer graces of a
> Claude, may be found many scenes truly terrific in their conception, yet so
> softened down, and the mind so much relieved by the intermixture of beautiful
> description . . . that the impression of the whole never becomes too strong,
> never degenerates into horror, but pleasurable emotion is ever the predominat-
> ing result. (I, 273)

The long descriptions of natural scenery are, then, according to Drake, essential parts of Mrs. Radcliffe's romances. These passages serve, in effect, as pictures to relieve the reader of emotions potentially too strong to produce the pleasure expected from a romance. The characters and readers are allowed to contemplate scenes from a distance much as they would view a painting and react appropriately to it.

Walter Scott, himself certainly one of the greatest writers of romance, includes Mrs. Radcliffe in his *Lives of Eminent Novelists and Dramatists;* like Drake, Scott praises highly Mrs. Radcliffe's abilities to paint these verbal scenes. In commenting on these passages in *The Mysteries of Udolpho,* Scott writes:

> . . . the interest is of a more agitating and tremendous nature [than in *The Romance of the Forest*]; the scenery of a wilder and more terrific description.[3]

Later Scott says, again comparing scenic descriptions in *The Mysteries of Udolpho* to those in *The Romance of the Forest:*

> The scale of the landscape is equally different; the quiet and limited woodland scenery of the one work forming a contrast with the splendid and high-wrought description of Italian mountain grandeur which occurs in the other. (p. 555)

In his discussion of *The Italian,* Scott finds inaccuracies in Mrs. Radcliffe's treatment of Italian history and manners, but this in no ways spoils the novel for him. Before quoting a passage in which Mrs. Radcliffe describes a scene on the seashore with distant vistas and graced with "picturesque luxuriance," Scott says:

> But if Mrs. Radcliffe did not intimately understand the language and manners of Italy, the following extract may prove how well she knew how to paint Italian scenery, which she could only have seen in the pictures of Claude and Poussin. (p. 560)

In addition to the quiet, reposed scenes of Claude and Poussin, the same novel has descriptions that remind Scott of the wilder scenes painted by another popular artist:

> There are other descriptive passages, which, like those of *The Mysteries of Udolpho,* approach more nearly the style of Salvator Rosa. (p. 561)

Then, in a summary comment, Scott maintains rightly that character is seldom a major concern with Mrs. Radcliffe and is of far less importance than setting:

The force, therefore, of the production, lies in the delineation of external incident, while the character of the agents, are entirely subordinate to the scenes in which they are placed; and are only distinguished by such outlines as make them seem appropriate to the rocks and trees which have been the artist's principal objects. (p. 563)

Both of these early critics of Mrs. Radcliffe commend her for her power to describe the beautiful scenery in her novels, and Scott suggests that when the novelist arrives at one of these descriptive passages plot and character are actually "subordinate" to the scenery in which they are placed. Plots devised by Mrs. Radcliffe allow her to exploit fully the sources of terror used by such predecessors in the Gothic tradition as Horace Walpole and Charlotte Turner Smith.[4] They all describe in considerable detail the ominous Gothic structures through which their characters, often seemingly driven by an insatiable curiosity, wander at night. The action of *The Castle of Otranto,* the first Gothic novel, takes place, as the title suggests, almost entirely in the castle itself; and Mrs. Radcliffe, in her first novel, *The Castles of Athlin and Dunbayne* (1789), has a title that suggests rightly that the action is largely confined to Gothic structures. Only seldom do the characters in this short and not especially interesting novel venture out into the fresh air and contemplate the beauties of nature surrounding the castles. Significantly, by the time Mrs. Radcliffe wrote her most famous—and best—novel, *The Mysteries of Udolpho,* the title again contains the name of a Gothic structure, but the castle here is not really the focal point of the novel. When Mrs. Radcliffe's novels are examined in the order they were written, it is obvious that with each she moves more and more of the action out into the open. There are, as stated earlier, few scenic descriptions in *The Castles of Athlin and Dunbayne.* In her second novel, *A Sicilian Romance,* published in 1790, Mrs. Radcliffe allows herself more room in which to work; and, as a result, the characters are more fully developed, and much of the action takes place outside, on the road. This enables Mrs. Radcliffe to describe in great detail the scenes that often serve to distract and console her characters. Also, her use of the word "romance" in the title prepares the reader for the quiet repose, the almost idyllic nature of the scenery through which the characters move. The third novel—again, significantly, with the word "romance" in the title—is *The Romance of the Forest,* published in 1791 and certainly her best work to date. Two other novels were published during her life, *The Mysteries of Udolpho* (1794) and *The Italian* (1797). In both, Mrs. Radcliffe is writing fiction of sufficient length to permit herself many descriptions of natural scenery. In these novels, in fact, her interest in description is so intense that only a casual attempt is generally made to describe the emotions of her characters. Rather, there seems to be an emotional distance between the scene and observer as Mrs. Radcliffe, actually, stops all action and movement of plot in order to indulge her taste for the picturesque. Samuel Monk describes the situation:

> Seldom, if ever, does she fail to relate the scene to the individual who beholds it, telling exactly what passions it stirs in a sensitive heart. But unlike her predecessors, she is also picturesque, and her objects show a conscious effort on her part to compose and group her objects and to flood them with light or darken them with shadows after the manner of Claude or Salvator. Thus, the two streams of tendency, the purely emotional response to the grand and the terrific, and the picturesque appreciation of nature, flow together in these truly remarkable books.[5]

Mrs. Radcliffe's facility at composing and grouping objects in natural scenery in much the same way as a graphic artist is seen in all of her works, even in the earliest novel and in her nonfiction. In *The Castles of Athlin and Dunbayne,* Osbert several times shows a refined taste for natural scenery:

> . . . the eye was presented with only bold outlines of uncultivated nature, rocks piled on rocks, cataracts and vast moors unmarred by the foot of the traveller. . . .[6]

Later, Mrs. Radcliffe again consciously groups the elements in her landscape in an effective manner, and here she shows an artist's interest in contrast and variety:

> The moon shone faintly by intervals, through broken clouds, upon the waters, illuminating the white foam which burst around, and enlightening the scene to render it visible. (pp. 185–86)

The frequency of much more carefully arranged and described picturesque scenes increases in *A Sicilian Romance* and *The Romance of the Forest,* but in *The Mysteries of Udolpho* and *The Italian* such passages create a gallery of verbal pictures. In both, well over half the action takes place in open country. Walter Scott maintains that Mrs. Radcliffe's characters are subordinate to setting, and Samuel Monk contends that she never fails to relate scenery to the emotions of the characters. Her characters do, certainly, react to the scenes and are often comforted by them. However, the reader feels that there is always a distance between character and scene that allows attention to be focused, in effect almost entirely, on the scene itself. There is no, or at best only the most superficial, effort to effect a strong relation of character to scene;

one never feels that setting is an extension of the character's emotions and feelings as in, say, Byron or the Shelleys. The immense, sublime scenery in which Prometheus is confined is not only an extension of his own superhuman being but also an appropriate backdrop for Shelley's monumental drama. Quite simply stated, no other setting would be appropriate. Setting and character are inseparable. Several times in *Frankenstein,* Mary Shelley has her own modern Prometheus placed among sublime nature, and, for the moment at least, Frankenstein is consoled emotionally by contemplating nature. In *Manfred,* the mountains and thundering avalanches are extensions of the hero's emotions, and the various scenes through which Harold passes are reflections of or foils to his own personality. These characters are involved in the settings. They do not simply contemplate and describe what is before them. One is never unaware of the imposing presence of the romantic hero in an appropriate setting, and a concern with scene never slows down the movement of action or insight into the characters. Distance and involvement are major concerns, and an awareness of this concern gets to the heart of a basic difference between Mrs. Radcliffe's use of the literally picturesque in nature and the way nature is generally used by the romantics. In describing a scene in *The Italian,* Mrs. Radcliffe says that it is viewed as through a "telescope reversed." [7] Indeed, all of her scenery is viewed in this way. Scenes are self-contained, confined; one is always aware of distance, both spatial and emotional. The romantic writers view nature through the small end of the telescope so as to bring themselves closer, literally into, their settings. In Mrs. Radcliffe's novels scenery is described in such great detail and with so very few personal, individualized reactions involving the characters that the action is halted and the scenes contemplated much as one would a painting. Later, with the romantics, sound was always a major part of the sweeping settings, but in passages from Mrs. Radcliffe only infrequently does sound detract from the quiet contemplation of her scenes, her verbal paintings. Almost without exception, one is aware of quiet and distance and of the novelist's concern for the picturesque. In *The Mysteries of Udolpho,* as the party moves toward Udolpho, Mrs. Radcliffe notes that they are actually weary from a steady succession of commanding scenes:

> . . . the travelers did not look back without some regret to the sublime objects they had quitted, though the eye, fatigued with the extension of its powers, was glad to repose on the verdure of woods and pastures. . . .[8]

Later there is a description complete with color, contrast, and deliberate arrangement, a composition to which Mrs. Radcliffe, for all practical purposes, gives a title:

The gay tints of cultivation once more beautified the landscape; for the lowlands were coloured with the richest hues which a luxuriant climate and an industrious people can waken into life. Groves of orange and lemon perfumed the air, their ripe fruit glowing among the foliage; while sloping to the plains extensive vineyards spread their treasures. Beyond these, woods and pastures, and mingled towns and hamlets stretched many a distant sail; while over the whole scene was diffused the purple glow of evening. The landscape, with the surrounding Alps, did indeed present a perfect picture of the lovely and the sublime—of "beauty sleeping in the lap of horror."(I, 160)

As they journey through the Alps:

. . . they quitted their carriages and began to ascend the Alps. And here such scenes of sublimity opened upon them, as no colours of language dare pencil. (I, 167)

When the group nears Turin, Mrs. Radcliffe indulges her taste for the picturesque and shows her ability to paint verbally:

As they advanced. . . the Alps seen at some distance, began to appear in all their awful sublimity; chain rising over chain in long succession, their higher peaks darkened by the hovering clouds sometimes hid, and at others seen shooting up far above them, while their lower steeps, broken into fantastic forms, were touched with blue and purple tints, which, as they changed in light and shade, seemed to open new scenes to the eye. (I, 171)

Then Emily is described not in the setting, but as contemplating it from without, from a distance. In this quotation sound is absent; the torrents are not described as making any noise. They are, rather, treated visually. They appear; they do not sound:

The solitary grandeur of the objects that immediately surrounded her—the mountain region hovering above; the deep precipices that fell beneath; the wavering blackness of the forests of pine and oak, which skirted their feet, or hung within their recess; the headlong torrents that, dashing among their cliffs, sometimes appeared like a cloud of mist, at others like a sheet of ice—these were features, which received a higher character of sublimity from the reposing beauty of the Italian landscape below, stretching to the wide horizon where the same melting blue tint seemed to unite earth and sky. (I, 169–70)

From an area described as "a sweet picture of repose," the group moves nearer to Udolpho:

This pass, which led into the heart of the Apennine, at length opened to day, and a scene of mountains stretched in long perspective, as wild as any the travellers had yet passed. Still, vast pine-forests hung upon their base, and crowned the ridgy precipice that rose perpendicularly from the vale, while, above, the rolling mists caught the sunbeams, and touched their cliffs with all the magical colouring of light and shade. The scene seemed perpetually changing, and its features to assume new forms . . . while the shifting vapours, now partially concealing their minuter beauties, and now illuminating them with splendid tints, assisted the illusions of the sight. (I, 229)

Finally, the castle itself comes into view, and Mrs. Radcliffe paints the scene complete with contrasts and a deep, remote background:

. . . though it was now lighted by the setting sun, the Gothic greatness of its features, and its mouldering walls of dark grey stone rendered it a gloomy and sublime object. As she gazed, the light died away on its walls, leaving a melancholy purple tint, which spread deeper and deeper, as the thin vapour crept up the mountain, while the battlements above were still tipped with splendor. From those, too, the rays soon faded, and the whole edifice was invested with the solemn darkness of evening. Silent, lonely, and sublime, it seemed to stand the sovereign of the scene. . . . As the twilight deepened, its features became more awful in obscurity. . . . (I, 230)

In *The Italian,* Mrs. Radcliffe's final novel designed for publication, she again describes scenery in the same way it would be viewed by a painter, scenery she could only have known from paintings. Like a painter, she often stresses a dark foreground and contrast:

To the south, the small opening led the eye to a glimpse of the landscape below, which seen beyond the dark jaws of the cliff, appeared free, and light, and gaily coloured, melting into blue and distant mountains. (I, 84)

One of the supporting cliffs, with part of the bridge, was in deep shade, but the other, feathered with foliage, and the rising surges at its foot, were strongly illumined, and many a thicket wet with spray, sparkled in contrast to the dark rock it overhung. Beyond the arch, the long drawn prospect faded into misty light. (I, 85)

In *The Italian,* Mrs. Radcliffe is especially fond of descriptions, reminiscent of Claude, of sunset scenes with dimly sketched mountains, castles and ruins crowning cliffs, and seascapes:

There appeared on a point of rock, impending over the valley, the reliques of a palace, whose beauty time had impaired only to heighten its sublimity. An arch of singular magnificence, remained almost entire, beyond which appeared wild cliffs, retiring in grand perspective. The sun, which was now setting, threw a trembling lustre upon the ruins and gave a finishing effect to the scene. (I, 93)

Mrs. Radcliffe guides her characters

> . . . to extensive prospects over plains and toward distant mountains, the sunshine landscape, which had so long appeared to bound this shadowy pass. The transition was as the passage through the vale of death to the bliss of eternity. (I, 134)

While imprisoned in the Convent of San Stefano, Ellena is comforted, like many heroines before her, by the views from her window:

> Ellena . . . found temporary, though feeble, relief in once more looking upon the face of nature; till, her spirits became gradually revived and elevated by the grandeur of the images of nature around her. She said to herself, "If I am condemned to misery, surely I could endure it with more fortitude in scenes like these, than amidst the tamer landscapes of nature. Here, the objects seem to impart somewhat of their own force, their own sublimity to the soul. It is scarcely possible to yield to the pressure of misfortunes while we walk as with the Deity, amidst his most stupendous works." (I, 182)

In another rather lengthy passage in which Mrs. Radcliffe describes the same area, both brush and pen are judged incapable of reproducing the total effect. Here Mrs. Radcliffe uses the image of the "telescope reversed":

> It was when the heat and the light were declining that the carriage entered a rocky defile, which showed, as through a telescope reversed, the distant plains, the mountains opening beyond, lighted up with all the purple splendor of the setting sun. Along this deep and shadowy perspective, a river, which was seen descending among the cliffs of a mountain, rolled with impetuous force, fretting and foaming amidst the dark rocks in its descent, and then flowing into a limpid lapse to the brink of other perspectives, whence again it fell with thundering strength to the abyss, throwing its misty clouds of spray high into the air, and seeming to claim the sole empire of the solitary wild . . . while the gloom and vastness of the precipices, which towered above, sunk below it, together with the amazing forces and uproar of the falling waters combined to render the pass more terrific than the pencil could describe or language may express. Ellena ascended . . . and she experienced somewhat of a dreadful pleasure in looking down upon the irresistible flood; but this emotion was heightened into awe when she perceived that the road led to a slight bridge, that, thrown across the chasm at an immense height, united two opposite cliffs between which the whole cataract of the river descended. (I, 184–85)

In much the same fashion, Mrs. Radcliffe describes the sea as viewed by the melancholy Ellena:

The moon, rising over the ocean, showed its restless surface, spreading to the whole horizon, and the waves, which broke in foam upon the rocky beach below, retiring in long white lines far up the waters. She listened to the measured and sad sound, and, somewhat soothed by the solitary grandeur of the view, remained at the lattice till the moon had risen high into the heavens; and even till morning began to dawn upon the sea and purple the eastern clouds. (I, 239)

And in one final passage from *The Italian,* Mrs. Radcliffe compares, as she often does, two types of scenes, two different visual effects:

The lawn, which was on each side bourdered by hanging woods descended in gentle declivity to a fine lake. . . . Beyond appeared the distant country, rising on the left with bold romantic mountains, and on the right, exhibiting a soft and glowing landscape, whose tranquil beauty formed a striking contrast to the wild sublimity of the opposite craggy heights. The blue and distant ocean terminated the view. (II, 245)

These passages quoted from several of Mrs. Radcliffe's novels, certainly representative passages chosen from many possibilities, illustrate the distinctive way in which the novelist views scenes from nature. There is almost always a feeling of distance between the character and the scene. Although the novelist does usually indicate a reaction in the character to the scene, this reaction is of only minor importance and often rather casually and predictably voiced. The scenes themselves, their colors, their balanced and ordered arrangement, their variety are Mrs. Radcliffe's major concern. Character and plot are, as Scott says, of secondary importance. Mrs. Radcliffe, her characters, and, certainly, her readers are to view the scenes, as she herself says, as through a "telescope reversed" in order to see a complete, framed composition. In two nonfiction works, *Journey Made in the Summer of 1794* and her *Memoir* published posthumously with *Gaston de Blondeville,* where Mrs. Radcliffe is in no way encumbered by plot, her treatment of scenery is precisely the same as in the novels. Again, the telescope is reversed.

Mrs. Radcliffe sets out with her husband and a party of close friends in the summer of 1794 with high hopes of actually viewing some of the sublime, picturesque scenery that she had known only through paintings but that she had already described accurately in four novels. As the group journies through Holland, the scenery is too flat and monotonous to offer much diversion. She is reminded of the quiet, static "Flemish landscape of the sixteenth and seventeenth centuries." [9] The party moves on to Germany where the scenery is generally agreeable. But at the German border, difficulties with passports are encountered, and, sadly, Mrs. Radcliffe is unable to continue on into Switzerland and Italy. The group then has a pleasant trip down the Rhine and finally fills out time by touring parts of England. The method of describing scenes in the *Journey* is the same used in the novels. They show a sense of composition, a sensitivity to striking colors, an infrequent use of sound—in sum, they are picturesque. The passages cited here, again selected from many possibilities, are, unlike those in the novels, in no way associated to plot, and therefore, only brief introductions are necessary.

In Bonn, Mrs. Radcliffe is impressed by the scenery around the Elector's Palace:

> The eye passes over the green lawn of the garden, and a tract of level country to the . . . Seven Mountains, broken, rocky and abrupt toward their summits, yet sweeping finely near their bases, and uniting with the plains by long and gradual descents that spread round many miles. The nearest is about a league and a half off. We saw them under the cloudless sky of June, invested with the mistiness of heat, which, softening their rocky points, and half veiling their recesses, left much for the imagination to supply, and gave them an aerial appearance, a faint tint of silver grey, that was inexpressibly interesting. The Rhine, that winds at their feet, was concealed from us by the garden groves, but from the upper windows of the palace it is seen in all its majesty. (p. 119)

Several times on the ride from Bonn to Godesberg, Mrs. Radcliffe comments at length on the views:

> Many a lurking village, with its slender grey steeple, peeped from among the woody skirts of these hills. On our left, the tremendous mountains, that bind the eastern shore of the Rhine, gradually lost their aerial complexion, as we approached them, and displayed new features and new enchantments; an ever-varying illusion, to which the transient circumstances of thunder clouds contributed. The sun beams, streaming through these clouds, threw partial glances upon the precipices, and, followed by dark shadows, gave surprising and inimitable effect to the natural colouring of the mountain, whose pointed tops we now discerned to be covered with dark heath, extended down their rocky sides, and mingled with the reddish and light yellow tints of other vegetation and the soil. It was delightful to watch the shadows sweeping over these steeps, now involving them in deep obscurity, and then leaving them to the sun's rays, which brought out all their hues in vivid contrast. (pp. 134–35)

> The three tallest points are now nearest to the eye, and the lower mountains are seen either in the perspective between them, or sinking, with less abrupt declivity, into the plains, on the north. The whole mass exhibites a grandeur of outline, such as the pencil only can describe; but fancy may paint the stupendous precipices of rock, that rise over the Rhine, the rich tuftings of wood, that mark the cliffs or lurk within the recesses, the spiry summits, and the ruined castles, faintly discerned, that crown them. (pp. 136–37)

One scene in the same area reminds Mrs. Radcliffe of the type of painting done by Claude:

> From the area of these ruins, we saw the sun set over the whole line of plains, that extend to the westward of Cologne, whose spires were distinctly visible. Beyond the hills of Sanctae Crucis, appeared at a league's distance, and the winding of the Rhine, gleamed here and there amidst the rich scene, like distant lakes. It was a still and beautiful evening, in which no shade remained of the thunder clouds, that passed in the day. To the west, under the glow of sun-set, the landscape melted into the horizon in tints so soft, so clear, so deliciously roseate as Claude only could have painted. Viewed as we then saw it, beyond a deep and dark arch of the ruin, its effect was enchanting; it was to the eye, what the finest strains of Paisiello are to the heart, or the poetry of Collins to the fancy—all tender, sweet, elegant and glowing. (pp. 138–39)

On the way to Andernach,

> The opposite shore exhibited only a range of rocks, variegated like marble, of which purple was the predominating tint, and uniformly disposed in vast, oblique strata. But even here little green patches of vines peeped among the cliffs, and were led up crevices where it seemed as if no human feet could rest. Along the base of this tremendous wall, and on the points above, villages, with each its tall, grey steeple, were thickly strewn, thus mingling in striking contrast the cheerfulness of populous inhabitation with the horrors of untamed nature. (p. 155)

A group of buildings in the Monastery presented

> . . . an object rendered sweetly picturesque, as the sun's rays lightened up its towers and fortified terraces, while the shrubbery below were in shade. (p. 155)

In the same area, Mrs. Radcliffe again notes interesting coloring:

> The light vapour that rose from the water, and was tinged by the setting rays, spread a purple haze over the town and the cliffs, which, at this distance appeared to impend over it; colouring extremely beautiful, contrasted as it was by the clearer and deeper tints of rock, wood and water nearer the eye. (p. 157)

From a bridge over the river Murg, Mrs. Radcliffe views the distant mountains in the region of Rastadt:

> They are here of a more dreadful height, and abrupt steepness than in the neighbourhood of Manheim, and, on their pointed brows, are frequently the ruins of castles, places sometimes where it seems as if no human foot could climb. The nearer we approached these mountains, the more we had occasion to admire the various tints of their granites. Sometimes the precipices were of a faint pink,

then of a deep red, a dull purple, or a blush approaching to lilac, and sometimes gleams of a pale yellow mingled with the low shrubs, that grew upon their sides. The day was cloudless and bright, and we were too near these heights to be deceived by the illusion of aerial colouring; the real hues of their features were as beautiful, as their magnitude was sublime. (p. 266)

Close to the border of Switzerland, Mrs. Radcliffe notices a young girl, striking in her native costume: "In these landscapes, the peasant girl, in the simple dress of the country, and balancing on her large straw hat an harvest keg, was a very picturesque figure" (pp. 272–73).

At this point in the *Journey,* the difficulties with passports prevent continuing on into Switzerland and Italy, and the party returns to England. The sight of Dover, "the whole appearing with considerable dignity and picturesque effect" (p. 369), impresses Mrs. Radcliffe greatly:

The height and grandeur of this cliff was particularly striking, when a ship was seen sailing at its base, diminished by comparison to an inch. From hence the cliffs towards Folkstone, though broken and majestic, gradually decline. There are, perhaps, few prospects of shore more animated and magnificent than this. The vast expanse of water, the character of the cliffs, that guard the coast, the ships of war and curious merchantmen moored in the Downs, the lighter vessels skimming along the channel, and the now distant shore of France, with Calais glimmering faintly, and hinting of different modes of life and a new world, all these circumstances formed a scene of pre-eminent combination and led to interesting reflection. (p. 369)

On a trip from Lancaster to Kendal, mountains

. . . rising from elegantly swelling ground, overlooked this enchanting vale, on the right, clouds rolling along its broken top, like smoke from a cauldron, and its hoary tint forming a boundary to the soft verdure and rich woodlands of the slopes, at its feet. The perspective was terminated by the tall peeping heads of Westmoreland Fells, the nearer ones tinted with faintest purple, the more distant with light azure; and this is the general boundary to the scene. . . . (p. 382)

In the region of Bampton,

Two mountains called Whiteside and Potters-fell, screen the perspective; Stone-crag is at the southern end, fronting Keintmoor-head. The vale seen beyond the broken ground we were upon, formed a landscape of, perhaps, unexampled variety and grace of colouring; the tender green of the lowland, the darker verdure of the woods ascending to mountains, the brown rough heath above them, and impending crags over all, exhibit their numerous shades within a space not more than two miles long, or half a mile in breadth. (p. 392)

This gay perspective, lighted up by a gleam of sunshine, and viewed between the brown lines of the nearer mountains, shewed like a miniature painting of a landscape, illumined beyond a darkened fore-ground. (p. 384)

Again the word "miniature" is used when an opening in the foliage "let in a gay miniature landscape, bright in sunshine" (p. 401). When the party arrives at Ullswater,

The mountains are all bold, gloomy, and severe. When we saw them, the sky accorded well with the scene, being frequently darkened by autumnal clouds; and the equinoctial gale swept the surface of the lake, marking its blackness with long white lines, and beating its waves over the rocks to the foliage of the thickets above. The trees that shade these eminences, give greater force to the scenes, which they either partially exclude, or wholly admit, and become themselves fine objects, enriched as they are with the darkest moss. (p. 418)

At Derwentwater, Mrs. Radcliffe admires the lake for

The soft undulations of its shore, the mingled wood and pasture, that paint them, the brilliant purity of the water, that gives back every landscape on its bank, and frequently with heightened colouring, the fantastic wildness of the rocks. . . . (p. 452)

The area around Barrowdale is especially attractive to Mrs. Radcliffe, and in several lengthy descriptive passages she creates detailed verbal paintings:

Not a path-way, not a crag . . . that sculptured their bold fronts, but was copied and distinctly seen even from the opposite shore in the dark purple mirror below. Now and then, a pleasure-boat glided by, leaving long silver lines, drawn to a point on the smooth water, which, as it gave back the painted sides and gleaming sail, displayed a moving picture. (p. 463)

As the sun-beams fell on different kinds of rocks, and distance coloured the air, some parts were touched with lilac, others with light blue, dark purple, or reddish brown, which were often seen, at the same moment, contrasting with the mellow green of the woods, and the brightness of sunshine; then slowly and almost imperceptibly changing into other tints. Skiddaw itself exhibited much of this variety during our ride. As we left Keswick, its points were overspread with purple azure; on our return, a tint of dark blue softened its features, which were, however, soon after involved in deepest purple. (p. 464)

These clouds disappeared before the strength of the sun, a fine downy hue of light blue overspread the peeping points of the most distant fells, while the nearer ones were tinged with deep purple, which was opposed to the brown heath and crag of the lower hills, the olive green of two wooded slopes that, just tinted by autumn, seemed to descend to the margin, and the silver transparency of the expanding water at their feet. (p. 474)

In two more representative passages as the *Journey* comes to a close, Mrs. Radcliffe actually uses the word "picture" to describe the scenery she has just viewed:

Nearly in the centre of these fells, which open in a semi-circle to receive the lake, a cataract descends, but, its shining line is not of a breadth to the vastness of its perpendicular fall. The village is sweetly seated under shelter of the rocks; and, at a distance beyond, on the edge of the water, the ancient hall, or priory, shows its turret and ivyed ruins among old woods. The whole picture is reflected in the liquid mirror below. (pp. 480–81)

The most impressive pictures were formed by the fells that crowd over the upper end of the lake, and which, viewed from a low station, sometimes appear nearly to enclose that part of it. The effect was then astonishingly grand, particularly about sun-set, when the clouds, drawing upwards, discovered the utmost summits of these fells, and a tint of dusky blue began to prevail over them, which gradually deepened into night. A line of lower rock, that extended from these are . . . of a dull purple, and their shaggy forms would appear gigantic in almost any other situation. (p. 482)

For several years after she gave up writing novels, Mrs. Radcliffe and her husband traveled often, but never, ironically, through the Alps and into Italy. Notations from the journal quoted in her *Memoir,* which was published with the first edition of *Gaston de Blondeville,* show Mrs. Radcliffe's continued fascination with natural scenery, with the picturesque. On 3 September 1797, the novelist and her husband are again at Dover:

The most grand and striking circumstances, as we stood on the point, were the vast sea view, the long shades on its surface of soft green, deepening exquisitely into purple; but above all, that downy tint of light blue, that sometimes prevailed over the whole scene, and even faintly tinged the French coast, at a distance. Sometimes too a white sail passes in a distant gloom, while all between was softly shadowed; the cliffs above us broken and encumbered with fortifications; the sea viewed beyond them with vessels passing from behind. . . .[10]

The next day:

Within land, the hills are brown, and bleak, and broken. The castle hills . . . scarred by roads and far from picturesque. (I, 22)

On 21 September 1798, on a "sweet, fresh morning," the Radcliffes

. . . left Cobham between seven and eight. Passed under a picturesque bridge uniting the grounds of Paine's hill; high, rough, broken banks, topped with lofty trees, that hang over a light rustic bridge. Then enter upon a wide scene of heath, skirted here and there with rich distances; afterwards; many miles of heath of a dull purple and dusty iron brown, with, sometimes, sudden knolls planted with firs; sometimes distances let in between bold hills. (I, 23–24)

Two days later:

> It is impossible to express the beauty of those soft melting tints, that painted the distant perspectives, towards Spithead, where sea and sky united, and where the dark masts and shapes of shipping, drawing themselves on the horizon, gave this softness its utmost effect. (I, 28)

> Here the governor had built a picturesque tower over his woods. Hence extended along the shore the fine woods of the rector of a village on an ascent, there the tower of the church, almost hid in wood, insists upon being painted. Here imagination has nothing to do; we have only to preserve the impression of the living picture on the memory in its own soft colours. (I, 30)

On 10 July 1800, at Capel on a tour of the southern coast:

> Upon the eminences views over the tops of oaks to mountainous hills and promontories, covered nearly to their summits with thick, woody, inclosures; when-ever the bank-trees opened, caught blue, peeping hill-tops, or mountainous lines coloured with a lovely bluish haze, and seen enchantingly beyond the dark, tufted foliage of majestic oak. (I, 33)

At Worthing:

> The whole southern sky, and the blue sea, extending from the Isle of Wight (its faint blue lands rising towards the west) to the white face of what we took to be Beachy Head. . . . Beneath, sloping towards the sea, a landscape of exquisite hues, of corn and thick hedge-rows of woods and intermingled villages. Farther on, the hills begin to whiten and rise into the high face guarding the entrance of Newhaven river which seems to fall into a fine bay. (I, 37–38)

At East Bourne:

> The sweet repose of the landscape and sea-bay to Hastings, and the grandeur of the various views, on all sides between the valleys of South-Downs and even above the summits, circling nearly the whole horizon with soft blue waves. Three miles of continual ascent or descent of almost treacherous hills, long and steep opening to vast distances, now obscured in ruin, but sublime in their obscurity. (I, 43)

> Have never seen such woody mountains before in England; they resemble the

forests of Wetteravia more than any I have seen, but with this difference, that these mountains are more pointing, abrupt and rocky, and that here the road often winds round the edge of the hills into deep and most picturesque glades, where comfortable cottages lie snug beneath noble trees. (I, 44)

Mrs. Radcliffe, once more on the Isle of Wight, again describes the hills:

One of the perspectives in front particularly fine, as we saw our road descending among the deep woods, and other woods rising up the hills and crowning the bold summit of an eminence, that seemed to rear itself over all the forest. The deep gloom of stormy clouds and fleeting lights of sunshine extremely various; the sun often shedding a misty glory over the solemn woods in the west, while sudden and awful shadows dwelt wide over other summits. Passed a most picturesque hamlet of green mossed cottages scattered round a little lawn, where the woods opened, but closed again in thicker shades. (I, 45)

On the packet for Yarmouth, Mrs. Radcliffe describes a scene in which she, in effect, gives the ingredients she considers essential for picturesque description:

Glided smoothly under a summer air: the evening splendid, and the scene most lovely. The Needles are vast dark blocks of rock, tall, but not pointed, standing out from the island in the sea. Hurst Castle, with its dark line of peninsula stretching athwart the channel. The Needles become more huge seen against the light, with the point of the Alum Rock in shade. These objects, with the high line of the Isle of Purbeck, faintly grey beyond, composed a perfect picture with most harmonious colouring. The light silver grey of the sea first met the eye, then the dark Alum Rock projected to meet Hurst Castle, whose towers were pencilled in deep grey beyond, which softened away to the heights of Purbeck, that closed the perspective. After sun-set, streaks of bright crimson appeared on the sky, behind clouds, black and swelling; the upper shore clear, though dark. (I, 48)

At Ryde:

The undercliff is wild and romantic, rather than grand; but the sea horizon from it, is often very grand. Upon the whole, I prefer rich beauty to wild beauty, unless accompanied by such shapes of grandeur as verge upon the sublime. Lovely sun-set; a roseate, melting into saffron and shades of blue; some light purple streaks. Below, the dark woody line of shore bending towards Cowes; the bay at its feet, purpled from the clouds. All this seen from our bed-room windows and between lofty trees. (I, 53–54)

On the grounds at Blenheim, Mrs. Radcliffe was

. . . delighted with the steep green slope, the water and bridge below, the abrupt woody bank opposite it, and, above all, the grandeur of the shades. Pass the bridge: on the right, the massy rocks of the cascade, but no water; on the left, the water winds beyond the woody banks; a highly tufted island, with a wooden landing near its margin, very picturesque. (I, 62)

In June 1805, Mrs. Radcliffe visits Belvedere House, the seat of Lord Heath, and is especially delighted by the art gallery. In the gallery are works by the very greatest artists, including Rembrandt, but it is a painting by Claude that obviously interests Mrs. Radcliffe more than any other:

In a shaded corner, near the chimney, a most exquisite Claude, an evening view, perhaps over the Campagna of Rome. The sight of the picture imparted much of the luxurious repose and a satisfaction, which we derive from contemplating the finest scenes of nature. Here was the poet, as well as the painter, touching the imagination, and making you see more than the picture contained. You saw the real light of the sun, you breathed the air of the country, you felt all the circumstances of a luxurious climate on the most serene and beautiful landscape; and the mind being thus softened, you almost fancied you heard Italian music on the air—the music of Paisiello; and such doubtless were the scenes that supplied him. (I, 65)

As Mrs. Radcliffe views this work of a favorite painter, there seems to be a kind of reversal of the usual situation. In earlier works, she had viewed natural scenes as if they were paintings; here, the pleasure she derives from viewing a painting by Claude is the same as that derived from "contemplating the finest scenes of nature." Often, these scenes in nature are intriguing when they are mysterious and leave something for a busy imagination to supply. Here, Claude makes her see, or imagine, more than the "picture contained." On 21 October 1812, the Radcliffes are at Malvern Hills:

The hoary crags, in vast masses, looked out from among the brown and red tints of the autumnal fern, and from the green earth, but the crags ceased below the summits, which were smooth and still green. Our view here commanded the vast expanse to the eastward, which we had seen from the inn; but we now saw over the broad Breedon Hill, which there bounded the horizon in one direction; and many lines were now visible beyond it. This view is great and comprehensive, but not sublime; the elevation reducing the importance of other heights, so that no single object remains sufficiently striking, either in form or character, to arrest attention, and break the uniform harmony of these rich and woody scenes. . . . (I, 86–87)

Hopefully, conclusions can be drawn from the examination of Ann Radcliffe's use of natural scenery other than the fact that she was acutely aware of the picturesque and as a rule arranged and constructed her scenes in much the same way and with the same concern for effect that characterize a painter. In her novels, certainly, the taste shown for the picturesque is far too refined to admire such things as poor Catherine Moreland's "horses, trees, hens, and chickens." But her novels are not simply a gallery of striking, arresting pictures based on the works of artists she knew and admired—Claude and Salvator Rosa—cleverly conceived and described; her verbal scenery serves to keep the characters and the reader from getting too close to the action and experiencing sensations and emotions too strong and potentially detrimental to the effect she wants. Hers is a special kind of Gothicism, essentially different from that of many other Gothic novelists. In her use of nature, she looks back rather than forward to the overwhelming, sensational, literally astonishing views of nature in the romantics. In Mrs. Radcliffe, the distance between character and scenery creates a general feeling of repose, of a kind of idyllic decorum. Twice she includes the word "romance" in titles. Actually, all of her novels are in the tradition of the romance and are as much concerned with such intangibles as atmosphere and mood as with plot and character. Her brand of Gothicism is not totally a direct descendant of *The Castle of Otranto*. True, she has villains in the tradition of Walpole's Manfred, distressed, sentimental female characters in the tradition of Matilda and Isabella, wronged women in the tradition of Hippolita, and often questions of fortunes and identity. But the really new and shocking improbabilities that produce the unique and almost surrealistic atmosphere in Walpole's novel are lacking in the works of Mrs. Radcliffe. There are no portraits stepping from their frames, no statues dripping blood, no skeletons dressed in the garb of a monk, no giant manifestations of any kind. What appears at first in Mrs. Radcliffe's fiction to be improbable is ultimately explained so that logic and reason prevail.[11] The depraved, demonic characters in Lewis's *The Monk* simply do not belong in the atmosphere of Mrs. Radcliffe's fiction; nor, certainly, would the strongly and mysteriously drawn characters in Charlotte Dacre's *Zafloya*. The transgressions of natural law by Mary Shelley's possessed Frankenstein would be out of place in Mrs. Radcliffe's novels. And the frantic world of Maturin's *Melmoth the Wanderer* is, indeed, an absolutely different world. As in the romance, the novels of Ann Radcliffe do not move beyond the bounds of taste and discretion, beyond what Clara Reeve calls in the introduction to her own attempt at Gothic fiction "judicious conduct" and the "verge of probability."[12] Miss Reeve's novel is a deliberate reworking of the kind of plot used by Walpole, but it is scrupulously free of what she considered Walpole's excesses and lapses in taste. Miss Reeve says: "The machinery is so violent, that it destroys the effect it is intended to excite (p. ix).

The destructive potential of violence and overwhelming emotion was, as we have seen, commented upon by Nathan Drake, who commends Mrs. Radcliffe for avoiding extreme violent effects by the use of "picturesque description" and "picturesque embellishment." These descriptions, these verbal pictures, in her novels serve to soften, as Drake says, terror, which "requires no small degree of skill and arrangement to prevent its operating more pain than pleasure" (I, 269). Edmund Burke in his *Enquiry* finds that fright and terror, when properly modified, can produce a pleasant emotion, but it must be modified:

> . . . if . . . pain and terror are so modified as not to be actually noxious; if the pain is not carried to violence, and the terror is not conversant about present destruction of the person . . . they are capable of producing delight, not pleasure, but a sort of tranquility tinged with terror . . . which is one of the strongest passions. (IV, vii)

An important distinction is made between horror and terror. Horror is associated with overwhelming emotion concerning destruction and great violence, the dominant emotions and sensations in the Gothic novels of such writers as Walpole, Lewis, Maturin, and Mary Shelley. Terror, technically, is a milder emotion, the dominant emotion in Mrs. Radcliffe's fiction. She clearly makes a distinction between these two related but vastly different emotions. In a dialogue intended for publication in *Gaston de Blondeville* but later published by Henry Colburn in the *New Monthly Magazine* under the title " 'On the Supernatural in Poetry.' By the late Mrs. Radcliffe," the novelist compares, through two speakers, scenes involving the supernatural in *Hamlet* and *Macbeth*. Of the scene in *Macbeth* with Banquo's ghost, she observes:

> There, though deep pity mingles with our surprise and horror, we experience a far less degree of interest, and that interest too of an inferior kind. The union of grandeur and obscurity, which Mr. Burke describes as a sort of tranquility tinged with terror, and which causes the sublime, is to be found only in *Hamlet;* or in scenes where circumstances of the same kind prevail.[13]

The dialogue continues:

> Terror and horror are so far opposite that the first expands the soul, and awakens the faculties to a high degree of life; the other, contracts, freezes, and nearly annihilates them. I apprehend that neither Shakespeare nor Milton by their fictions, nor Mr. Burke by his reasoning, anywhere looked to positive horror as a source of the sublime, though they all agree that terror is a very high one. . . . (pp. 149–50)

It is not necessary to examine in detail all of Ann Radcliffe's fiction and nonfiction to establish the fact that she approached natural scenery and described this scenery much as a painter would. Throughout her career she was vitally interested in the picturesque, an interest so strong that in works other than her novels it continues. These verbal paintings are in her novels functional in that they serve to maintain a necessary distance between character and scenery. Mrs. Radcliffe's characteristic use of natural scenery allows the reader, and to an extent, even her characters, to come not into a Gothic world of tasteless horror and violence, but into her own distinctive world of enchantment, of mild terror, and of, certainly, romance.

NOTES

[1]*Northanger Abbey* (New York: The Athenaeum Society, 1892), p. 7.

[2]*Literary Hours* (London: Longman, 1820), I, 270.

[3]*Lives of Eminent Novelists and Dramatists* (London: Warne, 1887), p. 555.

[4]Scott comments that Mrs. Smith's ability at describing natural scenery actually surpasses that of Ann Radcliffe: "The landscapes of Mrs. Radcliffe are far from equal in accuracy and truth to those of her contemporary . . . whose sketches are so very graphical, that an artist would find little difficulty painting from them."

[5]*The Sublime* (Ann Arbor: University of Michigan, 1960), p. 217.

[6]*The Castles of Athlin and Dunbayne* (London: Longman, 1811), pp. 8–9.

[7]*The Italian* (London: Cadell and Davies, 1797), I, 184.

[8]*The Mysteries of Udolpho* (London: J. M. Dent, 1949), I, 44.

[9]*Journey Made in the Summer of 1794* (London: G. G. and J. Robinson, 1795), p. 45.

[10]*Memoir*, in *Gaston de Blondeville* (London: Henry Colburn, 1826), I, 19–20.

[11]Only in *Gaston de Blondeville,* which Mrs. Radcliffe did not intend for publication, are there unexplained happenings.

[12]*The Old English Baron* (London: F. C. and J. Rivington, 1807), p. v.

SUE L. KIMBALL ✍ GAMES PEOPLE
PLAY IN CONGREVE'S
*THE WAY OF
THE WORLD*

WILLIAM CONGREVE'S PLAYS appeared at a time when gaming and gambling were truly a way of life in England. The years following the Restoration represented a period when the passion for gambling reached its greatest height, partially in reaction to the relaxation of the severe regulations imposed on gaming by the Commonwealth, and also as a result of the years spent by Charles's courtiers in France, where they had learned about "more games of hazard and skill than they had before suspected to be in existence; . . . on their return, they made no scruple of introducing them all to England."[1] All ladies and gentlemen gambled freely, tradition holding that Nell Gwyn lost £5000 at bassett in a single night (p. xiv). Catherine is credited with having introduced the game of ombre to England, and Queen Mary II was so keen a card player that she shocked her husband's Dutch subjects by playing on Sundays (p. xvi). Louis Kronenberger describes the gaming at White's, the best known of the chocolate houses, as the greatest " 'vice' of eighteenth century high life—greater even than the prodigious drinking." The play, says Kronenberger, was "frequent and steep," with women outdoing men in enthusiasm and endurance.[2]

Every gaming book of the period features discussions of methods of cheating, but the social stigma now attached to dishonest play was evidently lacking then. "In fact," says Hartmann, "so long as its exponents were not actually caught red-handed, it was regarded almost in the light of an embellishment to skillful play" (p. xiii). Charles Cotton, in *The Compleat Gamester,* published in 1674, and Theophilus Lucas, in *Memoirs of the Lives, Intrigues, and Comical Adventures of the Most Famous Gamesters and Celebrated Sharpers in the Reigns of Charles II, James II, William III, and Queen Anne,*[3] published in 1714, describe some of the methods: (1) "overlooking the adversaries' game," a ploy that Cotton promises "hath a great advantage, for by that means he may partly know what to play securely" (p. 56); (2) looking into one's partner's hand; (3) literally trimming the edges of certain cards in a deck to enable the "sharper" to be cut a "court" card by his unwary opponent; (4) placing marked decks of cards in drawers so they will appear to be new when brought out. I mention these methods and emphasize their apparent acceptability because the gamesters of *The Way of the World* employ analogous tactics with impunity. Mirabell seems at all times to be looking into the hands of his opponents; he looks into Millamant's hand when he chooses to do so, and he certainly plays with marked and concealed decks. The implication is that such maneuvering is not only acceptable but also necessary in a game with sharpers as unscrupulous as Fainall and Marwood.

Congreve's first comedy, *The Old Batchelor,* contains some imagery of croquet and of the hunt; a reference to plain-dealing, which was a seventeenth-century card game as well as a synonym for frankness; and a line by Belinda to Araminta, "But you play the Game, and consequently can't see the Miscarriages obvious to every stander by." [4] And in the "Epistle Dedicatory" to his second comedy, *The Double Dealer,* the playwright, describing its hero Mellefont as "a Gull, . . . a Fool, and cheated," ponders the question of whether all cheated men are gulls and fools (p. 115). In the play proper, Maskwell muses, "I have an After-Game to play that shall turn the Tables" (p. 185); the terms "dealing" and "gamester" frequently recur, and the Epilogue contains a specific reference to the dice game of hazard, with the implication that poets who write plays are hazarding their reputations with each effort (p. 212). A long dialogue between Cynthia and Mellefont is rampant with card-game imagery: marriage is a game; they will turn up a trump; a good hand is an accident to her—and a result of judgment or of card sense to him. Cynthia concludes, "Still it is a Game, and consequently one of us must be Loser," and Mellefont disagrees, "Not at all; only a friendly Trial of Skill, and the Winnings to be laid out in an entertainment" (pp. 140–41). Furthermore, *Love for Love* includes some fencing and tennis imagery, as well as references to a losing hand and to gamesters.

The opening chocolate house scene of Congreve's last comedy, *The Way of the World,* informs the rest of the play, establishing gaming as the playwright's metaphor for life and love. The comedy's prolific gaming imagery provides a thematic and structural emphasis on gaming as the world's way, and, finally, every character is at one time or another playing a game that may be a singles or doubles match, but that is usually part of a team effort. The audience of *The Way of the World* would, of course, have been familiar with the circumstances of the scene that begins with Mirabell and Fainall "rising from cards." We learn that Mirabell, though he has lost to Fainall, will "play on" if his competitor insists on further entertainment.[5] Fainall demurs:

> No, I'll give you your revenge another time, when you are not so indifferent; you are thinking of something else now, and play too negligently. The coldness of a losing gamester lessens the pleasure of the winner. I'd no more play with a man that slighted his ill fortune than I'd make love to a woman who undervalued the loss of her reputation.[6]

This speech of Fainall's is a most significant passage, not only because it is pregnant with dramatic irony, for reasons to be discussed later, but also because it establishes the motif on which the play's structure, theme, and much of its language build and introduces the idea that life is a game in the world of the play and elsewhere, with love, money, and their concomitant pleasures as reward to the winners.

Congreve introduces his gaming imagery in the Prologue, first describing poets as the unluckiest of fools, and then as

> . . . bubbles, by the town drawn in,
> Suffered at first some trifling stakes to win;
> But what unequal hazards do they run!
> Each time they write they venture all they've won. (ll. 11–14)

The word "bubble" acquired in the seventeenth century the meaning of "dupe" or "gull" and was frequently used to describe one easily victimized at cards.[7] An attaché at the British Embassy in Paris had warned his countrymen against gaming with the French because "Even the ladies do not want tricks to strip a Bubble." [8] About 1700, English manufacturers of cards began issuing decks with propaganda depicted on the backs; one such set entitled "All the Bubbles" warns against investing in spurious business ventures (p. 123). Congreve intimates in the Prologue that poets are gulled into writing plays by some "trifling stakes," despite the "hazards." The word "hazard," as it is used in two prologues by Congreve, would have been a gaming pun familiar to the audience, as the game of hazard is described in *The Compleat Gamester* as the "most bewitching game that is plaid on the dice" (Hartmann, p. 34).[9] Congreve's suggestion that poets "venture all they've won" is perhaps an oblique reference to Jeremy Collier's celebrated *Short View of the Immorality and Profaneness of the English Stage*,[10] a pamphlet that appeared in 1698, the year before the actual writing of *The Way of the World,* and to which Congreve later wrote a "vindication." [11] Undoubtedly, the playwright found the Puritan divine a threat to his security in the dramatic world, and much of the criticism of the play contains conjectures about the effect of Collier's attack on Congreve's decision to retire from the stage world after 1700. Interestingly, Collier fired a later salvo in 1713, entitled "Essay on Gaming," in which he deplored the bloodthirsty instincts fed by gaming: "When your bubbles are going down the hill, you lend them a push, though their bones are broken at the bottom." [12]

The Prologue continues with another gaming pun: "Should he [the poet] by chance a knave or fool expose,/That hurts none here, sure here are none of those" (ll. 35–36). The word "knave" by the sixteenth century carried a double meaning—an "unprincipled man given to dishonourable and deceitful practices," and also the "name given to the lowest court card in the deck, bearing the picture of a soldier or a servant." [13] "Expose" is a gaming term used to describe an inadvertently overturned card; an exposed knave in a whist game, for example, would result in a redeal, or if the exposure occurred during play, a penalty.

In Act I of *The Way of the World,* Witwoud relates that he has lost money to his fellow gamester Petulant, but Fainall consoles Witwoud with the remark:

> You may allow him to win of you at play, for you are sure to be hard of him at repartee; since you monopolize the wit that is between you, the fortune must be his of course (I.254–56)

To Mirabell, Witwoud explains,

> Petulant's my friend, and a very honest fellow, and a very pretty fellow, and has a smattering—faith and troth a pretty deal of an odd sort of a small wit. (I.260–62)

Witwoud continues the gaming motif with his pun on the word "deal": Petulant has been "dealt" a small amount of wit, or he has a great "deal" of it. Cotton describes a card game called plain-dealing as being "a pastime not noted for its ingenuity" (Hartmann, p. 68). Mirabell later remarks to Millamant,

> I say that a man may as soon make a friend by his wit, or a fortune by his honesty, as win a woman with plain dealing and sincerity. (II.417–19)

The delightful ambiguity here allows the choice between the card game or a straightforward manner as a means of winning the lady and is also a commentary on the times: devious means seem to be required for almost any undertaking, Millamant, well aware of her value as the prize in their game, urges him, "Well, Mirabell, if ever you will win me, woo me now" (II.429–30).

Also in Act I, Petulant "calls for himself" at the chocolate house, and then refuses to go, with the words, "Let it pass," and "pass on," phrases that he might have used at the whist table. When Mirabell threatens him, Petulant replies, "Let that pass. There are other throats to be cut." He is so casual in his suggestion that he might be offering a deck of cards to be cut, but what he is actually offering is information, which is Petulant's only contribution to the game of intrigue. Petulant, who is the witless fop, repeats the word "pass" so frequently that it seems to be a refrain associated with him, and he inquires "whose hand's out?" when Waitwell arrives with the black box (V.477).

In Act II Witwoud, who has been observing the game of wit in which Millamant and Mirabell are engaged, observes to the lady, "Very pretty. Why, you make no more of making of lovers, madam, than of making so many card-matches" (II.368–69), an expression that carries the dual meaning of cardboard matches and the holding of a pair or three of a kind in a game like gleek or picket. Witwoud later compares himself and Petulant to two battledores—or to participants in an early eighteenth-century version of badminton (III.358); what they bandy back and forth is witless banter instead of shuttlecocks. Shortly afterwards, Mrs. Marwood, in speaking to Fainall about his wife's virtue, remarks, "I dare swear she had given up her game before she was married," to which Fainall replies, "Hum! That may be. She might throw up her cards; but I'll be hanged if she did not put Pam in her pocket" (III. 574–77). The imagery here is that of the then popular gambling game of loo, or lanterloo, in which the Pam is the jack of clubs. Lynch's note indicates that "Fainall implies that although his wife might have given up other lovers, she has an 'ace' up her sleeve—Mirabell" (Lynch, p. 76*n*; Cotton, pp. 68–70).

Fainall tells Mrs. Marwood how he will dispose of Sir Wilfull: "He will drink like a Dane; after dinner I'll set his hand in" (III.594–95). Here Fainall may mean "I'll start him in his drinking," or "I'll take his 'hand' in whatever game comes up." And in referring to his wife's reputation, Fainall muses, "Bringing none to me, she can take none from me. 'Tis against all rule of play that I should lose to one who has not wherewithal to stake" (III.607–09). In this instance, Fainall cruelly notes that his wife has nothing in the way of a good reputation to lose; therefore convention decrees that he should not allow her in the game. In the parlance of poker, or its four-hundred-year-old antecedent, brag, she has no ante to put up, so she cannot play. This statement recalls Fainall's line from the chocolate house scene in which he indicates he will not "make love to a woman who undervalues the loss of her reputation."

In addition to its language, a further indication that *The Way of the World* is a consciously devised metaphor for gaming is Congreve's choice of quotations from the poets Waller and Suckling. First of all, the two poets represent opposing views about how to play the game of love and life—one arguing against, the other for, premarital or extramarital fruition. Millamant uses their poems, which deal with inconstancy in love, to prove that Sir Willful is incapable of playing any of the sophisticated games of wit that she enjoys; he not only cannot complete the couplet she offers him but does not even recognize it as poetry. Suckling, a writer for whom, according to Lynch, Congreve had a "more than casual esteem," had established a dialogue pattern in his play *Agalaura* that was much like a conversational game.[14] In the play, Agalaura's lover, at her request, and without knowing her reasons, agrees to give up his favorite diversion of gaming; yet she is required to assign him a new sin to replace this one (p. 53). The poet Suckling himself, known as "the most skillful and reckless player of his time" (Hartmann, p. xiii) is the only man credited with singly inventing a major card game—cribbage. He was a gambler who, according to rumors, arranged for the importation from France of specially marked decks for his own personal use and advantage (Hartmann, p. xiii). Waller, who may have been present when Queen Catherine tore the celebrated card at ombre, wrote a delightful little epigram to celebrate that occasion:

> The cards you tear in value rise;
> So do the wounded by your eyes.
> Who to celestial things aspire
> Are by that passion raised the higher.[15]

Interestingly enough, the lines Sir Willful fails to recognize are those of the inconstant lover, Suckling, while Mirabell completes a couplet by Waller, the more idealistic poet.

In order to observe the structure of the play as a game, it is helpful to determine the kinds of partnerships involved. Millamant and Mirabell are silent partners who work toward the same end, have the same desire, and have the same reluctance to acknowledge their desires publicly. Mr. Fainall's ostensible partner is Mrs. Fainall, who is actually allied in sympathy with Mirabell and Millamant. Mrs. Marwood is Mr. Fainall's actual confederate, and the one for whom he is scheming; at one point, Marwood intimates to Lady Wishfort that they (the two ladies) might escape to some rural, idyllic spot, but Marwood actually continues to work with Mr. Fainall because of their common aim, which is the frustration of all of Mirabell's plans. The Marwood-Fainall relationship should parallel that of Mirabell and Millamant but cannot, because it is extramarital and because Fainall and Marwood are selfish and completely unscrupulous. While there is some evidence that Mirabell abides by the rules in the game of life in this world, there is no rule that Fainall will not break if he can advance himself by doing so.

Witwoud and Petulant are partners of a sort. They complement, but do not compliment, one another, and there is definite evidence that the pair of them would represent but a single entry in any game. They are habitual, ineffective, halfhearted competitors for the game prize of Millamant and her fortune. Lady Wishfort wants a marital partner and refuses to admit that she has nothing to contribute to a connubial relationship. Even her fortune cannot outweigh the fact that she is no longer attractive as a marriage prospect; she is so blind to reality that she for a time has accepted Mirabell's advances as proof of her desirability. Foible and Waitwell appear to be a minor partnership—the second team necessary to support Mirabell in his game plan—but Foible, when examined carefully, is indeed, as Marwood calls her, the *passe-partout.* Sir Willful, a loner who serves as bumpkinlike contrast for his half brother, and an involuntary contestant for the first prize, willingly relinquishes it once Millamant is within his grasp, so that he can travel to find for himself "another way of the world."

Partnership understandings vary, as do audience understandings of partnerships. In the chocolate house scene, the audience impression is that Fainall is a good sport who is willing to terminate his game during a winning streak in order to give his opponent a chance on a luckier day. Later developments show, however, that although Fainall never acts from benevolent motives, he speaks the truth when he says, "The coldness of a losing gamester lessens the pleasure of the winner" (I.6–7). He enjoys the winning more when his victim writhes; a listless Mirabell affords Fainall no joy. The irony of Fainall's statement lies in the fact that he is actually expressing the sentiments of Mirabell, who is the same kind of competitor. Several critics have wondered why Mirabell holds for so long his ace-in-the-hole in the form of Mrs. Fainall's deed, when he could have produced it earlier. The reason is that, like Fainall, Mirabell finds no thrill in competing with a "cold gamester," or one who "slights his ill fortune," and he does enjoy toying with an overconfident Fainall. He wants to let Fainall believe himself to have won Millamant's fortune and then stymie the villain with one master stroke. Doubtless, Mirabell had dreamed early in the game of having everyone present for his revelation, as proves to be the case. The idea of delight in resistance is also reiterated in the song requested by Millamant in Act III:

> Then I alone the conquest prize,
> When I insult a rival's eyes;
> If there's delight in love, 'tis when I see
> That heart, which others bleed for, bleed for me. (III.346–49)

As do Fainall and Mirabell, Millamant thrives on spirited competition.

Although most twentieth-century critics admire *The Way of the World* as comedy, the concensus seems to be that its plot is nonexistent, or that if it exists it is too intricate to follow, and that audiences should simply admire the delightful characterizations and leave structure and plot alone. An examination of the games played reveals a plot that is a collage of intrigues not difficult to penetrate if observed from the vantage point of one character at a time. Almost everyone in the world of the comedy plays a game most of the time; with some games occurring simultaneously, it is profitable to begin with a minor character, Mincing, who is just clever enough to participate in the games of her mistress Millamant. In one of her more fanciful moments, Millamant complains about all the letters she has received from inept writers. To Witwoud, she complains:

> Nobody knows how to write letters; and yet one has 'em, one does not know why. They serve one to pin up one's hair. (II.325–27)

Witwoud is amazed to learn that Millamant's letters serve this purpose, but only because he has to keep copies of his correspondence.

Since Millamant's first move does not sufficiently impress Witwoud, she adds:

> [I use] only. . . those in verse, Mr. Witwoud. I never pin up my hair with prose. I fancy one's hair would not curl if it were pinned up with prose. I think I tried once, Mincing. (II.330–32)

Mincing never falters, never loses the timing of Millamant's exquisitely outrageous declaration, agreeing, "O mem, I shall never forget it" (II.333). To Millamant's addition, "Poor Mincing tift and tift all the morning," Mincing continues, " 'Till I had the cremp in my fingers, I'll vow, mem. . . . But when your la'ship pins it up with poetry, it sits so pleasant the next day as anything, and is so pure and so crips" (II.334–38). Mincing, a minor player, is a most effective gamester when involved by her mistress.

Petulant and Witwood are half men, a fact witnessed to by the ladies of the cabal: when they decide to enroll one man as a member, they admit the two fops. Petulant plays three games—the aforementioned one in which he hires women to call for him, or even calls on himself in disguise; a second, in which he plays at the courting of Millamant; and the third, a game of contradiction, in which Witwoud says "Black is black," and Petulant, "if he has a humour to do so," argues that black is blue. Witwoud also plays three games: in his first, he courts Millamant, but admittedly only because it is fashionable, not because he is genuinely interested in her; if he won her, he would not know what to do with her. His second game is that of superiority over Petulant, whom he calls an "enemy to learning." This form of amusement is necessary to Witwoud because participating in it with his alter ego feeds his foppish vanity. His third game is played with his newly-arrived-from-the-country-brother, Sir Wilfull, and consists of two ploys: the first is a form of blind man's buff and involves Witwoud's snobbishly hoping not to be recognized by his own brother, and further, not to be forced to acknowledge the relationship at all. In the second stage of this inter-fraternal match, Witwoud urges Petulant to bait his country bumpkin brother, much as if he were inciting a small dog to yip at a larger, shaggier, but harmless dog. To this diversion, Witwoud is a happy spectator.

One wonders why Mrs. Fainall bothers to play any games at all, since it seems that she has little to look forward to in the game of life and love, but she greets her villainous husband with dissembled affection, at the same time abetting her ex-lover Mirabell, for whom the personal stakes are great. As her part in the intrigue, she pretends to be Marwood's friend, warns Mirabell to enable him to evade Lady Wishfort, and finally prepares Mincing and Foible to vouch for any statements she might make about Marwood and Fainall. Though Mrs. Fainall plays on Mirabell's team because of her lingering love for him and her active distaste for her husband, she is not altogether cooperative with Milla-mant when she refuses to entertain Sir Wilfull and when she urges his attentions on Millamant. She seems to be not completely unselfish when she locks Sir Wilfull in the room with Millamant, and she would doubtless welcome the chance to reopen her affair with Mirabell.

Waitwell, Mirabell's servant, plays his assignment so well that he begins to think he actually is Sir Rowland, who has been "married, knighted, and attended all in one day" (II.499). In the guise of Sir Rowland, he flatters Lady Wishfort, rushes her, and attacks Mirabell as one who will "go out in a stink like a candle's end" (IV.468), all in one series of professionally delivered lines. Although he explains to Foible that his enthusiasm for his role is feigned (IV.499–503), he rises to every occasion as a worthy supporting player. It is the height of drama-tic irony that he declares himself ready to die for his truth—which is actually a lie—and also for his nonexistent innocence. In the game with Lady Wishfort, he plays along with her self-deception by suggesting that their union will produce an heir and departs to look for the all-important black box, with the grand exit line: "And may I presume to bring a contract to be signed this night? May I hope so far?" (IV.572–73).

Lady Wishfort's primary game is one of let's pretend. In her imagina-tion, she is still a youthful, desirable coquette, a contemporary of, and a rival of, her lovely niece Millamant. She is a female Dorian Gray who reverses the picture routine by trying to look like a younger portrait of herself. Her nervousness as she prepares to entertain her pseudosuitor is almost pathetic:

> *Foible:* A little scorn becomes your ladyship.
> *Lady Wishfort:* Yes, but tenderness becomes me best, a sort of dyingness. You see that picture has a sort of—ha, Foible? a swimmingness in the eyes. Yes, I'll look so. (III.149–52)

As part of her game, Lady Wishfort pretends to be concerned about losing her reputation when what she really does not want to lose is her lone candidate for matrimony. She has for years played a game we might call Puritan, as her library consists solely of Puritanic books, and she has attempted to suppress the sexuality of her daughter, Mrs. Fainall, whose dolls were all female and whose chaplain had to pretend to be a woman (V.176–80). Lady Wishfort's games are not at all benevolent in purpose: she has terrorized her male servants so much that the senior among them holds a tenure of one week, and she is not averse to poisoning the wine of Mirabell in her desire for revenge. She plays a game even with her speech; when trying to impress, she is the predecessor of Mrs. Malaprop, but when she is angry with Foible, her language is eloquent. Her ludicrous errors result not from ignorance, but from the desire to engage in the same snobbish game that involves lining up the coachman and postilion to serve as footmen and spraying them so they will not stink of the stable (III.4–7).

Fainall, who serves as the play's antagonist, if Mirabell is protagonist, plays the devious game of pretending to love his wife, although it is certainly not fashionable to do so. He has married her, he admits, "to make lawful prize of a rich widow's wealth" (II.184) and now encourages Mirabell to marry Millamant because Mrs. Fainall will then be Lady Wishfort's sole heir. When he learns, however, that Mirabell has made him an "anticipated cuckold," he lets desire for retaliation take precedence over greed and announces that he is no longer playing the role of husband, though he "wears the badge" (III.637). Along the way, Fainall indulges in a game of self-analysis, which he terminates with a bit of fallacious reasoning. His logic begins with the dismissal of wife, marriage, jealousy, and love and concludes with a kind of syllogism in which the major premise is that "Marriage is honourable" (III.611–12); the minor premise is that cuckolding comes from marriage; and the conclusion that therefore cuckolding should not "be a discredit" (III.613). As are many of the other gamesters in the world of this play, Fainall is deluded, but his delusion is not, like theirs, a refusal to accept reality; his delusion is caused by ignorance of facts. He thinks that he holds the trump card:

If the worst come to the worst, I'll turn my wife to grass. I have already a deed of settlement of the best part of her estate, which I have wheedled out of her. (III.625–27)

His confidence bolstered by possession of this worthless document, Fainall thinks he has won the game; he prematurely lays down his terms, refuses to compromise, and plays what he considers to be the winning card. He will manage Lady Wishfort's estate and will retain sole use of his wife's, or, he tells Lady Wishfort, ". . . your darling daughter's turned adrift, like a leaky hulk, to sink or swim, as she and the current of this lewd town can agree" (V.410–12). Fainall, unabashed by the accusations of Foible and Mincing, denounces his wife publicly and is not actually defeated until the formerly cold gamester Mirabell triumphantly produces the real ace-in-the-hole in the form of a deed of settlement that antedates Fainall's.

Mirabell masterminds many of the games, and a look at his technique reveals that he has not been the most scrupulous of gamesters: he has feigned a liking for Lady Wishfort to conceal his love for her niece; he has flattered the old lady by pretending to believe she is pregnant. But he has drawn the line at seducing her, and Mrs. Marwood has called his hand by revealing his motives to Lady Wishfort. This leaves Mirabell in an unenviable spot at a point in the game when he must devise a new strategy. He has also been Mrs. Fainall's lover but has married her to Fainall because he feared that she was pregnant. His latest design, or game strategy, is to cause his pretended uncle (actually his servant Waitwell) to woo Lady Wishfort. When the imposture is discovered, she will be so embarrassed that she will consent to Mirabell's marrying Millamant and her fortune. In short, he is trying to blackmail Lady Wishfort, which is exactly what Fainall is doing. Mirabell has played this kind of game enough that he knows not to trust Waitwell; to prevent his actually winning Lady Wishfort, he insures that Waitwell and Foible are married first. Mirabell and Fainall are reciprocally and with reason suspicious of one another, Fainall suggesting the existence of a Marwood-Mirabell relationship, and Mirabell a Marwood-Fainall liaison. Mirabell reads a significance into finding Millamant's door locked: he decides that she is making the pursuit more sporting, but his favorite game with her is that of repartee, an amusement that results in the famous proviso scene. He is fairly straightforward with Millamant in most instances, although he is not with Lady Wishfort. His last game with the older lady is one of sham-contrition; he asks for pity, lists his several sacrifices, and charms the older lady completely. After Mirabell's triumphant introduction of the deed of conveyance, he restores the contract to Mrs. Fainall in a gesture of forgiveness, the participants of the chocolate house scene now being reversed in position, with Fainall the dejected loser and Mirabell the sportsmanlike winner.

Sir Wilfull, the only character who plays no games at all until play's end, when he is conscripted by Mirabell, is unaware of conventional game rules, or even that there are such rules. He is bluff, hearty, straightforward, and so naive that he interprets his brother's unfriendly silence for unmitigated joy. He is guilty only of reverse snobbery, deploring his brother's "be-cravated and be-periwigged condition" and "Inns o' Court breeding" (III.456–57; 467). Sir Wilfull proves to be disarmingly shrewd, realizing that Witwoud has "served his time" as an apprentice-fop and is now ready to set up for himself (III.500). He is unaware, in a refreshing way, that he is breaking a long-standing game rule by making the grand tour after the age of forty and practical enough that he wants to learn French before he goes abroad. He is sensible, decisive, and, as he points out, not guilty of shilly-shallying. Incapable of participating in Millamant's quiz game because he has never heard of the poet Suckling, he contrasts with Mirabell, a skillful, sophisticated contestant who completes the Waller couplets smoothly. Yet Sir Willful is perceptive enough to recognize Millamant's refusal to walk with him as the result of town folks' having too many diversions available to them—plays and the like. His songs are all drinking songs—none of Suckling or platonic love for him as a subject—and when Sir Wilfull is really drunk, the only word to which he reacts is "wench." He finally consents to play the game simply to help Mirabell and Millamant in their final coup—to cause Fainall to expose his hand.

The remaining gamesters are ladies—and I have reserved a scrutiny of them until last because I believe that these ladies play a far more important role in the way of this world—or the world of this play—than has generally been accredited to them. As members of the ladies' cabal they are playing a female chauvinist game in which they whisper among themselves when they spy men, pretend to have the vapors, and affect silence without apparent provocation. Congreve allows no woman on stage during Act I except Betty, the waitress at the chocolate house; but we hear about the women, and the effect is one of real anticipation. Smith points out that the ladies had emerged historically as a faction to be reckoned with by influencing the subject matter and morals of drama by about 1674 and that by 1700 they had won their battle and gotten what they wanted.[16] He traces a gradual role reversal reflected in the plays themselves, with the woman subtly achieving a more assertive role, and describes Millamant as displaying an extraordinary independence. She tells Mirabell, "I shan't endure to be reprimanded nor instructed" (II. 408–09), and laughs, "What would you give that you could help loving me?" (II.412–13). Millamant, mistress of the quick retort and the evident inspiration for Mincing's ability with the *bon mot,* plays a sadistic game in which she professes a pleasure in giving pain, tells Mirabell that she converses with fools for her health (II.397–98), and causes him to describe a whirlwind as more tranquil and more steady than she. "A fellow that lives in a windmill has not a more whimsical dwelling than the heart of a man that is lodged in a woman" (III. 444–46), moans Mirabell. The games Millamant plays with her fiancé are frolicsome, but not really deceptive, since she is a plain-dealer. When Marwood tells Millamant that "the town has found" that Mirabell loves her, the young lady replies:

> The town has found it! What has it found? That Mirabell loves me is no more a secret than it is a secret that you discovered it to my aunt, or than the reason why you discovered it is a secret. (III.294–97)

She plays a catlike, almost vicious game with Marwood, toying with her as Mirabell is toying with Fainall, and discovering equal zest in the game. When Marwood declares, untruthfully of course, that she detests Mirabell, Millamant replies:

> O madam, why so do I—and yet the creature loves me, ha! ha! ha! How can one forbear laughing to think of it! I am a sybil if I am not amazed to think what he can see in me. I'll take my death, I think you are handsomer—and within a year or two as young. If you could but stay for me, I should overtake you—but that cannot be.—Well, that thought makes me melancholy.—Now I'll be sad. (III.322–28)

Millamant baits Petulant but plays no games unless she finds them amusing or worthwhile. With Sir Wilfull, she is frank; he stinks and she tells him so. She insists, however, that Mirabell "solicit" her as if she were "wavering at the grate of a monastery, with one foot over the threshold" (IV.141–43) and informs him that she intends to play her own game after marriage, which might involve remaining inviolate as her "closet." With him also Millamant plays a game of excessive delicacy, in which she cannot bear to think of "breeding" or endeavors toward that end. She too breaks the paramount rule by confessing to Mrs. Fainall that she loves Mirabell "violently."

Mrs. Marwood, incapable of holding her own with Millamant in a battle of sheer wit, uses another weapon. Her game is gossip, but it deserves a more malicious title than that, because what she spreads is often truth far better left untold. If plain-dealing does not serve her ends, she resorts skillfully to double-dealing. She reveals Mirabell's sham amour to Lady Wishfort, not out of friendship for the older woman, but because of her own suppressed desire for Mirabell. She tells Fainall of the premarital affair between his wife and Mirabell to incite Fainall to act quickly against Mirabell and suggests that he can besmirch his wife's reputation with her mother, thus winning all of the Wishfort fortune for himself. She deceives Mrs. Fainall, to whom she professes to be a sister in spirit, by claiming to despise men, especially Mirabell, at the same time acting as mistress to Mrs. Fainall's husband. Marwood receives an unexpected bonus for her own personal game plan when Lady Wishfort sends her to the closet, where she overhears Mirabell's entire plot revealed in a conversation between Foible and Mrs. Fainall. She discovers enough to cause her to realize that Foible is literally the "master key to everybody's strongbox" (III.203–04) and that Mrs. Fainall has a surfeit of appetite for Mirabell, rather than the want of appetite she professes (III.206–07). Marwood's next move is an attempt to circumvent Mirabell's carefully laid plan by proposing a Sir Wilfull-Millamant liaison to Lady Wishfort. Noting that Petulant and Witwood are a necessary accoutrement to Millamant's game— hangers-on to make the coquette appear desirable—she joins Millamant in the game of toying with them and pretending to "perceive" their debates to be "important and learnedly handled" (III.368–69). When Marwood stops the verbal tilting of Petulant and Sir Wilful before they reach the point of a physical exchange, her motive is not charitable; she simply wants to preserve Sir Wilfull for Millamant in order to thwart Mirabell's scheme. It is Marwood who contrives the letter to reveal Sir Rowland's identity, and it is also she who is not fooled by the announcement that Millamant will marry Sir Rowland. She manipulates Lady Wishfort into an agreement to pay Fainall to keep quiet, but she bows out quickly when her own reputation is at stake, announcing that she will ". . . meddle no more with an affair in which [she is] not personally concerned" (V.153–54).

Marwood is right about Foible; she is the key to the entire game. The servant is an apt pupil who plays along willingly with Mirabell as her coach and who adds a few innovations of her own, particularly when in the enemy camp of Lady Wishfort's chamber. Foible's prize for winning the game is essentially the same as that offered to other players—love and material reward—but hers carries an added twist. She has her man, who although a good enough dissembler, is not nearly so clever as she, and Mirabell has forbidden the consumation of their marriage until game's end. As to the fortune, Foible's is the most concrete prize of all—a farm, to which she can retire with Waitwell to live in the country where no games are necessary because all their neighbors will be plain-dealers like Sir Wilfull. Foible will have risen far above her humble beginnings as described by Lady Wishfort:

> Go set up for yourself again! Do, drive a trade, do, with your three-pennyworth of small ware, . . . an old gnawed mask, two rows of pins, and a child's fiddle; a glass necklace with the beads broken, and a quilted nightcap with one ear. . . . This was

your merchandise you dealt in, when I took you into my house, placed you next myself, and made you governante of my whole family! (V.9–20)

Lady Wishfort should perhaps have taken in a less capable, less conniving person. When she accosts Foible with the charge that she has been consorting with the enemy, Foible immediately attacks Mirabell, even fabricating a"fling at your ladyship" (III.79) by that gentleman. Foible flatters Mirabell (that "sweet, winning gentleman"), Lady Wishfort ("Your lover is impatient"), and Mrs. Fainall (the "pattern of generosity"). She encourages Lady Wishfort as coquette:

. . . a little art once made your picture like you; and now a little of the same art must make you like your picture. Your picture must sit for you, madam. (III.136–37)

The clever servant even pads the roster of liverymen, ostensibly to impress Sir Rowland with their sophistication and prosperity, but actually to cause Lady Wishfort to applaud Foible's attention to detail. She dares to employ double-entendre to her mistress; when invited to comment on Lady Wishfort's appearance, Foible replies, "[You look] most killing well, madam" (IV.13), when what she is really thinking is, "Like death itself." She caters to Millamant and Mirabell, allowing them to get together despite her mistress's orders. As the most effective game player of all, she recognizes Marwood's hand on a letter to Lady Wishfort and reacts quickly to tell Sir Rowland to claim that the letter is a plot of his nephew to discredit him. She further improvises to Lady Wishfort:

This was the business that brought Mr. Mirabell disguised to Madam Millamant this afternoon. I thought something was contriving, when he stole by me and would have hid his face. (IV.546–47)

Foible is a woman never to be outdone, a worthy competitor in any game, preferably in a dishonest one. Accused of disloyalty, she dissembles:

I'll confess all. Mr. Mirabell seduced me. . . . Your ladyship's own wisdom has been deluded by him; then how should I, a poor ignorant, defend myself? (V.23–26)

She impulsively decides to reveal her marriage to Lady Wishfort and to assure her, "He could not have bedded your ladyship; for if he had consummated with your ladyship, he must have run the risk of the law

. . ." (V.39–41). Foible knows all, and her timing is instinctively perfect. It is she who supplies Mirabell, through Mrs. Fainall, with the vital information that "Mrs. Marwood and he [Fainall] are nearer related than ever their parents thought for" (V.83–84). Foible feels perfectly free to reveal what she knows about the Marwood-Fainall affair, though she has been sworn to secrecy; her opponents have made a gross tactical error in selecting a book of poetry instead of a Bible as the book on which she took the oath.

Thus, while Mirabell directs much of the game of this play, acting in effect as player-coach, his star players are women: Millamant, whose name indicates a thousand-fold complexity, and Foible, whose name, ironically enough, literally means a "weakness of character," or the "weaker section of a sword blade," [17] but who proves to be much the stronger half of a pair without which the game might not have been won. Chief of the antagonists seems to be, not Fainall, but Marwood, who is consumed with the idea that she would mar Mirabell. The action of the play has indeed progressed like a series of games, with intricate moves and with a balance of raillery and seriousness appropriate to such a battle of wits. In *The Way of the World,* the gaming occurs on three levels: literally, in the card game at the chocolate house; figuratively, in the word play and maneuvering that takes place at Lady Wishfort's House; and finally on the stage itself, where a play is the playing of a game.

NOTES

[1] Cyril Hughes Hartmann, ed., *Games and Gamesters of the Restoration* (London: George Routledge and Sons, 1929), pp. ix–x.

[2] *Kings and Desperate Men: Life in Eighteenth Century England* (New York: Alfred A. Knopf, 1942), p. 70.

[3] Both of these books are reprinted and edited in Hartmann's work.

[4] Bonamy Dobrée, ed., *Comedies by William Congreve* (1925; rpt. London: Oxford Univ. Press, 1969), p. 45.

[5] Mirabell's "play on" recalls the famous opening lines from *Twelfth Night,* "If music be the food of love, play on." In this play, music is not the food of love; instead love is the end of the playing.

[6] William Congreve, *The Way of the World,* ed. Kathleen Lynch (Lincoln: Univ. of Nebraska Press, 1965), I. i. 4–9. All ensuing citations will refer to this edition.

[7] S. v. "bubble," *Oxford English Dictionary.*

[8] Roger Tilley, *A History of Playing Cards* (London: Studio Vista, 1973), p. 109.

[9] The poem accompanying the frontispiece to Cotton's book contains several puns on the hazards of the game.

[10] Significantly, this is one of the few books in Lady Wishfort's library.

[11] Congreve's reply to Collier is given in Sister Rose Anthony's *The Jeremy Collier Stage Controversy 1698–1726* (Milwaukee: Marquette Univ. Press, 1937), pp. 107–12.

[12] Quoted by Henry Jones (Cavendish) in *Card Essays* (New York: John Wurtele Lovell, 1880), p. 36.

[13] S. v. "knave," *OED.*

[14] Kathleen Lynch, *The Social Mode of Restoration Comedy* (New York: Macmillan Co., 1926), p. 78.

[15] G. Thorn Drury, ed., *The Poems of Edmund Waller* (1813; rpt. New York: Greenwood Press, 1968), p. 220.

[16] John Harrington Smith, *The Gay Couple in Restoration Comedy* (Cambridge, Mass.: Harvard Univ. Press, 1948), pp. 132, 135.

[17] S. v. "foible," *OED.*